IN THEIR
FOOTSTEPS

IN THEIR FOOTSTEPS

EXPLORERS, WARRIORS, CAPITALISTS, AND POLITICIANS OF WEST VIRGINIA

RODY JOHNSON

QUARRIER PRESS
Charleston, WV

Quarrier Press
Charleston, WV

©2005, Rody Johnson

All rights reserved. No part of this book may be reproduced in any form or means, electronic or mechanical, including photocopying, recording, or by any information storage and retrieval system, without permission in writing from the publisher.

Book and cover design: Mark S. Phillips

ISBN: 1-891852-41-8

Library of Congress Catalog Card Number: 2005900811

10 9 8 7 6 5 4 3 2 1

Cover photo: Author's collection

Printed in the United States of America

Distributed by:
West Virginia Book Company
1125 Central Ave.
Charleston, WV 25302
www.wvbookco.com

For our grandchildren

Katharine Lorraine Fields, Victoria Cherie Fields, Lissa Avis Fields, Caroline Margaret Fields, Ann Claire Johnson, Emily Avis Johnson, William Lewis Johnson, Alexander McMillan Johnson, Edward Boehm Johnson and those that may follow

Let us sing the praises of famous men, our ancestors in their generations. . . . There were those that ruled in their kingdoms and made a name for themselves in their valor . . . those who spoke in prophetic oracles; those who led the people . . . or put verses in writing; rich men endowed with resources . . . . Some of them have left behind a name. . . . But of others there is no memory . . . they and their children after them. But these also were godly men . . . their name lives on generation after generation.

       Ecclesiasticus 44:1-10, 13-14
       The First Lesson
       St. James Episcopal Church
       Lewisburg, West Virginia
       November 8, 2004

CONTENTS

Preface ix

Part I
Pioneer John Lewis and His Sons (1678-1811) 1

1. Staunton 3
2. The Founder 9
3. Lewisburg 23
4. Indian Fighters 27
5. Point Pleasant 41
6. Revolutionary Warriors 47
7. Sweet Springs 59
8. The Civilizer 65

Part II
Sergeant Patrick Gass of the
Lewis and Clark Expedition (1771-1870) 71

9. Wellsburg 73
10. The Voyage of Discovery 79
11. To the Pacific and Return 93
12. Journey's End 103

Part III
Captain John Avis, John Brown's Jailer (1818-1883) 107

13. Charles Town and Harpers Ferry 109
14. John Brown's Raid 113

15. Be Quick 121
16. War and Its Aftermath 129

Part IV
John D. and C.C. Lewis, Capitalists (1800-1917) 139
17. Kanawha Valley 141
18. Salt Kings 149
19. Slaves, Secession, and Scary Creek 159
20. Kellys Creek and Old Sweet 171

Part V
Governor George W. Atkinson, Republican (1845-1925) 185
21. Charleston 187
22. An Ideal Candidate 193
23. Elkins and Atkinson 203
24. The Governor's Term 211
25. A Southerner with Northern Principles 223
26. Judgment 229

Acknowledgments 237
Appendix — Family Trees 239
Abbreviations Used 242
Chapter Notes 243
Bibliography 256
Index 261
List of Illustrations 268
About the Author 269

PREFACE

They were explorers, warriors, capitalists, and politicians, representing two hundred years of American history. Between them they pioneered a new land, fought Indians, served in the Revolutionary War, participated in the Lewis and Clark Expedition, dealt with John Brown, fought in the Civil War, helped develop a capitalistic economy, and were governor of a state.

Their roots, like mine, lay in western Virginia. After sixty years of living elsewhere, I returned and wanted to know about the country, the history, and my ancestors.

Over the years my mother gave me books about the region, but I lived in Florida so had little interest. Then several years ago, I returned to West Virginia to summer in Lewisburg. I discovered that the past seemed much closer and more relevant. History surrounded me. Lewisburg itself carries the name of the brother of one of my ancestors. Nearby Old Sweet Springs, one of the original spring resorts, had once been in the family. A bust of my great-grandfather, an ex-governor, stands in the Capitol in Charleston. I live in a two hundred-year-old log house. The remains of a Confederate fortification stand on the hill above it. And West Virginians talk about their ancestors and the Indian attacks and the Civil War as if they happened yesterday.

Suddenly exposed to all this, I began to do more than thumb the pages of those dusty books on my shelves. I searched libraries, local museums, cemeteries, and visited historical sites. My wife, Katharine, is an artist, and, while she painted the Greenbrier Valley countryside, I sat nearby, reading all I could find.

The names of John Lewis, Braxton Davenport Avis, and George Wesley Atkinson had been familiar to me since childhood. John Lewis was a pioneer of the Shenandoah Valley, with vast land holdings stretching across the Alleghenies into what is now West Virginia. His sons were heroes in the French and Indian and

Revolutionary Wars. Braxton Avis, according to family legend, was the youngest drummer boy in the Confederate Army. I have a vague memory of my grandmother showing me a gray uniform that would fit a twelve-year-old boy. Wesley Atkinson was a Republican governor of West Virginia at the end of the nineteenth century. He wrote *History of Kanawha*, and his books are on my shelves.

I discovered a new set of men, men like John Dickinson Lewis, one of the Salt Kings of the Kanawha Valley and his son Charles Cameron Lewis, a capitalist who shunned the Civil War. I found very little information about Braxton Avis, but discovered that his father, Captain John Avis, had been Abolitionist John Brown's jailer. For some reason the family had never mentioned John Avis. Finally, in my mother-in-law's closet in California, I came across a newspaper clipping that tied a member of the Lewis and Clark Expedition to the family. He was Patrick Gass, a West Virginian from Wellsburg.

Though John Lewis' son William was called the Civilizer for his efforts on the frontier, each of these men, in his own contrary way, was a civilizer. The Lewises of the 1700s, tough Scots-Irishmen, helped conquer the wilderness and the British in the Revolutionary War. Patrick Gass, a coarse frontiersman, wrote a journal as he journeyed to the Pacific with Lewis and Clark. John Avis showed compassion for an abolitionist, yet he fought for his southern principles. The Lewises of the 1800s helped bring a roughshod capitalism to a remote valley. George Atkinson, a politician with a statesman's bearing, defended the rights of blacks and whites.

I wanted to follow the paths of these men through time, to walk in their footsteps, to stand where they stood, to visit and to know the places from their past. I explored Charleston, Lewisburg, Point Pleasant, Sweet Springs, Charles Town, Harpers Ferry, and Wellsburg in West Virginia and Staunton in Virginia. To get a feel for Patrick Gass' journey, I visited parts of the Lewis and Clark Trail in Montana.

The stories of these men are based on fact, as they were passed along orally and contained in writing in the eighteenth and nineteenth centuries. I have added a few scenes and some dialogue where the characters seem to demand it and have put that text in italics. These exceptions, as well as the sources where I found my information, are highlighted in chapter notes.

My journey begins in Staunton, Virginia where John Lewis arrived in 1732.

PART I

Pioneer John Lewis and his Sons
(1678-1811)

CHRONOLOGY

1603   The English establish Ulster and settle Scot Protestants in Northern Ireland.
1609   Colonists land at Jamestown.
1610   French Huguenots begin to immigrate to Ireland and England.
1678   John Lewis is born in Ulster.
1716   Governor Spotswood sees the Shenandoah Valley from the Blue Ridge.
1717   Scotch Irish begin immigration to America.
1729   John Lewis slays the Irish Lord.
1732   John Lewis and family settle in the Shenandoah Valley. George Washington is born in Virginia.
1736   Charles Lewis is born at Staunton.
1738   Augusta and Fairfax Counties are established west of the Blue Ridge.
1743   Thomas Jefferson is born in Albemarle County.
1749   The Loyal and Greenbrier Companies are formed.
1751   John Lewis names the Greenbrier River.
1755   Braddock is defeated by the French and Indians. Samuel Lewis is killed.

1756	The English initiate the French and Indian War
1757	Andrew Lewis leads the Sandy Creek expedition.
1762	John Lewis dies at Staunton.
1763	The Treaty of Paris concludes the French and Indian War.
1765	Britain imposes the Stamp Act. The Virginia House of Burgesses declares no taxation without representation.
1773	The Boston Tea Party occurs
1774	The First Continental Congress meets in Philadelphia. Charles Lewis is killed at the Battle of Point Pleasant.
1775	General Andrew Lewis defeats Governor Dunmore at Gwynn's Island.
1776	On July 4 the Continental Congress issues the Declaration of Independence. Washington crosses the Delaware.
1777	British forces capture Philadelphia. Washington spends the winter at Valley Forge.
1780	British capture the Charleston, S.C. garrison, including William Lewis.
1781	Washington and Lafayette defeat Cornwallis at Yorktown. Andrew Lewis dies.
1783	Great Britain and the United States formally end the Revolutionary War.
1789	George Washington is elected President. The Constitution is ratified.
1790	William Lewis establishes Old Sweet Springs.
1794	The Battle of Fallen Timbers ends the Indians' threat to the Ohio.

1

STAUNTON

John Lewis left Ireland because he killed his landlord. In 1732 he and his family arrived on a hilltop in the wilderness of the Shenandoah Valley near what is now Staunton, Virginia.

Entering Staunton from I-81, I stopped in front of a strip mall at a historical marker, titled "First Settler's Grave." It indicates that John Lewis' grave is one mile to the north and that he chose the site of Staunton. The marker notes that his sons "took an important part in the Indian and Revolutionary Wars."

I drove through the town's historic district, passed President Woodrow Wilson's birthplace and Mary Baldwin Women's College, crossed Lewis Street, and came to Gypsy Hill Park. There stood a twenty-foot-high obelisk dedicated "To the Memory of John Lewis." At the base was a replica of the inscription on his grave. However, I wanted to see the site itself. After a bit of searching, I found someone in Staunton who directed me to the location of the Lewis home and the grave.

Since childhood, I have known of John Lewis. The Lewis name is prevalent in my family. My grandmother was Anne Lewis Johnson, and four subsequent generations of Johnsons have used Lewis as a middle name. I could see similarities between my father and his brothers—strong, athletic, outdoorsmen who hunted and fished—to their Lewis ancestors. As a child I pictured my dad and my Uncle Howard as pioneers exploring the mountains. Had they lived in the eighteenth century, they would have fought Indians and served in the Revolutionary War as bravely as they participated in World War II.

Northeast of Staunton, I turned off a state road onto a gravel lane. The John Lewis house sat on a hill, nearly hidden among tall oak trees. Nearby were a large red barn and fields with grazing cattle. As I approached, the house looked more like something out of the 1930s than the 1700s. I was disappointed. Similarities to a late 1800s photograph that I had seen were gone except for the basic, two-story rectangular log house with chimneys at each end. The house was sheathed in brick with a wing attached at the back. In front was a small, open porch. A stone shed stood just outside the kitchen door.

The house I remembered from the picture was log with stone chimneys. It had an attached, separate structure with the first story of stone and the second story of timber. John Lewis added the "Fort" section for protection against the Indians, but it must have been removed during the brick renovation.

I went to the front door and rang the bell. A dog barked inside. The door opened, and there stood a pleasant, young fellow. I introduced myself and told him I was looking for John Lewis' grave. The fellow smiled. He said his name was Sean Thompson. His expression indicated that I was not the first person to knock on this door because of John Lewis. We talked about the house for a few minutes. Sean said the place had been in his family since 1907. "The old house is within these walls," he said. "That stone store house off the kitchen was built from the old fort part of the home."

I asked again about John Lewis' burial site, which I knew was nearby. Sean pointed to the next hill, topped by a lone, leafless tree and said, "You'll see a fenced-in spot just beyond that oak."

Back in the car on the main road, I soon turned off on a narrow lane and passed an old farmhouse. Parking near a locked gate entering a pasture, I could see the hill with the tree. I climbed a fence expecting a farmer to yell at me for trespassing. I waded across what must have been Lewis Creek and headed up the hill through a herd of curious cows. Near the lone tree was a rusty, black iron picket fence. I removed a small limb that had replaced a lost lock and entered the enclosed area. There, between two hedges, lay a marble slab with three red flowers blooming beside it. The gravestone read:

> Here lie the remains of
> JOHN LEWIS
> Settled Augusta county, located the town of Staunton, and furnished five sons to fight the battles of the American Revolution.
> He was the son of Andrew Lewis and Mary Calhoun and was born in Donegal County, Ireland in 1678 and died Feb'y 1, 1762, age 84 years.
> He was a brave man, a true patriot, and a friend of liberty throughout the world.

Photo by the author

At the bottom a Latin inscription, based on Paul's First Epistle to the Corinthians, read: "Mortality relinquished, he lives clothed in immortality." This marble slab had been laid over the original limestone in 1850.

From this burial spot, I could see the red brick of the Lewis home tucked among the trees. To the west lay a distinct line of mountains, the Alleghenies; and to the east stood the hazy Blue Ridge Mountains. The two ranges mark the boundaries of the Shenandoah Valley. Except for the hum of traffic on I-81, a mile away, the hilltop was quiet. John Lewis' family—his wife, Margaret Lynn, and his sons, Thomas, Andrew, William, and Charles, had buried him here almost 250 years ago.

Before leaving Staunton, I stopped at the Museum of American Frontier Culture, unique because of its three eighteenth century houses brought from Ireland, England, and Germany. Reconstructed as farms, they reflect how the settlers lived before coming to the New World. A log house and farm of the early nineteenth century shows how the settlers lived after arriving in the Shenandoah Valley. The Ulster house interested me the most. John Lewis and his wife, Margaret Lynn, may have lived in something similar in Ireland. This farm consisted of a cottage with whitewashed sandstone walls and a thatched roof of rye straw. Next to it stood a long barn with a stable for the horse, a place for the cow, and space to store the cart and the turf. There were also a pig sty and a hen house.

John Lewis and Margaret Lynn married in 1715 (he was thirty-seven; she, twenty-two).[1] Their families came from different places and for different reasons to the Ulster Province in Northern Ireland to settle in the 1600s. Margaret Lynn's family originated in the Scottish Lowlands. She was the daughter of William Lynn and Margaret Patton. Her father was called the Lord (or Laird) of Loch Lynn, the place from which his family came across the Irish Sea. Her mother's family, the Pattons, lived in County Donegal as early as 1626.[2]

Poor soil and constant battles with England made Scotland a terrible place to live. The English wanted to rule Ireland and Scotland. In the hope of controlling the Irish, the English encouraged the Scotch to colonize Ulster by offering them cheap land. So the Scotch moved in great numbers to Northern Ireland and thus became known as Scotch-Irish.

The Lewises were neither Scotch nor Irish. They descended from French Huguenots, who began leaving France in the 1600s and who came to Ireland by way of Wales.[3] Catholic France prevented the Huguenots from practicing their religion as they wished. While John's father, Andrew, was French, his mother, Mary Calhoun, was Irish.

A visit to Ireland a few years ago amazed me; it seemed to be West Virginia surrounded by water. The land, with its cattle and sheep and hilly country, appeared almost identical to my home state. The people projected the same friendliness as those at home. I shouldn't have found that surprising. At least half the people of western Virginia can claim Scotch-Irish ancestors. My trip to Ireland and some knowledge of its history gave me a feel for why some 250,000 Scotch-Irish came to America in the eighteenth century.

The English pushed the Irish off their land, colonizing the North with tough, ornery Scotsmen. The Irish revolted in the 1600s. Oliver Cromwell came from England and put down the revolt, bringing peace for a time. James II succeeded Cromwell and reestablished Catholicism. William of Orange defeated James in Ireland at the Battle of the Boyne, again restoring peace. In less than fifty years, the Scotch-Irish lived through several wars interspersed with short periods of peace. In 1702, however, Queen Anne assumed the throne and reinstated High Church rules. Only Anglican priests, not Presbyterian ministers, could conduct Scotch-Irish marriages and funerals. The Scotch-Irish Presbyterian beliefs came from John Calvin: God was sovereign over kings. The English kings placed themselves above God.

At the same time, greedy English landlords raised rents on the land. Queen Anne banned the import of Irish woolens and linens so they would not compete with English goods. Drought and smallpox ravaged Ireland. Religious persecution continued.

America, consequently, sounded like a wonderful place. Reports from those who had gone before promised a New World with an abundance of fertile land, wild game, and forests for wood to build houses. People were allowed to worship as they wished. John Lewis' neighbors began an exodus to this new land. After killing his landlord, Lewis was forced to go.

As I drove out of Staunton, I thought about the strength of character it takes for a people to uproot themselves from their homeland—to risk their lives crossing a dangerous ocean to settle in an unknown land. From my point of view, 250 years later, it is hard to imagine undertaking such a journey. But a few years ago I saw the remains of a homemade raft washed onto a Florida beach. It had been used by Cubans to come to this country to escape Communism. I believe the same desperation and courage that drove my Irish ancestors centuries ago continues to drive brave refugees all over the world.

2

THE FOUNDER

"John Lewis, remove yourself from my property immediately or my men and I shall remove you by force," yelled Sir Mungo Campbell, Lord of the Manor. John, his wife Margaret Lynn, and Samuel, his brother, stood behind the barred door.[1]

That evening, sitting at supper, they had heard distant voices. John left the table and peered out the window. A crowd of ruffians approached. John slammed the front door and secured it with a crossbar. Margaret Lynn sent the children into a back room. Samuel, who was ill and had been staying with the Lewises, rose from his cot.

Margaret Lynn Lewis knew that there would be trouble. John held a lease on property named Campbell's Manor in the County of Donegal, and their landlord had demanded that they vacate it. John had originally obtained the lease from an honorable man who was called "lord" because he owned much land. He was English, not Irish. At that point in time, the English had taken most of the land in Ulster from the Irish. But the lord died, and his estates passed to his oldest son, Sir Mungo Campbell, a man of despicable character, who was deeply in debt and drank heavily. He resented the Lewises' prosperity. They paid their rent on time and met all the requirements of the lease, but that made no difference to him. He demanded that they pay more rent, a demand designed to force them into relinquishing the lands. John went to the lord's manor house to talk with Sir Mungo but found him drinking with his companions. They hurled abuse at John, but he remained calm. Having had his say, he left quietly.

Blows struck the heavy wood door of the Lewis cottage followed by cursing and mumbling. John grabbed his only weapon, a shillelagh. Margaret Lynn feared for her family. The roar of a gun shot blasted through the cottage. Samuel fell to the floor. Margaret Lynn saw blood flowing from her hand. A musket had been fired into their home through a crack in the wall, killing Samuel.

John broke into a rage, his red hair extending in all directions. Margaret Lynn had never seen him this way. With wild eyes, he opened the door, charged through, and swung his shillelagh. He split Campbell's skull with a hard wooden cudgel. He swung again and split the skull of Campbell's servant. The rest of the attackers threw down their arms and ran.

Screaming, Margaret Lynn ran to John. Blood covered his hands, and pieces of Campbell's head speckled his shirt. The two villains lay at his feet.

She had little memory of what happened next. Friends arrived, advising John to flee. Though he had defended himself and was clearly in the right, this man of the middle class had little chance against the English authorities and the power and connections of the young lord. Margaret Lynn could not stand the thought of John leaving, but there was no choice. He could be hanged.

John wrote a letter for the authorities, describing the incident and the necessity of defending his family. Then he dressed in a friend's clothing, disguising himself. Margaret Lynn bravely held her children to her as he departed, heading for the port of Londonderry.

Such is the story, passed down over the years, of John Lewis slaying his landlord.

Until the slaying, John had no intention of going to America. His lease was long term, and he had been fortunate with his crops. With a bounty on his head, no choice remained except to join the hundreds of other Scotch-Irish crossing the Atlantic in 1729.

After John left, Margaret Lynn received a message from her merchant brother in Portugal. John had passed through there and reached America. Her brother arranged for Margaret Lynn and the children to sail from Londonderry to Philadelphia. They boarded a ship packed with three hundred passengers, all crowded below deck. The air was foul, their clothes damp, and the food poor. They slept on straw mattresses. During the day, if the seas remained quiet, they were permitted to go on deck for fresh air. Margaret Lynn was allowed one trunk with a few clothes and family heirlooms. The trip took three months. Panic spread throughout the ship when it was thought that they were lost. The food was nearly gone. And then ahead they saw the green coast of America. Imagine their arrival in the New World.

Margaret Lynn and her children stood at the crowded rail of the ship as they moved up the Delaware River, waiting to catch the first glimpse of Philadelphia. Margaret Lynn was excited and nervous. Surely John will be at the dock, she thought. Watching the riverbank covered with trees, she thanked God that they were no longer on the terrible ocean. She held the hand of her daughter Anne, who had been born just before John left. The rest of her children—Samuel fifteen; Thomas, thirteen; Andrew, eleven: William, seven; and her namesake Margaret Lynn, five – ran about the deck, playing with the other youngsters. Their voices rang out in a manner that she had not heard for a while. They, too, were ready to see their father.

Houses appeared along the river. Margaret called her children to stand beside her. As they sailed into Philadelphia, she saw brick and stone buildings, squares, and straight streets. People walked about. With a population of 10,000, it was the biggest city she had ever seen. Some said it was second in size only to London in all of the English lands. Ahead at the docks two other ships disembarked people from Ulster.

Their ship approached the wharf. People crowded the dock. Margaret Lynn searched the crowd for John. Suddenly, Samuel, her oldest son, pointed, crying out," There he is! There he is!"

She saw John, taller than most, waving his hand. It had been two years since they parted.

Margaret Lynn might have wished to live in Philadelphia. The city already had a library and gas streetlights, thanks to Benjamin Franklin, who had just begun publication of his Poor Richard's Almanac. But John Lewis did not feel it wise to stay. "We must go to the frontier where we can have land again and where the English authorities will have trouble finding me if, indeed, they are still looking."

So the Lewis family moved to Lancaster, along with many of the other Scotch-Irish. They stayed there through the winter of 1731. However, they found the land expensive and becoming crowded. John heard of a large, unsettled valley in Virginia. He visited Williamsburg, the capital of the Virginia Colony, to find out more. On his return he told Margaret Lynn that Williamsburg did not impress him, except for the College of William and Mary and the Governor's House, which had a marble floor. Nonetheless, he decided that Virginia was where they should go. There, hundreds of thousands of acres beyond the Blue Ridge Mountains lay uninhabited.

Fifteen years earlier, Governor Spotswood led an expedition of his cronies across the Blue Ridge. It was reported that they viewed the Shenandoah Valley through an alcoholic haze and then beat a quick retreat back to Williamsburg. The governor presented each of his friends with a golden horseshoe memento to commemorate their courage.² He then wisely signed a treaty with the Iroquois nation, ensuring that the Indians would not cross the mountains and harass the colonists or their plantations. Thus, the Valley was not settled. It waited for John Lewis, his family, and others to become its early settlers.

On horseback and on foot, John, Margaret Lynn and their five children headed south during the summer of 1732. It was the year of George Washington's birth. A few other settlers followed the same route at the same time, but went no farther than present-day Winchester. The Lewises crossed the Susquehanna River, waded the Potomac, and followed a narrow Indian trail through woods so thick that they and the horses had to walk single file. Then the country opened up. Densely forested mountains rose on either side of the wide, empty valley. Fields of blue grass and white clover spread before them. The Indians had hunted there for years and burned the land each season before returning west across the mountains to their winter home beyond the Ohio. The open ground attracted the buffalo, which the Indians hunted. The Lewises may have seen groups of buffalo feeding on the abundant grasses.

Following the North Fork of the Shenandoah River and pushing on a bit farther, the Lewis family came to a hill near a clear spring with a creek running below. John and Margaret Lynn decided to settle at that spot. Because of its beauty, John named the place Bellefont.³ They held no legal title to the land, but it did not matter in the uninhabited wilderness. They set up tents and began to build a home.

On the hilltop by the spring, John and his sons constructed a log house. It rose two stories, made from logs cut from chestnut trees in the nearby woods. They notched the logs so they would lock in place. They rolled logs up poles to position them for the second floor. With the boys still young, John probably needed the help of some of the neighbors who had followed them into the Shenandoah. They chinked the spaces between the logs, using a concoction of mud and moss. To cover the roof, shakes or clapboards were cut from logs and overlapped like shingles.

Most log houses measured twenty feet by sixteen feet, but the size of the available trees was the determining factor. The house may have started out with a dirt floor but later would have a wooden

John Lewis Home. Called Bellefont and Fort Lewis, the home is located near Staunton. *Courtesy Ronald Steffey*

floor made from rough slabs of timber smoothed by a broad ax. A door was cut in the center of the front wall with a window on either side. The door hung on wooden hinges with a cross bar to lock it. It opened into the hall (living room) where the family gathered, cooked, and ate. Next to the hall stood the parlor, John and Margaret Lynn's sleeping quarters. A portion of the parlor may have been walled off as a chamber for the two girls, Margaret Lynn and Anne. In the back corner of the hall, a ladder and later, perhaps, a narrow stairway led up to the loft where the boys slept. The loft had three windows on each side. The windows closed by sliding a shutter across the opening. Parchment may have been used to allow some light to enter, but later would be replaced by glass ordered from Philadelphia. At each end of the house stood a stone fireplace, one in the hall for cooking and one in the parlor for warmth.

Early settlers like the Lewises made their own furniture and farm implements from the wood around them – walnut, oak, and maple. Mattresses were stuffed with goose feathers. Unable to bring their glass, china, and silverware from Ireland, the family used pewter plates, cups, and wooden bowls. Margaret Lynn would soon have a spinning wheel to make yarn for cloth. With some help from her two daughters, she milked the cow, made butter, did the washing, and preserved what they grew for the winter. The Scotch-Irish did not consider it proper for the women to work in the fields.

John and his boys chopped down trees and removed the stumps to prepare the fields. At first, life was far more primitive than in Ulster. But for food, there were deer, turkey, wild fruit, nuts and berries, plus trout from the streams. John and his sons planted corn, sweet potatoes, beans, squash, and pumpkins, although they preferred hunting to farming. In autumn, they shot game to be stored as meat for the winter. As John and the boys hunted and explored the Alleghenies, they learned the habits of the wildlife and soon knew every mountain, valley and stream in the area almost as well as the Indians did. They even dressed like Indians, wearing loose deerskin hunting shirts, pants, and moccasins. They carried a knife or a leather-encased tomahawk hanging from their belts.

The Indians who sometimes passed by were peaceable enough. Their only interests seemed to be hunting or fighting other tribes. Occasionally, they stopped without invitation. On these occasions Margaret Lynn would offer them food and drink. Afterwards, they smoked their pipes and then quietly disappeared into the woods. Their ability to speak English was limited. On arriving, they would say, "I am come," and when they left, "I go."[4] Their intentions were never clear. Margaret Lynn was glad when John added a half stone, half wood extension at one end of their log house to provide protection in case the Indians attacked. Bellefont, then, soon became Fort Lewis.

Four years after John and Margaret Lynn's arrival in the Valley, they had their seventh child, their New World baby, Charles. Margaret Lynn was forty-three; John was fifty-eight. Charles' brothers and sisters ranged in age from eight-year-old Anne to twenty-year-old Samuel. By that time, sixty other families lived in the area.

John Lewis was a vigorous man. With his family settled, he pursued his interest in obtaining land. In 1736, the year of Charles' birth, King George II granted William Beverly of eastern Virginia 118,000 acres of land lying between the Blue Ridge and the Alleghenies. The English wanted to see the land settled, hoping that would prevent the French from moving into Virginia from the west. They also wanted it to be a place from which settlers could move westward into the Allegheny Mountains. Some Scotch-Irish settlers believed that the eastern Virginia Anglicans wanted the Irish Presbyterians to protect them from the Indians. Of course, Beverly wanted to sell land to those already there and to bring new settlers to his property, which he called Beverly Manor. He became a frequent guest at Bellefont and became beholden to John for entertaining and encouraging settlers to buy land. Margaret Lynn was expected to feed the many passers-by. But John received his reward, the right to acquire 2,000 acres for fourteen pounds, thus becoming the largest landowner in the manor. The colonial government appointed John to the position of captain, expecting him to protect the expanding population. They sent him muskets and pistols to accomplish the task.

Margaret Lynn's first cousin, James Patton, also became involved in Beverly Manor. As a sea captain, he had met William Beverly at Beverly's plantation on the Rappahannock River. Cousin James, not particularly discriminating in his choice of passengers, hauled settlers, indentured servants, sometimes even convicts sent by the English government and slaves to eastern Virginia. On the return trip to England, he carried tobacco bales from the plantations and furs from west of the Blue Ridge. But Cousin James was looking for other ventures, and he, Beverly, and John became partners. John and James liked to compete with each other. To keep peace, they worked the opposite ends of their land ventures. Patton concentrated on the James, Roanoke, and New Rivers to the south, and John worked the Cowpasture, the Jackson, and the Greenbrier Rivers north to the headwaters of the Potomac.

Another visitor to Bellefont was Benjamin Borden, an agent for Lord Fairfax. John met Borden in Williamsburg and invited him to come to Augusta County to hunt. On one of their forays they captured a buffalo calf that Borden tamed and took to Williamsburg to Governor Gooch. The pet so pleased the governor, who generously gave land to those he favored, that he granted to Mr. Borden property bordering Beverly Manor.

John wanted to develop land of his own. He obtained a grant of 30,000 acres west of Beverly Manor on the Cowpasture River with the requirement that he settle one family per 1,000 acres. He received another 30,000 acres even farther west and put it in the name of his sons Thomas and Andrew, aged twenty-one and nineteen at the time. This was the Lewis Grant. Thomas and Andrew, with young Charles tagging along, later surveyed the property before the French and Indian War interrupted their work. From the Lewis Grant, Charles, at age fourteen, received 1,000 acres in the Cowpasture River Valley. There he would later settle and raise a family.

Further expanding his land interests, John became a charter member of both the Greenbrier and Loyal land companies. The

Loyal Company's 800,000 acres bordered North Carolina and extended in a generally northwestern direction across southwest Virginia into the Alleghenies. John served as chief sales agent. The Greenbrier Company tract went even farther west than the property that Thomas and Andrew received, extending into what is now West Virginia. John listed himself and sons William and Charles as members of the company.

John originated the Greenbrier name, which would be attached first to a river, then a company, a county, and later a famous resort hotel.[5] At the ripe age of seventy, John and son Andrew were exploring to the west in the Alleghenies. They were working their way along a river. John and his horse, according to the story, became entangled in a thicket of briars. I imagine John saying, *"Goddamn it. We're going to name this river the Greenbrier. Andrew, write that name down in your surveying notes."* Margaret Lynn probably told John that at his age he should stick to the sales end of the land ventures and leave the exploring to his boys.

Son Thomas surveyed the southern boundary of Lord Fairfax's six million acres in order to resolve the continuing squabbles over the boundary between Beverly Manor and the Fairfax lands. Thomas—with forty men and assisted by Peter Jefferson, Thomas Jefferson's father—spent a winter defining a seventy-five mile line from the source of the Rappahannock in the Blue Ridge across the Shenandoah Valley to the source of the Potomac in the Alleghenies. George Washington also joined Thomas' surveying team.

Andrew surveyed as well. He spent several years laying out the 50,000-acre Greenbrier tract, keeping 4,000 acres for himself. He discovered a spring that became known as Lewis Spring. Eventually this became the site of Lewisburg.

In 1740 famine hit Ireland. More Scotch-Irish came to America, many migrating from Philadelphia down the Old Wagon Road into the Valley. This boosted John's land business. With the expanding population, the Virginia Colony formed Augusta to the south and Frederick to the north as the first two counties west of the Blue Ridge Mountains. Augusta's boundaries, in theory, extended infinitely west to the Mississippi River.

When at last a semblance of government came to the wilderness, John and Thomas became two of the original Justices of the Peace of Augusta County. The county court began to dispense justice. One of the first cases involved one of Thomas' slaves, a man named Hampton. The man attempted to rape a white woman. To prevent any further activity of this nature, Thomas asked if Hampton might be "dismembered."[6] The court approved, providing that a skillful person did the "dismemberment".

Establishing a town became the next step. While John sometimes gets credit for choosing the location (two miles from Bellefont), it was Mr. Beverly who built a rough log courthouse on that spot. Thomas, as county surveyor, prepared a layout with forty-seven lots, including the streets of Beverly, Frederick, and, of course, Lewis, all of which exist today. In fact, as the town expanded, Washington, Jefferson, and Madison Streets were added beyond and parallel to Lewis Street, an indication that Lewis came before the nation's founders. By 1749, the town had been named Staunton after Governor Gooch's wife, Lady Staunton. At this time the population of the Virginia colony was 80,000, with only a few hundred of that number settled west of the Blue Ridge.

The Presbyterian Church also had arrived in the Valley. After all, the Scotch-Irish came to America for religious freedom. A Presbyterian minister, Mr. James Anderson of Philadelphia, preached the first sermon to be heard in the county of Augusta in the hall at Bellefont. He lived with the Lewis family, preaching the gospel and traveling about the county. Governor Gooch, despite being an Episcopalian, approved of Anderson's visit. The Church of England had long been established in eastern Virginia, but there seemed to be no concern in Williamsburg about the Scotch-Irish Presbyterians starting their own churches in western Virginia. No Episcopalian priests ventured beyond the Blue Ridge so there was little choice but to let the Presbyterians worship as they wished. In Ulster it would have been different. The settlers established meeting houses like Tinkling Spring. These houses served as schools with the ministers as teachers. Margaret Lynn and John, however, sent William and Charles to eastern Virginia to be educated by a Reverend Waddell. In 1749, Augusta Academy, a more formal school, was instituted a few miles to the south of Staunton. Lewis men served as its early trustees. The school later became Liberty Hall and eventually Washington and Lee University.

The Reverend John Craig, who started the Tinkling Spring Meeting House, had some problems with John and Colonel James Patton, the former ship captain and partner with John in Beverly Manor. The two men squabbled with each other about the land business and on matters pertaining to the church. Each had a different opinion as to how and where the meeting house should be built. The arguing went on for years. Reverend Craig wrote that he "could neither bring them to friendship with each other nor obtain both their friendships at once."[7] Later, Colonel Patton was murdered by Indians. The Reverend, however, had made peace with Patton before his death, and afterwards, he wrote; "Col. Lewis was friendly to me till he died."

Bellefont remained a busy place with many people visiting. Imagine the marriage of daughter Margaret Lynn, her mother's namesake, to William Long.[8] The Scotch-Irish loved weddings and people would have come from all around. Horses and wagons filled the field next to the house. A wedding became an excuse, though hardly needed, to consume much corn whiskey. Per the marriage custom, the young fellows raced on horseback at breakneck speed for a bottle of whiskey with a white ribbon around its neck. John, the father of the bride, probably stood in a field on the next hill over from the house with the bottle in his outstretched hand as the riders cantered toward him. The one arriving first got to kiss the bride. It is probable that one of the Lewis brothers won, but he would not have been much interested in kissing his sister. After the wedding ceremony, the women spread a feast on wooden tables surrounding the house. John spoke. Toasts were made, and, following another custom, one of the bride's shoes was stolen. In addition to the corn whiskey, the men consumed great quantities of blackberry wine and spruce beer. Some mixed whiskey with the beer. Afterwards, everyone danced. The couple bedded down in an upstairs room accompanied by shouts and loud jokes about the size of the family they would have. The evening ended with a shivaree, a serenade of the bridal couple by beating on skillets and pots.

While a social structure existed in Ireland, the class system had been left behind in the migration to western Virginia. All the settlers were much alike in that they had to start with nothing, clear the land, build their houses, and plant the fields. That a family had wealth or a distinctive heritage, as did Margaret Lynn in Ireland and Scotland, meant nothing in the wilderness. But social differences gradually reappeared based on what a person accomplished as an individual. Though the Lewis family left behind whatever distinctions they held in Ireland, they gained status in the colonies, through John's leadership and later those of his sons. In eastern Virginia the social distinctions were already well developed. But the people—

who had plantations, lives as ladies and gentlemen, the Anglican Church, and the College of William and Mary—had arrived in America a hundred years before the Scotch-Irish. As John proved in his dealings with Governor Gooch, Mr. Beverly, and Mr. Borden, Scotch-Irish men were capable and proud, and could handle themselves in both the colonial capital of Williamsburg and in the wilderness of the Alleghenies.

Despite John's age, his dignified position in Augusta County and in the land companies, he could still get himself into trouble. In Staunton, probably at a tavern, John laid down his shillelagh on a table. A fellow from the other side of the Blue Ridge picked it up to admire it. He was a Tuckahoe, a name applied to those from eastern Virginia.[9] The name came from a root eaten by early settlers in the lowlands along the coast. This led to a confrontation that may have gone like this:

"Tuckahoe," John said, "the custom in this part of the country is that when you pick up another man's weapon you must either fight or retreat."

The Tuckahoe responded, "I'll be dammed if I will retreat and, if you so wish, Sir, I am ready to fight."

"So be it," said John.

The two men went outside. Each cut himself a long hickory stick. They stood facing each other with cudgels touching. A group of onlookers gathered. At the ready the Tuckahoe swung mightily. On contact with John's weapon, the Tuckahoe's stick broke. The loose end hit John in the head. He fell to the ground, and the fight was over. John may have told Margaret Lynn that the knot on his head came from bumping into a tree. But in Staunton the truth would have been known. His sons certainly suggested that he was a bit old to be engaging in cudgel matches.

At first the Indians didn't bother the settlers as they passed through to hunt in the Valley. But by 1750, as more people arrived, the Indians realized that they were being pushed out of their hunting grounds. The French had taken over the land in the Ohio Valley, and they encouraged the Indians to join them in fighting the English settlers who were moving farther west.

As the Indian threat increased, John became a colonel with responsibility for the militia of Augusta County. Every man over twenty-one, except civil officials and Quakers, served. Each man kept a gun, gunpowder, and ammunition at his home. Each would go to his church meeting house for muster and training. All the Lewis sons except Thomas, a civil official and thus exempt, joined the militia. That was just as well. It was said of Thomas that with his poor eyesight he couldn't tell an Indian from a settler at twenty paces. The Lewis home now became Fort Lewis and served as a shelter to the neighbors who feared Indian attacks.

Supposedly, the Indians attacked Fort Lewis.[10] At the time, all the Lewis sons were away on the frontier and the servants were gone. John Lewis, at eighty, stood at a porthole on the fort end of the house and fired away with Margaret Lynn reloading his guns at his side. The couple withstood a six-hour assault, and John shot several of the intruders. Then the servants returned and the Indians raced away. This story may be an exaggeration as there is no record of any Indian raid so close to Staunton. Instead, an Indian party may have approached the house asking for supplies as they typically did. Perhaps, when the Indians became insistent, some shots were fired from the fort to encourage their departure.

John Lewis died in 1762 at the age of eighty-four. His family buried him on the hill beyond the house. People came from all around, even as far away as Williamsburg. They praised John as a man of "heroic courage," "formed to excel in war," "an ardent friend of progress," "wise in his conceptions," "equally adapted to peace," "irreproachable in his public and private morals," "courteous, affable and eloquent, fond of society, and a splendid conversationalist."[11] Margaret Lynn knew him as impetuous, stubborn, vigorous, tall and muscular, with a manly beauty. At age fifty, he had started a new life in a new world and became a leader in its development.

After his death historians called John Lewis "The Founder" and the "Lord of the Hills." His sons carried his legacy forward—developing the frontier, fighting the Indians in the French and Indian War, serving in the colonial government, and participating in the Revolutionary War.

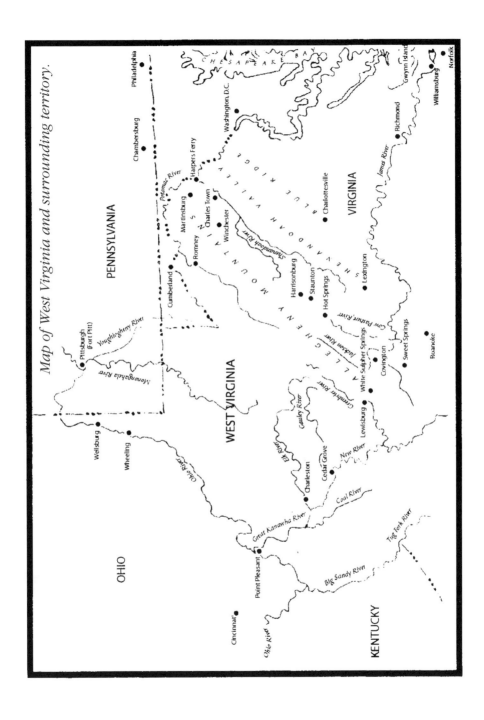

3

LEWISBURG

Two routes lead into West Virginia from Staunton. One is the interstate, the other a winding, two lane state road. Parts of both carry the Lewis name.

On I-81 out of Staunton, the southbound lane is the John Lewis Highway, the northbound lane, the Andrew Lewis Memorial Highway. Just before Lexington, I-64 splits off from I-81, leaving the Shenandoah Valley, and heading into the Alleghenies. As I drive westward, I feel as if I am going into another world, that I am going home. There is an attraction to the mountains that I didn't know existed until I returned to West Virginia after many years in Florida. I-64 follows creeks, crosses rivers, sweeps around the sides of mountains, overlooks deep valleys, passes between high ridges, and climbs over the Eastern Continental Divide, before entering the Greenbrier Valley and Lewisburg. It is certainly one of the prettiest seventy-mile stretches of interstate in the United States.

John Lewis and his sons traveled a more direct route as they explored and surveyed their Allegheny lands. By foot and horseback, they headed west from Staunton, entering the mountains at Buffalo Gap. Following animal and Indian trails through thick forests, they crossed the Cowpasture River valley between mountain ridges 3,000 to 4,000 feet high. They climbed over Warm Springs Mountain into Warm Springs Valley and followed the Jackson River south to present-day Covington. At Covington, they turned west to climb the Divide, passing through the same gap I-64 travels to reach the Greenbrier River. By the late 1700s, this route became the pioneer path to the Kanawha River and on to Ohio and Kentucky. It was one of the spurs westward from the Shenandoah Valley's Great Wagon Road.

Returning to Lewisburg from Staunton, I took the two-lane road that follows the old trail. It is named the Andrew Lewis and Charles Lewis Highway. It runs through one of the Lewis land grants. Andrew, Thomas, and Charles served time in small frontier forts in the area, one of which was Fort Dickinson. Adam Dickinson settled there and built the fort. His son, Colonel John Dickinson, served with Charles at the Battle of Point Pleasant, and Adam's granddaughter married Charles' son. A roadside marker notes that the fort was attacked by Indians in 1756.

A few miles off the highway, upstream on the Cowpasture River, Charles built his home. Like his father's place near Staunton, he named it Fort Lewis. I visited the site, which is now the Fort Lewis Lodge. The two-story building is uniquely attached to a silo and has adjacent cabins. Nearby, an old home sits on a knoll where Charles Lewis built the original house and fort. From there Charles could view the Cowpasture Valley and his 950-acre farm acquired in the 1750s.

After stopping at Fort Lewis, I returned to the Lewis Highway, which winds its way up Warm Springs Mountain. From the top looking eastward, I noticed the valley appeared almost empty. There probably aren't many more people living there now than in Charles' time. But on the western side where Warm Springs and Hot Springs are situated, it's different. In this valley I passed the old brick Bath County Court House; the original springs, still available for baths; the elegant country estates with their white fences that sweep up the lower reaches of the surrounding mountains; the brick tower and cupola of the Homestead Hotel, rising majestically above the trees; and the surrounding, manicured golf courses. Like the Greenbrier, the Homestead is one of the original old Virginia spring resorts, and both are still popular, two hundred years later.

Andrew Lewis is credited with discovering Warm Springs and Hot Springs. The Lewis family acquired the initial legal title to the area in 1751 with the agreement they establish a hotel. With brother Thomas and partner, Thomas Bullitt, Andrew built the first Homestead, probably nothing more than a log house. Settlers stopped there as they headed west. Bullitt ran the hotel. Andrew quickly departed the partnership to deal with more pressing military matters. A roadside marker in Warm Springs states that the county court first met in 1791 at the house of John Lewis' widow Margaret, who donated two acres for public use. While this acknowledges the Lewis presence, it's inaccurate. Margaret Lynn had died eighteen years earlier in Staunton.

Driving on, I stopped at a marker on a mountain overlook. It indicated that through the valley below immigrants passed, going west to the Kanawha Valley and the Mississippi basin. In Covington

I drove by the huge paper mill and got on I-64. I crossed the Jackson, which flows by way of the James River east to the Atlantic. In a half hour I passed over the Divide and crossed the Greenbrier, flowing west by way of the New, the Kanawha, into the Ohio.

I entered Lewisburg on Washington Street, lined with tree-shaded lawns and large, pre-Civil War homes. Men with salt fortunes built some of these houses so their families could escape the summer heat of the Kanawha Valley, a hundred miles farther west.

I live a few blocks off Washington Street in a modified, two-story log house, located in a meadow on the edge of town. The log portion dates back to 1800. Sitting in the living room with its stone fireplace, hand-hewn log walls and rough beams, it's easy to visualize the past.

Settlers arrived in the Greenbrier Valley as early as 1760, but were driven out by Indian attacks. Chief Cornstalk massacred families in 1763 near Muddy Creek Mountain just west of Lewisburg. The settlers returned, but two hundred Indians attacked nearby Fort Donnally in 1777. Colonel Samuel Lewis, son of Andrew, rushed to the rescue and saved the settlers. Names from those times, like Arbuckle, Stuart, and Tuckwiller, are still common in the community today. With the Indian menace gone, Conestoga wagons, pulled by oxen and carrying people and supplies westward, rumbled through the newly established town. During the Civil War the area changed hands several times. At the Battle of Lewisburg in 1862, the Yankees defeated the Confederates in a fight that raged across the town. Advancing Confederate soldiers marched by the log house that I now live in, as they positioned themselves for the battle. The stone remains of a Confederate gun emplacement lie up the hill, overlooking Lewisburg.

Downtown Lewisburg's extensive historic district includes, on the east side, the General Lewis Inn and the Osteopathic School, formerly the Greenbrier Military School. On the west side is a campus-like setting surrounded by historic buildings: the community college, formerly Greenbrier Women's College; Carnegie Hall, named for its benefactor, Andrew Carnegie; the Old Stone Presbyterian Church and its cemetery, the first church established west of the Alleghenies; the North House historical museum, and the 1834 library building. Up the hill is a Civil War cemetery.

The main street has changed over the years. Gone are the grocery store, drug store, auto dealership, and department stores, all of which have joined Wal-Mart on the outskirts of the community.

Photo by the author

Instead, there are antique and gift shops, real estate offices, restaurants, City Hall, and the Greenbrier Valley Theater for performing arts. Many of the businesses are situated in buildings with early 1800 dates on their fronts. This four-block stretch remains a busy place.

By the library is a historical marker commemorating the founding of Lewisburg in 1782 and "Gen. Andrew Lewis who mustered troops which participated in the Battle of Point Pleasant, 1774." What that sign doesn't mention is that Andrew had been to the Lewisburg area almost twenty-five years earlier on one of his surveying jaunts and had discovered the Lewis Spring. It is located just beyond Lewisburg's main intersection of Washington and Jefferson Streets at the rear of the courthouse in the Lewis Spring-Andrew Lewis Park. This once prolific spring attracted the first settlers, and they built cabins around it. The spring has been enclosed in a small stone building for almost two hundred years and is considered unsafe. The grate covering the entrance to the stone building is locked, but water still bubbles up inside. This small park was the site of Fort Savannah, one of the early Indian forts on the frontier. It was later named Camp Union, the place where General Andrew Lewis, Colonel Charles Lewis, and a thousand western Virginians rendezvoused before marching across the mountains and down the Kanawha to battle the Indians and their leader, Chief Cornstalk, at Point Pleasant.

There, on the banks of the Ohio, Andrew gained military fame, and his younger brother Charles lost his life.

4

INDIAN FIGHTERS

Charles Lewis felt a knife prodding him in the back as the Indians pushed him along. The deerskin thongs around his wrists cut into his flesh. The rocky trail bruised his bare feet. Indians walked ahead, behind, and alongside him, taking him farther westward to their village across the Ohio. Charles had been hunting in the mountains west of his Staunton home, and the Indians had ambushed him. There had been tales of Indian attacks, but he did not think they would attack in the area where he hunted.

The path that the party followed broke out of the trees and ran along the top of an embankment that dropped down into a creek bed. Charles sensed his chance. He ducked his shoulder and rammed one of his captors in the chest, knocking him flat. Charles leaped over the side of the embankment. As he tumbled down the bank, he broke his bounds with a great surge of strength. He plunged through a stream. The Indians were close behind. He leapt over a fallen tree, tripped, and collapsed into tall grass. The Indians jumped the tree but didn't see Charles, and ran ahead into the woods, looking for him. Their yells receded into the distance. Charles stayed still. After a while, he started to rise but suddenly froze. Coiled by his body lay an enormous rattlesnake. The snake's fangs almost touched his face; the rattle buzzed by his ear. Then sudden quiet. He felt the snake slither across his legs and move off. Charles figured the snake must have thought him dead. Barefooted, unarmed, and with little to eat, Charles trudged back across the mountains to Bellefont.

This youngest son of John Lewis may have been the first Lewis to have had a serious run-in with the Indians.[1]

In 1749, a French expedition placed plate markers along the Ohio. They put one at the mouth of the Kanawha, claiming all lands drained by that river for France. The French controlled Canada, the Mississippi to its mouth, and the Ohio Valley. They feared the

British settlers would advance into their territory and had convinced the Indians to help them in holding back the colonists. In that same year, Indians attacked settlers at Drapers Ferry near present-day Blacksburg, Virginia. That was the first attack launched across the mountains. Beginning to feel the pressure from a migration of people who insisted on settling on their hunting grounds, the Indians, encouraged initially by the French, started a war against the settlers on the Allegheny frontier that lasted forty years.

The Indian attacks and the French land ambitions led Governor Dinwiddie, who had replaced Governor Gooch in Williamsburg, to send twenty-one-year-old George Washington across the Ohio to warn the French that they must withdraw. The French refused. The governor ordered Washington to return with a group of Virginia volunteers. Amongst these men was Andrew Lewis, recently appointed a captain of militia. Thus began a relationship between Andrew and George that would last through the Revolutionary War. At Great Meadows the Virginia volunteers built Fort Necessity, a small stockade located south of what is now Pittsburgh. A thousand French and Indians attacked the fort. George Washington's force fought bravely and barely held out. Many were killed on both sides. Andrew was wounded. A heavy rain fell and the French called a truce. Andrew may well have avoided a massacre as the forces mixed after the truce. One of the militiamen raised his gun to shoot a nearby Indian. Andrew deflected the gun, saving the Indian's life.[2] The French let the Virginians go, and Andrew returned to the Augusta frontier to build forts that would help protect Staunton and the county from possible attacks.

The following year, 1755, Samuel Lewis and his younger brothers, William and Charles, as part of four hundred Virginia militia, marched with General Braddock's army of 1,400 Redcoats toward Fort Duquesne, now Pittsburgh, to fight the French and the Shawnees.[3] As a captain, Samuel led a company that included William and Charles. Andrew, at the time, was stationed in one of the frontier forts to the south. George Washington rode with Braddock as his aide.

Braddock's army marched into the thick forests of the Allegheny Mountains following the trail leading to Fort Duquesne.[4] The woods in August were stifling. Sweat poured down Charles' back. He and William walked side by side with Samuel, their commander, as the Virginia volunteers led the way. Behind followed the Redcoats and

Portrait of Andrew Lewis, from the *West Virginia Historical Magazine*, 1904

their general, Braddock. Charles, now nineteen, said to Samuel, "That English general wouldn't know a Shawnee if he saw one."

"Colonel Washington and I have talked with him," said Samuel. "We told him this was not the way to attack the Indians, that you don't march an army en mass through the mountains, but he won't listen. He thinks he is fighting the French on the plains of Europe, two great armies facing each other along a battle line where they fight like gentlemen. He doesn't know that you must fight the Indians with Indian ways – surprise attack, burn their villages, kill them. He doesn't understand the word ambush."

"This army sounds like a herd of stampeding buffalo. Every Indian east of the Mississippi must know we are coming," said Charles.

They marched on. The Redcoats, in their formal uniforms, stepped stiffly along, rifles on their shoulders, eyes straight ahead. Samuel, Charles and William in their buckskins, with the rifles at the ready, looked from side to side. The ambush was inevitable.

The force crossed the Monongahela River; Samuel's company led the way. They proceeded up a ravine that cut into the face of a cliff. Charles sensed trouble. He looked at Samuel. Suddenly, rifle shots ricocheted amongst them. The French and Indians lay concealed in the grass on top of the cliff. The troops sought cover. Braddock tried to reform his Redcoats and the volunteers. The Indians rushed down from the heights into the ravine, attacking with tomahawks. Braddock attempted to wheel his forces about to face the enemy, but they were caught between the cliffs and the river. Close infighting with bayonets, tomahawks, and scalping knives resulted in a horrible slaughter. Charles and William found their brother Samuel dead with a gunshot wound to his chest. General Braddock was wounded and died. Charles suffered a flesh wound. The militiamen, led by Colonel Washington, finally established a defensive line, preventing a further massacre and allowing an escape by swimming and rafting across the river.

William and Charles brought Samuel's body home to Bellefont where he was buried on the hill. There, his father would later join him.

The Lewis family received another shock when Indians killed Margaret Lynn's cousin James Patton. He was on land business, visiting at Drapers Meadows on the New River. While he was writing at a desk in the Draper home, the Indians burst into the room. Patton, being a large man of great strength, rose and swung his broad sword, killing two Indians. But another Indian, whom he could not reach, shot him. The Indians shot Mrs. Draper in the arm and crushed the skull of her infant child. Three other settlers were killed. After stealing all the weapons and burning the house, the Indians kidnapped a man, two women, and two children. One of the women was Mary Draper Ingles who became a frontier legend by escaping from the Indians on the Ohio and finding her way across the mountains and down the New River Gorge to return the seven hundred miles home in forty days.[5]

Within the year after Braddock's Defeat and the Drapers Meadow massacre, the Colony of Virginia mounted an attack against the Indians. Led by Andrew Lewis, three hundred men of the Virginia militia and one hundred friendly Cherokees marched from southwest Virginia into the mountains, with a plan to follow Sandy Creek to the Ohio, and to attack the Indian villages across the river. The area, a trackless wilderness, lay along what is now the border between West Virginia and Kentucky. No Redcoats accompanied the force, and this time the Indians would not know the Virginians were approaching.

Trouble came quickly. Andrew became disgusted when Captain Hogg's company joined the force late. During the wait for Hogg, the men consumed their fifteen-day food supply. Game was scarce. The force became bogged down in the winter snows of February and by flooding creeks. The men turned mutinous, and Hogg believed that he should be the leader. Andrew wanted to proceed, but received orders from Governor Dinwiddie to cancel the expedition. Utterly disgusted and with a disgruntled army, Andrew turned the force around to troop back home over three hundred miles of mountains. The men became so desperate for food that they boiled tugs of hide from their buffalo robes. Thus came the name of Tug Fork of Sandy, which they followed on their return trip.[6]

The officials in Williamsburg criticized Andrew, but only through his leadership did the men get back home. Andrew was an impressive man, tall and well-formed, but "austere and reserved and seldom known to smile."[7] At times he appeared haughty to his men, and they did not always understand his ways. However, a Cherokee chief with the expedition wrote the governor that in battle there was no other man that he would rather be with than Andrew Lewis.

Braddock's Defeat and the Sandy Creek Expedition became preludes to the French and Indian War. Britain finally decided to take the French intrusion into the Ohio more seriously and, because of other problems between the two European countries, declared war on France in 1756. Historians called this the Seven Years War in Europe and the French and Indian War in America.

The British appointed George Washington the Commander-in-Chief of the Virginia forces, and he selected Andrew as a major under him. The Virginians rarely fought a battle, other than protecting their frontier from the Indians. Charles served as a lieutenant, stationed in one of the forts along the Virginia Colony's frontier.

Andrew, however, became immediately involved in the war. He led a group of men to build a road over the mountains so that a large English force under General Forbes could again try to capture Fort Duquesne. British Major James Grant of the Scots Highlanders convinced his immediate superior to let him lead a preliminary attack on the fort. Andrew thought this unwise but was ordered to join Grant. Andrew's men marched in the rear, since the British considered the Virginians inferior to their own troops. On approaching the fort, the Indians charged out of ambush and attacked Major Grant and his Highlanders. Andrew left men to protect the baggage and rushed forward to help Grant. Andrew fought a hand-to-hand battle with an Indian, whom he killed. But he eventually had to surrender to save his life. Grant also surrendered, and both he and Andrew became prisoners of the French.

Grant, seeking a scapegoat for the loss, sent a message to the English general saying that the defeat, which had a similarity to Braddock's, was Andrew's fault. The French captured the messenger and read the report in front of Grant and Andrew.

Andrew looked at the English major and said, "You lying bastard." Andrew then unsheathed his sword, "I'll take care of you. Pull your sword." Grant didn't move. Andrew spat in Grant's face.[8]

At Bellefont, John and Margaret Lynn Lewis received a message from George Washington. Their son Andrew was missing and presumed dead. Margaret Lynn thought that she had lost another son. Andrew's wife, Elizabeth, was pregnant with her fourth child when she received the news. The baby was born shortly thereafter, and Elizabeth named him after his missing father.

Time passed; another message arrived, stating that Andrew was alive. He and his French captors had marched from Fort Duquesne to Lake Erie, paddled the 150-mile length of Lake Ontario, and then traveled down the St. Lawrence River to Montreal. The journey took several weeks. Later, the French moved Andrew to Quebec. The next year, English General Wolfe attacked Quebec and, while defeating the French, lost his life. This defeat led to an exchange of French and English prisoners; one was Andrew. He came home after a year away, rejoined the Virginia Regiment, and spent time in Tennessee, attempting to keep the Cherokees at peace.

The English won battles in New York and Canada and regained Fort Duquesne. These losses and other defeats in Europe led the French to end the war and to sign the Treaty of Paris in 1763, giving to England the Territory of Canada, the Ohio Valley and all other land east of the Mississippi.

The war with France may have been over, but the Indians remained a continuing menace as the settlers again pushed westward into the Alleghenies and beyond. Shawnee Chief Cornstalk, leading sixty braves, approached the Greenbrier settlements at Muddy Creek and Big Levels near what would become Lewisburg. The Indians acted friendly, but then killed or captured every man, woman, and child. They wiped out both communities, including fifty people at Big Levels. Cornstalk moved eastward to hit the Jackson River settlers (near Covington), and farther on to the Kerr Creek settlements at the edge of the Shenandoah Valley (near Lexington). These attacks resulted from a confederation of Indian tribes in the Mississippi Valley led by Chief Pontiac. The Indians also laid siege to Fort Pitt, the former French outpost of Fort Duquesne.

In 1763, King George stunned the Virginians. He placed a ban on all settlements west of the Allegheny Mountains, hoping to maintain peace with the Indians. Most of the Loyal Company and all the Greenbrier land, which Andrew now worked, lay west of the divide. The settlers ignored the ban. They stayed on their land but refused to pay their quitrents or rents. Since the King said the land belonged to the Indians, not them, the settlers felt they had no obligation to pay. Andrew, his brother Thomas, and their partner, Thomas Bullitt, ignored the ban as well. They went ahead with their plans to develop Warm Springs and Hot Springs.

At the end of the French and Indian War, Andrew quit his service with the English military, disgusted that he had never been promoted beyond the rank of major. He returned to his land business. But Augusta County recruited him to be county lieutenant to put together militia forces to continue to protect the frontier. The

Indian threat became so bad again that the movement of people down the Shenandoah Valley all but ceased. The killing could have been worse in Augusta, where, by then, two thousand families lived. But with experienced Indian fighters like Andrew and Charles and the line of forts through the mountains, the county remained protected.

With the men Andrew recruited, the English launched another expedition, this one commanded by Colonel Henry Bouquet. It was to counter the continuing Indian wars led by Chief Pontiac. Andrew stayed behind, but Charles served as one of the three captains of the Virginia volunteers. Andrew's son John was also a member of the 1,500-man force. They marched across the Ohio to the Forks of the Muskingum River, north of what is Marietta, Ohio. The size of this army so overwhelmed the Indians that they declared peace. They released all the settlers they had been holding prisoner, some for as long as ten years. Charles led home a group of fifty women and children, many of whom he knew. They arrived on Christmas day.

With John gone, Margaret Lynn continued to live at Bellefont with her fourth son William and his family. William was very different in personality from his brother Andrew, though they had done some exploration together, particularly in the Sweet Springs Valley. William was vigorous, handsome of face, and fond of books. He attended medical school in Philadelphia, where he met his wife, Anne Montgomery. He and Anne returned to Bellefont just in time for him to participate in Braddock's Defeat. Afterwards, he stayed close to Bellefont, managing his elderly parents' affairs. Thirty years later he would serve in the Revolutionary War, despite his age and being described as being quiet and domesticated.

The second son, Thomas, lived at Lynnwood across the valley on the western edge of the Blue Ridge next to property owned by George Washington and James Madison. He had married Jane Strathers from eastern Virginia near Fredericksburg. With his bad vision, Thomas concentrated on his municipal and legislative duties and, like Andrew and Charles, served in the House of Burgesses in Williamsburg.

Andrew, with his wife, Elizabeth Anne Givens, would soon move to a place on the Roanoke River in Botetourt County (near Roanoke). Andrew was elected from Botetourt to the House of Burgesses, which with his land business, kept him busy.

Margaret Lynn's namesake, daughter Margaret Lynn, lived in Staunton

Photo by the author

with her second husband, William Crow. Also born in Ulster, daughter Anne married Michael Findly, and moved to Pennsylvania.

The youngest member of the family, Charles, had recently married Sarah Murray who was from New York. They built a home on a knoll on his land by the Cowpasture River. As a boy, he had accompanied Thomas and Andrew on surveying trips in that area and later had been stationed nearby at Fort Dickinson. He considered the area fairly safe from the Indians until Pontiac started his war and the Shawnees, under Cornstalk, raided the Greenbrier and Jackson River settlements not too far to the west. Charles converted his home to a palisaded fort, and, like his father, called his house Fort Lewis. As the baby of the family, Charles was a special favorite of all. He was a slimmer version of his brothers, the most easy-going and quick to smile. He inherited the amiable and charming traits of his father but not the pugnaciousness.

The Lewis family enjoyed a wonderful surprise shortly after Charles and John, Andrew's son, returned from their expedition with Colonel Bouquet. Young John received a letter from English General Gage, notifying him that he had been given a commission

Detail of painting of Charles Lewis that hangs at the Hubbard House. *Courtesy Charles Stacy*

in the regular English army. His father, Andrew, had wanted such a commission as well but had never received one. Nor had George Washington received one either. The English seemed to look down on their frontier soldiers. In fact, the English referred to Andrew as Paddy because of his Irish background. However, young John's commission showed that, indeed, English General Gage and Colonel Bouquet respected Andrew's military role and had honored him through his son. It was unfortunate that John Lewis had not lived long enough to join in the family celebration at Bellefont with his grandson.

Margaret Lynn could look upon her sons and grandsons and be proud. From the marriages of her children, came over forty grandchildren. Of course, she feared for her sons and grandsons. The Indian attacks continued, and the troubles with England never seemed to cease. The English had imposed taxes (the Stamp Act and the Townsend Act) on the colonies to pay for the war with the French and Indians. The colonies, however, declared that there could be no taxation without representation. In Boston, British soldiers killed protesting colonists. Virginia boycotted English goods. Andrew, as a representative in the House of Burgesses in Williamsburg, supported Patrick Henry who said, "If this is treason, make the most of it." If war came with England, Margaret Lynn knew that her sons and grandsons would fight.

In 1773, Margaret Lynn Lewis died and joined her husband, John, and son, Samuel, on the hill by Bellefont. Almost a hundred years later, it was reported that Margaret Lynn's long lost diary had been found. It appeared as, "The Commonplace Book of Margaret Lynn Lewis" in a North Carolina magazine. It described, among other things, her husband, John, slaying the "Irish Lord," the kidnapping of a daughter "Alice" by an Indian chief's son who wanted to marry her, and Charles's death at Point Pleasant. Many Lewis descendants greeted this document with great excitement. But according to an article in the *Richmond Times Dispatch* in 1948, the document was a hoax.[9] Margaret Lynn had no daughter named Alice, and she had died the year before Charles was killed so could hardly have known of his death. The document was attributed to Fanny Farmer, a name used by Mary Jane Seith Upshur, who contributed to the literary magazines of the time.

King George's ban on westward expansion continued for several more years. In the meantime the colonial government in Williamsburg, with undoubtedly some prodding from House of Burgess Delegate Andrew Lewis, wanted to establish a western boundary for Virginia and get rid of the confusion over the King James' ban. The legislature appointed Andrew and his friend Dr. Tom Walker, who ran the Loyal Company, to meet with Sir William Johnson, the King's Superintendent of Indian Affairs in the North. The purpose was to buy land from the Iroquois and to set a permanent boundary with the Cherokees.

During the negotiations at Sir William's estate in upstate New York, Andrew made quite an impression. The governor of New York said, "He looked like the genius of the forest, and the very ground seemed to tremble under him as he walked along."[10] The Iroquois agreed to sell their land. However, the Cherokees still had a right to part of the Iroquois land. So Andrew went to Tennessee to meet with the Cherokees. He found that John Stewart, the King's Superintendent of Indian Affairs in the South, had already negotiated a treaty with the Cherokees. This treaty drew a line from eastern Tennessee straight north to the Ohio, cutting by more than half the land supposedly obtained from the Cherokees. Loyal Company land extended beyond this line and had settlers on it. Andrew was livid. With Williamsburg's support, he went to see Stewart, but to no avail. He even convinced the Cherokee chief, whom he knew from the Sandy Creek Expedition, to agree to move the line, but Stewart wouldn't budge.

Stewart sent an emissary to Williamsburg, and the governor decided to no longer fight the issue. After a two-year squabble, a treaty was signed in 1770, placing Virginia's boundary no farther west than the mouth of the Kanawha. The feelings between Andrew and Stewart remained so strong that the two men considered a "gentlemen's redress" or duel. Fortunately, the distance separating the men, South Carolina to Virginia, discouraged further animosity.

Meanwhile, Charles prospered on his 950 acres on the Cowpasture River.[11] In 1773 he produced 2,374 pounds of hemp, the highest total in that part of Virginia. His work force consisted of six black slaves, two mulattos, and a white indentured servant. He had 45 cattle, 43 sheep, and 50 hogs plus 26 horses. The will and inventory he had prepared listed furniture valued at $117, a $10 looking glass, a $30 brown suit, and a watch given to him by his father valued at $30.[12] On September 11, 1774, his wife, Sarah, had their sixth child, Charles Cameron Lewis. His father had already left to march to Point Pleasant.[13]

In the early 1770s, settlers—ignoring treaties and established boundaries—moved ever westward into the Ohio Valley. The Indians continued their resistance. They penetrated as far east as the Cowpasture and fired on Fort Lewis from the bluff along the river. Charles was away, and his cousin-in-law was killed. The Indians screamed for the defenders to come out of the "Lewis hog pin" and fight. Prudently, they did not.[13]

Charles reflected on the situation in a July 9, 1744, letter to Colonel William Preston:

> Of no doubt but you have heard of ye engagement that Capt. Dickenson is had with ye Indians. He had one man killed and his Lieutenant Wounded. a fewe Days ago ye Indians fired at Wm Mcfarlen Neere ye Warm Springs and wounded him slitly. Ye inhabitants of our Frontier is in ye Greates Confusion. they are gathered in forts. I have ordered out Several Compneys of Militia which I am in hops will put a stope to thir intended Hostilities. I hear that ye Assembly is to Meet ye 11th of Next Month when I hope they they will fall on som Method to put an End to ye War.[14]

Governor Dunmore of Virginia ordered Colonel Andrew Lewis to gather a force that once and for all would put down the Shawnees and the other Ohio Indians. The plan was for Andrew and his Virginians to move down the Great Kanawha River to the Ohio and for Dunmore to lead a force south down the Ohio River from Fort Pitt. The two forces would join together at Point Pleasant and march on the Shawnee towns along the Scioto River.

Charles was directed to form a regiment of militia from Augusta County and meet Andrew and the regiment from Botetourt County at Camp Union on the Greenbrier River, which is now the town of Lewisburg. The combined force consisted of 1,000 men and four hundred packhorses to carry supplies. The men included veterans of Washington's surrender at Fort Necessity, Braddock's Defeat, the Big Sandy Expedition, the capture of Fort Duquesne, and Bouquet's march into the Ohio wilderness.

The advance party of 600 men, the packhorses, and 100 cattle, under Colonel Charles Lewis, left Camp Union on September 6, 1774, and marched over the mountains to the Mouth of the Elk (present-day Charleston). There, they built canoes and proceeded down the Great Kanawha to the point where it met the Ohio River. They completed the 160-mile trip from Lewisburg in nineteen days and set up camp at the junction of the two rivers to wait for Dunmore. The juncture of the calm waters of the Kanawha and the Ohio, the thick forests, and the early fall colors led the men to name their camp Point Pleasant. As each day passed, Andrew became more disturbed by the governor's delay in joining the two forces. Meanwhile, Dunmore with his 1,300-man army from northern Virginia moved down the Ohio with the supposed intent of meeting the Shawnees at the mouth of the Hocking River for peace negotiations. He sent a message to the Shawnees, but a report came back that they had gone south to talk with the army at Point Pleasant. Finally, on October 9, Andrew received a message ordering him to cross the Ohio with his troops and meet Dunmore closer to the Indian towns.

On the early morning of October 10, 1774, two soldiers who were out hunting deer two miles from camp between the Ohio and Clear Creek came upon a mass of Indians. One of the soldiers was killed. The other raced into the camp at Point Pleasant declaring that he had seen the enemy standing side by side in a mass covering four acres. The Indians intended to drive Andrew's army off the point and into the two rivers. Andrew listened quietly as he lit his pipe, and then ordered two columns of 150 men each to go investigate. Charles commanded one column, Colonel William Fleming the other. The columns, 200 yards apart, marched briskly up the river, fearing little since they believed they had such an overpowering force. The men carried muzzle-loading long rifles, tomahawks, and scalping knifes. Their uniforms consisted of regular frontier garb-fringed hunting shirts, leggings, caps, and moccasins. In contrast,

Charles wore part of his dress uniform, a scarlet waistcoat. Some criticized him for being so conspicuous. But he wore the coat, not out of negligence or any great vanity, but because he wanted to put some spirit into his men.[15]

The two columns advanced a half mile, and with the dawn just coming, the Indians began to shoot from behind trees and bushes. The men broke ranks and sought protection. The Indians advanced with screams and yells. Charles stood his ground at the head of his column in a clearing, encouraging his men to retaliate and hold their ground.

A shot hit Charles in the stomach. He handed his gun to one of his men, grabbed his stomach, and walked back to camp.[16] *He said to the men he passed, "I am wounded but go on and be brave." Charles met Andrew, coming forward, who looked at his younger brother and said, "I expected something fatal would befall you."*

Charles replied, "It is the fate of war." He entered his tent, laid [sic] *down, and died.*[17]

5

POINT PLEASANT

On a muggy, overcast August morning, Katharine and I left Lewisburg, heading for Point Pleasant. We drove on Route 60, known as the Midland Trail, the path that General Andrew Lewis and his western Virginian Army followed to their battle with the Indians. It took them nineteen days to cover this route that bisects the state of West Virginia. It took us three and a half hours.

Colonel Charles Lewis led the first contingent of Andrew's army out of Camp Union at Lewisburg across Muddy Creek Mountain due west to near Green Sulphur Springs. He then turned north, crossing what is now I-64. We followed his trail a bit to the north on Route 60, slowed down to follow a truck over Sewells Mountain. Charles proceeded along Meadow Creek through less rigorous terrain.

East of Fayetteville, our paths met where he marched and we drove along Route 60 to Ansted near Hawks Nest and the overlook into the New River Gorge. Charles and his men, swinging north, skirted Gauley Mountain, picked up the Buffalo and Indian Trail along Rich Creek, and followed it up the Gauley River. We continued along Route 60 past Kanawha Falls just below where the New and the Gauley Rivers meet to form the Kanawha, and then proceeded on to Cedar Grove. Charles, to the north of us and still on the buffalo trail, left the Gauley, followed Bells Creek, crossed a ridge and proceeded down Kelly's Creek to the Kanawha. He crossed land on which his great-grandson, C.C. Lewis, would develop coal mines in the late 1800s. At Cedar Grove on the Kanawha River, our paths met. There, a marker commemorates the passage of Andrew and Charles on their way to Point Pleasant.

We were half way. Our paths would coincide, following the Kanawha from Cedar Grove to Point Pleasant. A few miles outside of Charleston at Malden, another marker said, "Buffalo Salt Licks, a favorite spot for animals and Indians." It referred to the mouth of Campbells Creek where Mary Draper Ingles, kidnapped by the

Indians, had made salt for them in 1755. Charles and his men stopped there as well to replenish their salt supply. Colonel John Dickinson, also on the march to Point Pleasant, would later be granted this land. His daughter would marry Charles's son, and their son, John Dickinson Lewis would have a salt well and live on the property.

Just east of Charleston, Katharine and I drove on I-64 to pass through the capital city of West Virginia. On the west side of downtown, where the Elk River enters the Kanawha, or Mouth of Elk as it was called in Charles' time, he and his men built canoes for the army to ride down the Kanawha to their destination. Charles could have never conceived what this area would look like over 225 years later—metropolitan and industrial sprawl filling the valley for thirty miles. I wondered what it might look like 200 years later. Crossing over to the south side of the river, we exited the interstate and followed the Kanawha through an ever-widening valley of bottomland, the final forty miles into Point Pleasant. We followed the route to Charles' doom.

The Point Pleasant Battle Monument is a state park located where Andrew's army camped. We left the car and walked out onto a grassy expanse with a tall obelisk in the middle. Here the Kanawha meets the Ohio. The spot's Indian name of "Tu-Endie-Wei" means "the point between two waters."

The obelisk commemorates the western Virginians who fought the Indians. On one side of the obelisk is a plaque entitled "The Influence of the Battle of Point Pleasant Upon Subsequent History." It says that the victory resulted in a treaty with the Indians that again put Virginia's border at the Mississippi and added the territory northwest of the Ohio to that colony. This allowed the expansion into Kentucky and on westward. Thus, with this expansion, the new nation's western border became the Mississippi. It could have been the Allegheny Mountains if the Indians had maintained control. In addition, the treaty kept the Indians quiet for three years, enabling Virginia's fighting men to fully participate in the Revolutionary War rather than being tied up protecting their frontier from the Indians.

Interestingly, Lord Dunmore is not mentioned on the plaque. There is some historical conjecture that Lord Dunmore, in not arriving at Point Pleasant with his army, had schemed with the Indians, hoping they would defeat the cantankerous western Virginians and weaken the strength of the Virginia Colony's ability to oppose England. With the Stamp Act of the 1760s, the relationship between

Photo by the author

the Colonies and England rapidly deteriorated. Consequently, it has been claimed by some, even by such a notable figure as Teddy Roosevelt in his book *The Winning of the West*, that Point Pleasant was the "opening act" of the Revolution and, therefore, its first battle.[1] This notion is particularly popular among western Virginians. "The Battle of Bunker Hill" followed several months later in 1775.

Plaques on the other sides of the obelisk reflect the men who fought the battle and honored the 81 killed and the 140 wounded. Like many western Virginia families, the Lewises were well represented at the battle. John Lewis' two sons (Andrew and Charles), his four grandsons, and the husbands of his two granddaughters fought there. Son Charles was killed, as were the two sons in law.

Colonel Charles Lewis' wife, Sarah, had a brother and three step brothers at Point Pleasant. Her brother was killed, as was one of her stepbrothers. A stepbrother who survived,

Photo by the author

Charles Cameron, was the namesake for Charles and Sarah's son, Charles Cameron Lewis, born September 11, 1774, a few days after his father departed for the battle. He was the first of many Charles Camerons to follow.

Of those that fought at Point Pleasant, seven, including Andrew, became generals in the Revolutionary War and six commanded regiments. If Charles had lived, he too would have been among those military leaders.[2] Participants also showed political leadership, becoming governors of the states of Virginia, Kentucky, Tennessee, Georgia, Indiana, North Carolina, and Mississippi.[3]

From the obelisk Katharine and I were attracted to a circular, almost ground-level structure close to the Kanawha riverbank. It was the magazine where General Lewis' army had stored their munitions. In front was a small stone marker: "Colonel Charles Lewis, 1736 -1774. Died in Battle." I wondered if he was buried by the magazine.

On the Ohio River side of the park stood another monument. It was inscribed with one word: "Cornstalk." After the Battle of Point Pleasant, Cornstalk became the great statesman of the Indian nations. Andrew participated in negotiations with him and held him in esteem even though they had been former enemies. As an orator, Cornstalk was considered by some to be an equal to Patrick Henry.[4] Cornstalk lay buried in this park, killed three years after the Battle of Point Pleasant. He came to warn the frontier soldiers, stationed here, of new Indian uprisings. Instead of being grateful, the soldiers held him hostage. Indians killed a hunter across the Kanawha. In revenge, a soldier whose family was massacred by Cornstalk in Greenbrier County instigated his instant murder. Cornstalk's death accelerated the Indian uprisings.

Also in the park is a lead plate that predates everything else. The French placed it there in 1749, claiming the territory for France.

On the site is a hand-hewn log house that had been a tavern outside the fort. It is now a museum and is similar to the original part of our house in Lewisburg. We entered and were greeted by Gloria Rousch, a member of the Colonel Charles Lewis Chapter of the Daughters of the American Revolution. After she told us some things about the site, and I mentioned that I was a descendent of Charles, she said, "I am in love with Charles. He was the handsomest and most charming of the Lewises, and he would have been the most famous if he had lived." Her face beamed. From her enthusiasm I almost thought he was still with us, not dead for over two hundred years. She brought out a copy of the Lewis genealogy and found my name.

I asked her, "Is Charles buried here?"

"Yes, he was, and there is a marker out there, but then his remains were moved to the Lewis farm on the other side of town. Andrew had been given that land here for his service in the French and Indian War. Charles' family had land in Kentucky. In 1800 the families swapped with each other, and the farm has been owned by the Charles Lewis heirs ever since."

"Didn't I see in the Charleston paper that the family just put that farm up for auction?" I asked.

"They did and that's a shame. I read the family got $3 million for it. Mr. Charles Cameron Lewis, Jr. died in 1998. He was in his nineties and had run the farm all these years. No one else in the family wanted it. Mr. Charles was a fine gentleman. He's the one who gave me this Lewis genealogy."

"I'd like to go out there and see Charles' burial spot."

"Well, you could do that. I don't know whether the new owners have taken over or not."

Gloria gave us directions. We drove through Point Pleasant to the north edge of town. We turned on an unmarked gravel lane that ran past some farm buildings, and then made a circle in front of an exquisite house set in the middle of rolling farmland. A new pickup sat in the driveway. I went to the front door and knocked. A slim, attractive woman in her forties came to the door. I explained that I was looking for Charles Lewis' burial spot.

"Let me get my husband," she said.

A trim fellow with pleasant features came forward and introduced himself as John Lewis Slidel. I apologized for bothering them and asked about Charles Lewis' gravesite. "Well, he's not buried here on the farm. He's at the historic site," said John.

"The lady at the park thought his remains had been brought here."

"The only people buried here are his son and grandson, Lieutenant Charles Cameron Lewis and Charles Cameron Lewis, Jr. When I'm here, I try to keep the gravesite up, but we've been too busy lately. It's over by the railroad, and kids walking the tracks move the stones. I can tell you how to get there."

John then invited Katharine and me in and showed us the house. It was built in 1866 and was of Italian revival architecture. We admired the large, high-ceilinged rooms, the walls paneled in cherry from trees on the farm, the moss green wallpaper in the entryway, and the banister laced with fretwork.

John told us about the farm. It was 1,300 acres, the largest dairy farm in West Virginia at one time. It stretched from the hills to the east across Route 62 to the Ohio with a mile of riverfront. John said he had spent summers on the farm as a child. His mother had been raised on the property. His uncle, Charles Cameron Lewis, Jr., had run the farm and had recently died. He had been the eighth generation of Charles Cameron Lewises. And there would be no more. He had never married and so had been the last Charles Lewis male heir in that line. John mentioned that he had inherited the original Charles Lewis' pocket watch. We wondered about Charles Lewis' gun, which was supposed to be among his descendants somewhere.

John said that less than thirty days remained until the house closing. He and his wife had come over from Maryland to pack up things. He said it was a shame that the place was going out of the family. The descendants were scattered all over the country, and none of them were interested in living there. They had tried ways to develop the property, but nothing seemed to work out. He was pleased that the house had been bought by a couple with a big family, who lived across the river in Ohio.

Katharine and I thanked John for his graciousness and went to find the burial site. Down another gravel road Katharine spotted stones sticking up in the brush under some trees. I walked through waist-high weeds to the site. The railroad tracks were just beyond; farther on behind a distant line of trees lay the Ohio. The stones sat piled up one on top of another. One had an indecipherable inscription. Was Colonel Charles Lewis buried there or was he at the historic site? I hoped that he, who had died a hero's death, was not under that pile of stones, but rested in a more pleasant spot by the rivers in that grassy park.

6

REVOLUTIONARY WARRIORS

With the death of Colonel Charles Lewis, the Virginians at Point Pleasant fell back toward their camp. In contrast to the pleasant fall day, the battlefield became a scene of horror.

> the ring of rifles and the roar of muskets . . . the flashing knives—the fight, hand to hand – the scream for mercy, smothered in the death groan-the crushing through the brush-the advance-the retreat-the pursuit, every man for himself . . . a shriek-the collecting again of the whites, covered with gore and sweat, bearing trophies of the slain, their dripping knives in one hand, and rifle-barrel, bent and smeared with brains and hair, in the other . . . .[1]

The voice of Cornstalk rose above the cries of the wounded and the shrieks and howls of the Indians as he rallied his forces.

The Virginians used a trick of holding out their hats from behind trees to attract Indian fire. They would drop their hats, and the Indians would rush out to scalp the victims. The Virginians, all better shots than the Indians, would then shoot or scalp them.[2] The ferocity of the fighting continued. The Indians stood firm behind logs and fallen trees on a line angling from the Ohio to the Kanawha with the Virginians caught between the two waters. General Andrew Lewis began worrying that the battle could be a stalemate. Neither side could advance, nor would they retreat. If he could not dislodge the Indians by nightfall, his forces would be at a serious disadvantage.

Upstream on the Kanawha, a mile from the point, Crooked Creek winds inland between high banks and weeds parallel to the Ohio. Andrew dispatched three companies to the creek. The men moved up the stream between its banks. Slipping around the enemy line, they attacked from the rear. The Indians thought that militia reinforcements had arrived, and they fell back to the top of a ridge.

By early afternoon the Virginians drove the Indians off the ridge, and two hours later they had the enemy in full retreat. The bodies of the dead floated down the Ohio. Most of the Indians escaped across the river on rafts. With nightfall coming and an exhausted army, Andrew made no attempt to pursue his enemy.[3]

The next morning Andrew and the Virginians crossed the river into Ohio to meet up with Lord Dunmore's army and to march on the Indian towns. A messenger arrived from Dunmore, ordering Andrew to halt. In no mood to pay attention to the governor, Andrew continued. Near Dunmore's camp, he found the short, stocky governor in frontier attire accompanied by a tall, stately Indian. Andrew stared in disbelief. It was Cornstalk. Behind Andrew, his men began to grumble. They shouldered their rifles, aiming at the Indian with whom they had been battling to the death only a few days earlier. Dunmore advanced smiling, his hand extended to congratulate Andrew on the brave performance of his men in battle. Expressionless, Cornstalk stood quietly by Dunmore's side. Andrew ignored the extended hand. Dunmore explained that he was making a peace treaty with Cornstalk and that Andrew must return to Camp Union and disband his troops.[4] In shock, Andrew turned his force around and headed back to the Ohio. The men were an undisciplined group at best and were ready to rebel. They wanted to return and attack the governor and his Indian friends. If nothing else, they had been promised horses and booty from the Indian towns that they were to attack. However, Andrew's good sense prevailed. He marched his reluctant army back to Point Pleasant where he released his men to return to their homes across the mountains. For Andrew and his army this was a poor conclusion to a victorious battle. In time, Andrew would gain his revenge.

What had Dunmore been up to? Andrew began to suspect that the governor had been aware of Cornstalk's plans to attack; yet Dunmore had not informed him nor rushed to his aid. Did Dunmore want the Virginians to be defeated? The representatives of these men were resisting British rule in the House of Burgesses in Williamsburg, and there was already talk of revolution. The Virginia Colony strongly opposed actions by the British Parliament – the Stamp Act, taxing documents to pay for the French and Indian War, and the Townsend Act, imposing taxes on imported goods. The Colonies took the position: "No representation, no taxation."

In the months prior to the Battle of Point Pleasant, several things

Statue of Famous Virginians at Capitol Square, Richmond, Virginia. George Washington is on horseback. Andrew Lewis is second figure from left. *Photo by the author*

were impacting relations between the Colonies and Great Britain. Parliament annexed for Quebec all territory across the Ohio, taking it away from Virginia. This action, like the Proclamation Line of 1763, was designed to suppress the westward movement of the colonies. After the Boston Tea Party, the British closed the port of Boston. In sympathy, the Virginia House of Burgesses declared a day of fasting and prayer. Dunmore immediately dissolved the session. In the meantime, the first Continental Congress was meeting in Philadelphia.

Many Virginians, consequently, believed Dunmore's actions were indeed part of an English scheme against the colonists. As a result of the victory at Point Pleasant, however, and much to the chagrin of the British, the Virginians ignored all proclamations and acts against crossing the Ohio. Settlers, without Indian intervention, reinitiated their westward expansion, adding to Virginia the new county of Kentucky.

Andrew met Cornstalk at Pittsburgh the next year in peace talks. They had not confronted each other directly at Point Pleasant, only afterwards in the strained meeting with Dunmore. But in Pittsburgh these two warriors, now seeking peace, gained great respect for each other. Cornstalk, like Andrew, was an awe-inspiring man. Andrew thought Cornstalk the most dignified Indian he had ever known. This respect for a former foe contrasted to Andrew's feeling for his English contemporary, Lord Dunmore.

In March 1775, Andrew Lewis and brother Thomas attended the Virginia Convention in Richmond to address the problems with the British. Andrew represented Botetourt County and Thomas, Augusta County. Patrick Henry gave his "Give me liberty or give me death" speech. The convention replaced the House of Burgesses in Williamsburg, which had been dissolved by Dunmore. Brother William Lewis, though not in attendance, participated in the preparation of a declaration from Augusta County that was presented to the Convention:

> Many of us and our forefathers left our native land and explored this once savage wilderness, to enjoy the free exercise of the rights of conscience and of human nature. These rights, we are fully resolved, with our lives and fortunes, inviolably to preserve: nor will we surrender such inestimable blessings, the purchase of toil and danger, to any ministry, to any Parliament,

or any body of men on earth, by whom we are not represented, and in whose decisions, therefore, we have no voice.[5]

The full Augusta resolution was printed on a satin cloth and distributed throughout the colonies. Meanwhile, in Massachusetts, Paul Revere made his famous ride to warn the colonists of the British attack on Concord. The Battle at Bunker Hill followed, and the Second Continental Congress convened in Philadelphia, appointing Andrew's friend, George Washington, the Commander of the Continental Army.

In the fall of 1775, William Lewis joined the 1st Virginia Regiment as a lieutenant. His low rank reflected his lack of fighting experience compared to his brothers, Andrew and Charles. He was fifty-years-old, and up to this point in his life he had contributed in more peaceable ways by serving in local government in Staunton and Augusta County.[6] However, the situation with the British was a different matter. He now felt it his duty to fight for the freedom he had declared in the Augusta resolution.

Governor Dunmore declared martial law in Virginia. He established shipboard headquarters near Norfolk and began building up British and Loyalist forces in that area. Meanwhile, Virginia established its own state government in Richmond and began operating completely free of British rule. In their first Revolutionary skirmish, the Virginians defeated Dunmore's forces at Great Bridge. Dunmore retaliated by burning Norfolk in January 1776 and then hid out with his fleet in the nearby Elizabeth River.

With Dunmore's buildup, and much to Andrew's chagrin, the legislature elected popular and politically brilliant Patrick Henry to be commander-in-chief of the Virginia forces. Andrew was given command of a regiment under Patrick Henry. He refused the commission. He wrote a letter to George Washington, saying he could not serve faithfully under a man who had had no military experience. Early in 1776, Andrew was appointed a brigadier general, a rank surpassing Patrick Henry, and the great orator resigned. All Virginia officers and their units had changed from state to Continental commands. From his headquarters in Williamsburg, Andrew took charge of Virginia's forces, which he had to recruit and train. This included the 1st Virginian with William in its ranks. In the meantime Andrew was keeping track of Dunmore's maneuvers.

In May, fearing an attack by Virginia ships coming down the

James, Dunmore moved his fleet as if to sail out of the Chesapeake Bay into the Atlantic. Instead, he suddenly turned back up the bay and established headquarters at Gwynn's Island, a place he thought could be easily defended.

Andrew, surprised by the maneuver, felt sure that the British were going to bring in more forces by sea to end Virginia's rebellion. Fearing that he might be lured into a trap, Andrew sent only a part of his troops to Gwynn's Island to engage Dunmore. The island lay two hundred yards off the mainland, but with no artillery and an insufficient force, the Virginians had little impact on the British. Over a month's time Andrew expanded his army, calling up 1,300 militiamen and gathering some artillery. He arrived opposite Gwynn's Island and saw 500 British troops bivouacked there. He collected boats and rafts from the local inhabitants so that he could assault the island.

In the channel between the island and the mainland, the British warship *Otter* stood ready to repulse an attack. This ship was notorious for its raids on the unarmed plantations along the Chesapeake. Overnight the *Dunmore*, the ship that housed the former governor's headquarters, replaced the *Otter*. Unknown to the British, Andrew had at the ready two eighteen-pound cannons. He personally fired the shot that began the surprise attack on the ship. Cannon fire damaged the *Dunmore* and wounded the governor before the ship could be towed away. The *Otter* came to the rescue but was also damaged. Lord Dunmore, learning that the British were not going to reinforce him and attack Virginia, but instead would be going to South Carolina, fled the island. Andrew did not have sufficient boats to attack across the channel and inflict further damage. He could only watch as the British ships hoisted anchor and sailed away. However, he must have felt great satisfaction in running Dunmore out of Virginia. This action also resulted in freeing Virginia from any further attacks by the British for the next three years.[7]

In May of 1776, the Virginia Convention authorized its delegates to the Continental Congress to support independence. The convention established a state constitution and a bill of rights. Patrick Henry was elected the state's first governor. Meanwhile, in Philadelphia, Thomas Jefferson wrote the Declaration of Independence. On July 4, 1776, the Continental Congress signed the document.

At the end of that summer, the 1st Virginia Regiment and William marched north to New Jersey to join General George

Washington's Grand Army, which was badly in need of reinforcements.[8] Andrew requested a transfer himself so he could join Washington, but John Hancock, President of the Continental Congress, replied that his greatest service would be to stay in command where he was, to defend Virginia in case the British returned. The British left Virginia alone in the initial years of the war, allowing Andrew to recruit forces to fight in the North.

The Continental Congress's failure to promote Andrew to major general disappointed him further. He did receive a letter of condolence from George Washington. When Washington was being urged to take command of the Continental Army, he had suggested that his old friend Andrew be considered instead. Whether this was a sincere gesture is not known. Unfortunately, Andrew had antagonized many people, both fellow officers and politicians, during his military career. Bored by lack of action, Andrew retired from the Continental Army in 1777.

Meanwhile, during that same year, William served with General George Washington's army, attempting to defend New York City. Outnumbered by the better trained and far better equipped British, Washington retreated out of New York north to White Plains, then south to New Jersey, and finally into Pennsylvania. Though the British had all but whipped the Americans, the British did not pursue. On Christmas day, General Washington and his troops crossed the Delaware in a snowstorm to surprise the British at Trenton. They chased the Redcoats to Princeton, outflanked them, and caused them to retreat from the field. The Continental Army spent the winter of 1777 in the New Jersey hills, encouraged by their victories.

The British moved on Philadelphia in the summer of 1777. The Continentals tried to stop them at Brandywine. William held the position in General Peter Muhlenberg's 1st Virginia Regiment of brigade inspector, a proper role for a man of his age. Muhlenberg, a Lutheran pastor from the Shenandoah Valley, had recruited men from his pulpit by stripping off his clerical robes to display his militia uniform. At Brandywine, he led the initial attack, drove deep into the enemy, took one hundred prisoners and then fought his way out. But the British outflanked and defeated Washington's army and took Philadelphia. Washington countered by attacking the British at Germantown in horrible fog. With no visibility, the Continentals fired on their own troops, and the attack ended in disaster.

In that year, when Andrew retired from the Army, he suffered another blow. His former adversary, Chief Cornstalk, whom he had come to admire, was murdered at Point Pleasant. The unwarranted killing incensed and saddened Andrew. Cornstalk's death so infuriated the Indians that after three years of peace they again went on a rampage. The following spring they attacked Fort Donnally in Greenbrier County. Andrew's son Samuel led a detachment from nearby Camp Union at Lewisburg that saved the fort. But the Indians pressed on and attacked as far east as the Roanoke River.

In the winter of 1778, William Lewis, his son John, and his nephew Thomas, Jr., son of his brother Thomas, sat huddled in their ragged great coats on a bunk in a crude log lean-to set in a hollow at Valley Forge.

The wind howled outside. Snow blew in between the cracks and collected in small piles on the frozen dirt. A fire blazed in the middle of the floor, smoking up the hut. They had not eaten that day and were waiting to go collect some soup and barley. The British were twenty miles away, residing in warm houses, eating well at their winter quarters in Philadelphia.

White vapor came in puffs from William's mouth as he said, "I fear for my family in Virginia, Anne and the children living alone. I miss them."

"Father, they'll be fine. The British have shown no indication of invading Virginia. My two younger brothers are growing up, and they help take care of things," said John.

"They are good boys, but they soon will be joining the Continental Army," said William as he wrapped his arms around himself to keep out the cold.

"I heard that Uncle Andrew has left the army, " said Thomas.

"Yes," said William, "he has served his time. Hopefully, he will enjoy some peace with his family now."

"Uncle William, will we ever be able to throw the British out of America?" asked Thomas.

"If our army can survive this winter, we have a chance. General Washington is a great leader. The French are going to help us. We may not win many battles, but if we can hang on, the British will lose their will to fight." William stood up. He coughed, and then coughed again.

"Father, are you all right?" asked John. "There are so many men that are ill. And so many that have died."

"John, I'm fine. It's just the smoke. I have lived fifty years and have many more to go. Let's get something to eat."

The men stood, put on their hats, and pulled their coats around them. William pushed back the deerskin door, and the three men stepped out into the dark day and the blowing snow.[9]

With morale low, discipline poor, men starving, dying from disease, and deserting, Washington's army of 11,000 was rapidly shrinking. This was the low point of the war, but the situation began to improve. In February 1778, the French and Americans signed a treaty of alliance. Frenchman Marquis de Lafayette, whose father the British had killed during the French and Indian War, arrived at Valley Forge to help train the dispirited men. A Prussian baron taught the troops about European military formations. Discipline improved, replacements arrived, and the supply operations became more efficient. William and the men felt encouraged. In June the Continentals marched out of Valley Forge, a new army.

With France's entry on the Continental side, the British panicked, realizing that they now had to fight on many fronts to defend their empire. They abandoned Philadelphia and moved to New York City. Washington's army followed the British north, attacking them at Monmouth, New Jersey in June 1778. Both William and son John were there. The battle ended in a draw, an improvement for the Continental Army over its performances of the previous year.

On the frontier, the Indians, with Cornstalk dead and encouraged by the British, continued to attack settlers who crossed the Appalachians into Ohio and Indiana. George Rogers Clark, leading Virginia militiamen, countered the attacks by burning Indian settlements in Indiana and Illinois. Virginia annexed much of the land that Clark captured and named it the County of Illinois.

While William marched with Washington's army, Andrew, his military career over, continued to serve his country and his state. After Cornstalk's death, he and his brother Thomas were appointed United States commissioners to negotiate a treaty with the Delaware Indians at Pittsburgh. The treaty allowed American forces to proceed through Ohio to attack the British at Detroit. The attack never occurred, but the treaty had significance because, for the first time, an Indian tribe aligned itself with the Americans rather than the British.

The Delawares wanted to form a state and be a part of the

United States. Governor Thomas Jefferson asked Andrew and Thomas to resolve Virginia's boundary dispute with Pennsylvania over a strip of land along the Ohio, now known as the West Virginia panhandle.[10]

With the French in the war, the British gave up battling in the North. The people there were uncontrollable. The British decided to retake the colonies by invading the South, thinking that Southerners were more sympathetic to their rule and would join with them. A British army sailed from New York and landed at Savannah, capturing the city at the end of 1778. By mid-1779 the British controlled all of Georgia. In October Congress appointed General Benjamin Lincoln to lead the Continental Army in the South.

As part of this transition south, William, now in his fourth year in the Continental Army, became a major to the 10th Virginia Regiment. The unit consisted of half army regulars from Virginia and South Carolina and half South Carolina militiamen. Lincoln, with French assistance, tried to no avail to retake Savannah. Although the French had scared the British by entering the war, joint attacks by French and American forces had yet to be successful. General Lincoln moved to Charleston, South Carolina. With Savannah in their hands, the British now wanted Charleston. They transported 8,000 men by ship from New York and slowly closed in on the city, holding the Continental Army under siege. British ships entered the harbor and bombarded the city. General Lincoln planned an escape, but the local authorities demanded that the army stay. In May 1780, with the British ready to storm the Continental lines, Lincoln surrendered to save the city from destruction. William was one of 5,500 men taken prisoner, the biggest Continental loss of the war.

As the situation continued to deteriorate, George Washington sent a new army south. British and Continental armies battled back and forth in South and North Carolina. The British, under General Cornwallis, whipped the Americans at Camden; the Continentals won at Kings Mountain. At Cowpens, in January 1781, the American forces routed the British. Cornwallis retaliated at Guilford Courthouse and drove the Americans from the field. Small battles continued. Meanwhile, William remained a prisoner in Charleston, South Carolina.

Cornwallis next moved into Virginia and sent raiders, led by Colonel Banastre Tarleton to attack the central part of the state.[11] Known as "Bloody" Tarleton for his indiscriminate slaughter of American troops in the South, he almost captured the state's second governor, Thomas Jefferson, at Charlottesville. Jefferson, however, managed to slip away. The Virginia legislature fled westward across the Blue Ridge to Staunton. This marked another low point in the war for the new country. George Washington wrote in his diary, "instead of having the prospect of a glorious offensive campaign before us, we have a bewildered and gloomy defensive one."[12] It was the seventh year of the war.

With William away, his wife, Anne, and their younger children still lived at John Lewis' old home, Bellefont, near Staunton. Like their father, the oldest sons, John, twenty-three and William, twenty, were off at war.

Colonel Samuel Lewis, Andrew's son, arrived at Bellefont at midnight by horseback. He quickly dismounted and pounded on the door.

"Aunt Anne, Aunt Anne, " he yelled. "Open up. It's me, Samuel, your nephew."

The door opened. Anne stood there in her nightgown and sleeping bonnet, holding a candle. "Gracious, Samuel, what's all the commotion at this hour?"

"Where are the boys, Aunt?"

"They are upstairs in bed."

"Call them, Tarleton is coming."

Awakened by the noise, her children quickly joined her in the front door. Alexander, seventeen, William, fifteen, and the little girls, Agatha and Elizabeth, stood by her side. A baby cried in the background. It was Charles, named for his uncle who had died at Point Pleasant.

"I fear the British will come over the Blue Ridge through Rockfish Gap from Charlottesville and attack Staunton," said Samuel.

Anne turned to her two young sons and said, "Go my children. I spare not my youngest, my faired-hair boy, the comfort of my declining years. I devote you all to my country. Keep back the foot of the invader from the soil of Augusta or see my face no more.13 "

Within minutes the boys dressed, grabbed their muskets, saddled their horses, and cantered off with Samuel to join the local forces at Rockfish Gap.

When later told of this event, George Washington said, "Leave me but a banner to plant upon the mountains of Augusta, and I will rally around me the men who will lift our bleeding country from the dust, and set her free."[14]

Tarleton did not come over the Blue Ridge. And King Louis XVI of France diverted a large portion of the French fleet to support the Americans. The tide of battle changed. The British, fearing an attack on New York by Washington and the French, ordered Cornwallis to take up a defensive position at Yorktown and to prepare to send his troops north. Despite winning many battles, the British had failed to meet their objective of conquering the southern colonies.

A French fleet entered the Chesapeake while Washington headed south with a large army. Cornwallis was trapped. In October 1781, 8,000 British troops surrendered at Yorktown, effectively ending the Revolutionary War. Two Lewises, John and Thomas, Jr., both sons of Thomas, fought at Yorktown. With the war over William Lewis was released from prison in Charleston, South Carolina and returned home to Virginia.

The British had had enough. After seven years of fighting, they gave up in frustration. They had won battles at Bunker Hill, Long Island, Brandywine, Germantown, Camden, and Charleston, but—as at Valley Forge—the Americans would not fold. Win or lose, they were always ready to fight again. Parliament finally realized that their army would never conquer the Americans. The British feared they would lose other parts of their empire with so much of their fighting forces tied up in America.

General Andrew Lewis died in September 1781, at age sixty. In the last two years of his life, Andrew continued to serve Virginia as a member of the governor's council under Governors Thomas Jefferson and Thomas Nelson. He acted as the military adviser to the governors and worked to recruit men and supplies to fight the British in the South.

Andrew developed a fever while riding home to Botetourt County from the state capital in Richmond. He died on the way. Three weeks later the Continentals beat the British at Yorktown.

Peace negotiations began the next year. Congress approved a treaty in September 1783, which established boundaries for the thirteen states that extended west to the Mississippi, north to Canada, and south to Florida.

In that year of the treaty, William at age fifty-eight left Bellefont, where the Lewis family had lived for fifty years. He, his wife, Anne, and their children moved to the Sweet Springs Valley, to develop a community and a resort and to bring civilization to a remote part of the western Virginia mountains.

7

SWEET SPRINGS

Sweet Springs lies in a valley alongside Peters Mountain on the Virginia-West Virginia border. William Lewis first came there in 1754 with his brother Andrew, exploring the land. Some thirty years later, after the Revolutionary War, William returned to establish one of the most famous of the old Virginia spring resorts. His brothers, Andrew and Charles, were the warriors; William was the civilizer.

I have known Sweet Springs since childhood. I have a vague recollection of hunting squirrels there with my father when I was five years old. Old Sweet, as we called it, was a family institution; my parents talked about it over the years. In our home in Florida, where I was raised, pictures of the resort hung on the wall. In the past, during infrequent trips to West Virginia, I would drive down to Old Sweet. Thirty years ago, I remember seeing elderly people meandering about the lawn. At that time it was the Andrew Rowan Memorial Home, a state institution for the aged. When I visited some years later, I found the facility abandoned. A wire fence surrounded the property, and grass grew high around the buildings.

But now, having returned to West Virginia to spend the summers, I wanted to know more about this place that enamored my family for so many years.

The trip from Lewisburg takes about a half hour. It was an unusually warm June day. I could smell the freshly cut hay that lay rolled in bales in the fields that sweep part way up the surrounding ridges. Midway down the valley among the farms, a clump of trees appeared. In front and alongside the road sat the old Romanesque, brick springhouse. The wire fence no longer surrounded the property, and the grass was freshly mowed.

Across a lawn, shaded by a grove of trees, lay the Jefferson Building with its red brick walls and four white porticoes, built in 1833. This Roman Classic, 100-yard-length building had been designed, some thought, by Thomas Jefferson. Jefferson had popularized the architecture with his Monticello home in Charlottesville, which was based on Roman villas in the Italian countryside. The Jefferson Building looked as if it could have been part of the University of Virginia though it seemed to me bigger than most of the structures there.

I later learned that the Jefferson Building was not designed by Jefferson but had been constructed by one of his master builders, William B. Phillips. Phillips had been the "principal brick mason" for the Rotunda, the serpentine garden walls and one of the Pavilions on the Lawn at the University of Virginia.[1]

Parking in the circle driveway of crumbling asphalt, I got out of the car. Despite my past visits, I had forgotten the magnificence of the Jefferson Building. I stood and stared upward, scanning its front. Looking more closely, I saw the white paint peeling off the porch railing that ran the length of the building and off the brick columns of the porticoes.

On the other side of the lawn, four brick cottages lined a driveway. Two had partially collapsed; bricks lay on the ground all about. Standing nearby was a man in his seventies; I introduced myself. He was Warren Coleman, the new owner. He told me that he had seen an ad in the *Wall Street Journal* in 1996, saying that the old resort would be sold at auction. This intrigued him. He drove up from his home in North Carolina. Coleman had been in the landscaping business in Charlotte and, as a sideline, liked to restore historic structures. He decided he had to have the old resort and for a bid of $300,000 bought it. I asked him why he wanted this particular site.

"How many places designed by Jefferson are in private hands?" he said.

That seemed to be the answer. He had three men working. They had fixed the Jefferson Building so that it wouldn't leak and be subject to further deterioration. He planned to rebuild two of the cottages so they would be livable, and to restore the bathhouse and spring. I asked Warren Coleman what use he might have for the facility.

"I don't know," he said. "The kitchen from the old people's home is still in good shape. I could make this place a cooking school. Chefs could come from Europe. Or it could be an athletic rehabilitation center. I don't have it on the market. I'm in no hurry. I just want to slowly restore the place to its original grandeur. Of course, it would take millions to really fix it up."

Warren Coleman and I walked the grounds. A long, dilapidated log building looked as if it might have been the original slave quarters. White wooden cottages stood near the bathhouse. One of these was the George Washington Cottage where the first president supposedly stayed during a visit. And I knew from my family that one had been the Johnson family cottage, used in the early 1900s.

On our tour, Warren and I stopped at the bathhouse. It surrounded a large, silt-filled pool. We looked down a well into a spring that bubbled up a small flow of water. Some of the internal walls of the bathhouse had collapsed, and it would take a major effort to restore the building and pool.

For the first time in fifty years, Old Sweet Springs was in private hands. The State of West Virginia had bought it in 1941 and made it a tuberculosis sanatorium, then converted it to a home for the elderly. The state had even extended the Jefferson Building, adding the fourth portico. About 1990, it was closed and the property given to Monroe County. The county hoped to convert it into a drug rehabilitation center, but that endeavor failed. The bank foreclosed, and Warren Coleman bought what he calls Jefferson Place.

William Lewis started Old Sweet in 1790 as a resort to capitalize on its spring waters, which were thought to have curative powers. It was similar to Hot Springs, now the Homestead, and White Sulphur Springs, now the Greenbrier Hotel, both within thirty miles. Unlike Old Sweet, the Homestead and the Greenbrier survived, perhaps because of better management and direct railroad access after the Civil War. Of course, William's brother Andrew had preceded him in the resort business as one of the founders of Warm Springs and Hot Springs in 1760.

Old Sweet remained in the William Lewis family until just prior to the Civil War. William's grandson John expanded the place, adding the Jefferson Building to replace the rough log cabins. But John fell into financial trouble, could not make the loan payments, and finally sold the resort. It came back into the Lewis family in 1900, this time on the Charles Lewis side.

My great uncle, Cam Lewis, bought it. He added electric lights, a telephone line, and a nine-hole golf course. He, too, had financial troubles. His father, my great-grandfather, Charles Cameron Lewis or C.C., as he was called, bailed his son out and another son took charge. The family story that C.C. Lewis won the resort at a poker table was unverifiable. After C.C.'s death, the family found a buyer in 1920, and the Lewis connection to the resort ended for good.

Photo by the author

Old Sweet struggled through the 1920s and 1930s. A movie called *Glorious Betsy*, the story of a love affair between Napoleon's brother and a Baltimore belle with shots of the Jefferson Building sparked new investor interest, but then it was sold to the state.

With Old Sweet gone, my family still traveled to Sweet Springs but stayed with Cousin Sadie at her farm where she took in guests. She was a distant cousin, a descendant of William Lewis. It was at her place that I had accompanied my father on the squirrel hunt. My Aunt Pye Johnson tells a story about my Uncle Howard, her husband, visiting Cousin Sadie. He had walked in the back door, wearing dirty boots.

"Don't come in here with those boots on," she said.

"But Cousin Sadie, you let the sheep come in."

"That's OK. They live here; you don't."

On my next trip to Sweet Springs I met Lynn Spellman. Lynn is a direct descendant of William Lewis and the last Lewis left in the vicinity. She and her husband live in a farmhouse on the main road going through the valley. In her house are two paintings. One is a portrait of Governor John Floyd, a Virginia governor of the 1830s. His daughter, Leticia, married into the Lewis line and thus he, too, is an ancestor of Lynn's. His son, John B. Floyd, also a governor of Virginia, is notorious for his poor leadership as a general during the Civil War, attempting to defend what is now West Virginia from the advancing Yankees.

The other painting is of an imposing antebellum home called Lynnside where three generations of Lynn's family lived. Its architecture reflected the Jefferson tradition of an Italian country villa. Its brickwork, however, differs from the Jefferson Hotel, indicating that William Philips did not build it.[2] The remains of that house sit directly across the road from the porch where Lynn and I sat talking. Trees and tall grass almost obscure the still standing brick walls.

Lynn, a pleasant, unassuming woman of about fifty, told me the story: "The house caught fire one night in 1935. The volunteer fire department rushed to the village of Linside, twenty miles away, rather than to Lynnside, the house. Our family had no insurance and no money to restore the house so they had to move into the tenant house across the road, which is where we are sitting today."

After my visit with Lynn, I inspected the stately old remains. The brick house was almost square, with tall windows and two towering chimneys. The portico was gone, lost in the fire. Trees and vines almost covered it. I peeked in a broken window. The ceiling had fallen in and the rooms were full of trash. I stood there quietly wondering about the grandeur that once belonged to this family.

Somewhat depressed, I walked through a field and up to the top of a hill where the family cemetery stood. From that height, I looked down on Lynnside shrouded by trees and farther up the valley to the back of the Jefferson Building. On top of the hill, gravestones protruded above the uncut grass. A few trees provided some shade. In the middle of the graveyard lay a mound of rocks. A white board leaned against the rocks with the names William Lewis and Anne Montgomery Lewis painted on it. I found a marker for their son John and even one for the first Governor Floyd.[3] In the midst of the family stood a plain headstone marked "Faithful Slaves, Tom & Dinah." And a very modern tombstone, much out of place on this site, showed that Cousin Sadie had died in 1962. The graveyard represented two hundred years and seven generations of William Lewises.

I still occasionally check on Old Sweet. The workmen finished refurbishing one cottage and have started on another, but I don't see Warren Coleman there very often. I remember that first day we talked. Warren said, "I don't own this place. It belongs to the people. I'm a caretaker. You don't own history."

8

THE CIVILIZER

William and Andrew Lewis stared in amazement. They had walked up a creek, heard water cascading on rocks ahead, and then saw through the trees a waterfall, a hundred feet wide and fifty feet high. They had entered Sweet Springs Valley.[1]

Starting from their home in Staunton, four days earlier, the two brothers had waded the Cowpasture River, climbed over Hot Springs Mountain, and followed the Jackson River downstream, and then wandered up Dunlap Creek. They climbed up and around Beaver Dam Falls and found Sweet Springs Creek at the top. Farther on along the creek they came to a spring. They were in the midst of a heavily forested valley.

William's discovery occurred in 1754, when he was thirty years old. He has been described as a studious man, at times pious, but like his father, tall, robust, and handsome. As brave as his brothers, he was however less disposed toward combat. From that time on Sweet Springs Valley would be a part of his soul, and because of his association with this valley, he would be known as the Civilizer.

On another visit to Sweet Springs, as the story goes, William and a friend were chased by Indians. The two men hid in the spring along the creek. The water felt so relaxing that they stayed all night, and the next day William emerged cured of a prevailing case of rheumatism. And there were other stories: a colt bitten by a rattlesnake survived after plunging into the water; the same was said later of a snake bitten dog that belonged to the Lewises. Thus, came the reputation of the magical powers of the spring water.

Word spread eastward. By the beginning of the 1800s at least seventy-five spas or resorts appeared at springs in the western Virginia mountains. These included Warm Springs and Hot Springs already developed by Andrew Lewis and run by a nephew. Medical science was in its infancy, and some believed that these waters, with their high mineral content, cured diseases. The real cure, if any, came from the cooler, clearer air of the mountains as compared to the heat of the coastal lowlands where cholera and yellow fever prevailed. The Europeans were already strong believers in the curative power of spring water, and flocked to Bath and Brighton in England and Aix la Chappelle in France. The spring at Sweet Springs, heavy in carbonic acid that gave it a briskness, and being thermal, was said to be comparable to the springs in England.

While a captive at Charleston, South Carolina, during the last two years of the Revolutionary War, William had plenty of time to think of this mystical valley. Perhaps, because of his medical training in Philadelphia and his experience with the powers of the spring, he decided to start a resort. In 1783, he and his family left the homestead at Bellefont and started anew at Sweet Springs on 8,000 acres, which he had inherited from the estate of his father.

William had retained his strong religious beliefs and faith in the Ten Commandments throughout the Revolutionary War, and he carried them with him to his new endeavor at Sweet Springs. His son Tom had returned from serving with General Anthony Wayne after the defeat of the Indians in the Ohio country.

On a Sunday morning, Tom saw wild ducks gliding on Sweet Springs Creek. He grabbed his gun and slipped along a fence until he was in range of the ducks. He raised the gun to shoot then felt the swift strike of a stick across his shoulder. He looked up and there stood his father who had just returned from a church service. William said to his son, "I will teach you, sir, that you shall not profane the Sabbath day here." [2]

It wasn't until 1790, with the Indians no longer a threat to western Virginia, that guests began to arrive in any number. By then the resort probably included a few log cabins and a log hotel with a porch running its length. There was no springhouse at that point, and guests bathed and drank from a "muddy pool." Descriptions of the time varied. An English visitor wrote:

> We had a good deal of Genteel Company from different parts of the continent. . . . We had a regular ball every week, besides tea parties. . . . Our accommodations I can't say were as good as the Hotel de York in Paris as there was only one inn and upwards of

two hundred people. . . . we had plenty of good eating . . . great appetites which the waters created. . . . Our lodging was in Logge Cabins, and mattresses and some bed to lay on.[3]

Another guest, Dabney Minor of Orange, Virginia, had different thoughts, "During my stay there, there were upon an average of fifty boarders. Price of board $7 per week. You will suppose from this that we fared sumptuously. Quite the reverse. The living was barely tolerable." Mr. Minor, however, did care for the "nobility of the scenes."[4]

In 1797, George Washington visited the resort. He had completed his eight years as the first President of the United States and arrived with his wife Martha, or perhaps it was his mother; the record is not clear. Thus, there was always a Washington Cottage at Sweet Springs. George and William's son John were good friends from their Revolutionary War days at Valley Forge and Monmouth. It is presumed that Thomas Jefferson visited frequently both before and after his presidency. Old Sweet, as its guests would always call it, had arrived.

William had ideas for the place that reached beyond its being just a resort. He planned a town called Fontville. It covered thirty acres and was divided into one-half-acre lots that were to be sold at auction. It never got past the paper stage, despite William building a stone courthouse and a jail to establish a "backwoods legal circus" as part of its promotion. The ladies used the courthouse for a parlor; gambling tables were set up by the judge's dais, and guests slept in the jailer's house. Court was held there beginning in 1795. It covered five counties that spread westward to Kanawha County and the Ohio River.

Thomas Jefferson sued Aaron Burr in the Sweet Springs court for $200. Both owned property on the western frontier, as did many prominent citizens of the time. According to Jefferson, one of Burr's tenants with "force of arms" ejected Jefferson's tenant. This suit occurred in 1802, shortly after Jefferson became President by a vote of the House of Representatives. He and Burr had ended up with the same number of electoral votes in the election of 1800. Burr became the Vice President. It is doubtful that either participated in the trial, though both undoubtedly had visited Old Sweet and been guests of the Lewises. In 1807, the court moved to Lewisburg to escape the "comic opera" atmosphere that surrounded it.[5]

The next year William turned the management of the resort over to son John. William's wife, Anne, had died and was buried on the hill overlooking the valley. William joined her on that hilltop six years later at age eighty-seven.

John ran the place until his death in 1823. However, it took William's grandson, John B. Lewis, a former West Point cadet, to give Old Sweet its greatest legacy. He was also responsible for almost bringing financial ruin, and letting it out of the Lewis family.

Under John B. Old Sweet underwent an expansion that helped the resort surpass the other Virginia spas, including the nearby "White" at White Sulphur and the "Hot" at Hot Springs. The Grand or Jefferson Hotel, built by Jefferson brick master, William Phillips, replaced the log structures. This grand building was completed in 1833 at a cost of $60,000. A publication of the time said it had "proportions such as were not to be seen anywhere else in the mountains."[6]

Another observer described the structure as "a beautiful long brick building with three Greek porticos, standing in a grove of what was still backwoods America . . . three stories high, the lower story . . . arcaded in the familiar manner of Southern houses. On top of this arcade ran the long piazza, unroofed except for the three high porticos that crossed it . . . everyone sighed over these splendors, over the Greek porticoes, and the tasteful Greek cornices, the three black walnut flights of stairs, and the $60,000."[7]

Notes by Dr. William Burke were even more verbose: "Dr. Lewis has just now finished a house which for architectural beauty and accommodations is superior to any house for the same use in the United States, that I have seen." Burke described the baths: "The water is 73 degrees. . . . In plunging into these waters, one experiences a slight shudder . . . succeeded by a delightful glow. . . . Few mineral waters have acquired such fashionable and well-merited celebrity as the Sweet Springs.[8]

One guest gazing in wonderment at the expansive brick facility, said of John B. in a letter to a friend, "Poor fellow, I'm afraid his means will fail." And fail they did. John B., with a debt of some $34,000, had difficulty making the payments and was forced to sell the resort and the property.

The last significant land holding of the Lewises' 100,000-acre Greenbrier Company was gone. However, John B.'s brother, William, who had married Governor Floyd's daughter, retained 1,000 acres as collateral for a loan to John B. It was on this remaining land that William built his mansion, Lynnside.

By the end of the eighteenth century, John Lewis' sons, with the exception of William, were gone: Samuel at Braddock's Defeat in the French and Indian War; Charles at Point Pleasant at the beginning of the Revolutionary War; and Andrew, serving Virginia to his last day, just before the Revolutionary War ended. Thomas died in 1790 at his home next to the Blue Ridge in Rockingham County.

William, in surviving his brothers, experienced a lifetime that spanned the immigration from Ireland, the settlement of the Shenandoah Valley, the French and Indian War, the Revolutionary War, the founding of the United States, and the beginning of its subsequent growth. He lived under his country's first four presidents: George Washington, John Adams, Thomas Jefferson, and James Monroe. He personally knew Washington and Jefferson, and perhaps Monroe.

While called the Civilizer for his efforts in western Virginia, William Lewis lived to witness the expansion of the United States far beyond that frontier. Thomas Jefferson doubled the size of the United States with the purchase of the Louisiana Territory in 1803 and then sponsored the journey of exploration by Meriwether Lewis and William Clark to the Pacific Ocean.[9]

PART II

Sergeant Patrick Gass of the Lewis & Clark Expedition (1771-1870)

CHRONOLOGY

1700 Benjamin Gass arrives in Pennsylvania from Ireland.
1771 Patrick Gass is born in Falling Springs, Pennsylvania.
1789 George Washington is elected president.
1792 Patrick is drafted to defend settlers from Indian attacks.
1799 Patrick rejoins the army after five years as a carpenter.
1801 Thomas Jefferson becomes the third president.
1803 May: The United States purchases the Louisiana Territory from France.
August: Patrick joins the Lewis and Clark Expedition at Fort Kaskaskia, Illinois.
November: Patrick leads the construction of Fort Dubois.
1804 May: The expedition starts up the Missouri.
August: After the death of Sergeant Floyd, Patrick is elected to fill his position.
September: The Teton Sioux threaten the expedition.
November: The corps establish winter quarters at Fort Mandan, North Dakota.
1805 April: The expedition departs Fort Mandan.
June: The corps arrives at the Great Falls in Montana.

September: The expedition crosses the Bitterroot Mountains.
November: Lewis and Clark reach the Pacific Ocean.
1806 March: The corps departs Fort Clatsop.
June: The expedition again crosses the Bitterroots and splits forces.
August: Lewis and Clark rejoin at the mouth of the Yellowstone River.
September: The expedition arrives at St. Louis.
1807 Patrick's journal is published.
1809 Meriwether Lewis commits suicide.
1812 Patrick reenlists in the army and fights in the War of 1812.
1814 Meriwether Lewis' journal is published.
1832 Patrick at age 60 marries 20-year-old Maria Hamilton.
1849 Maria dies of the measles, leaving Patrick with six children.
1861 Patrick tries to enlist in the Civil War.
1870 Patrick Gass dies at age 99 at Wellsburg.

9

WELLSBURG

I found Patrick Gass of the Lewis and Clark Expedition mentioned in a clipping tucked in an old family Bible in my mother-in-law's house in California. Trying to find out something about him, I discovered to my amazement that he was a West Virginian. My wife Katharine now joined me in having a West Virginia lineage. Patrick had lived in Wellsburg most of his life. He was a third-generation American. His grandfather, like John Lewis, came to the colonies through Philadelphia from Ireland. But the Gasses came thirty years before the Lewises and, like so many of the first Irish to arrive, initially lived in Pennsylvania. Although Patrick would travel with another Lewis from Virginia on his expedition, the family ties between John Lewis and Captain Meriwether Lewis, if any, were quite distant.

Through the Wellsburg Genealogical Society, I learned that Patrick's great-grandson Eugene Gass Painter lived nearby. We decided to visit.

We pulled into the parking lot at the Shop and Save alongside Route 2 in Wellsburg where we were to meet Eugene Gass Painter. I stepped out of the car, and simultaneously, a sprightly, older gentleman hopped out of an adjacent car. I said, "Mr. Painter." He broke into a smile and extended his hand. I introduced Katharine. They were second cousins, many times removed. Katharine told Mr. Painter how we happened to find out that her family had a tie to Patrick Gass.

"Well, Patrick Gass was my great-grandfather," said Mr. Painter. "His youngest daughter, Rachel, was my grandmother. She lived here all her life, never went more than fifteen miles away from where she was born. Patrick and I were born on the same day, June 12, 138 years apart. You all won't mind waiting a minute before I show you around, will you? My son Gene is coming here. I'm eighty-seven, and I want Gene to take over this family history business when I'm gone. I want him to meet you."

We told Mr. Painter about going to Montana with our four granddaughters and seeing the Lewis and Clark Interpretive Center in Great Falls. We had also driven over the Lolo Pass into the Bitterroots, the mountains on the Montana/Idaho border, which Patrick had described in his journal as being so difficult to cross. Mr. Painter told us about his visit to South Dakota for a Lewis and Clark festival, where he gave a talk about Patrick.

"You know," Mr. Painter said, "no one knows what happened to Patrick's original journal. Some said that fellow who published it might have kept it. If so, it's never been found. Here's what I think happened. One of his daughters who lived along the river had it. There was a flood that rose as high as the second floor of some of the houses in Wellsburg. I think that journal is in the bottom of the Ohio out there, or maybe it floated on down the river."

I mentioned to Mr. Painter that I thought Patrick's journal was more direct and easier to read than the flowery writings of Meriwether Lewis, which were more the style of the time.

"Well. I don't know," said Mr. Painter. "The story is that he had only nineteen days of schooling in his life. But he certainly taught himself to read and write. That journal was supposedly pretty crude so the schoolteacher here in Wellsburg who published it must have done some editing. You know that Patrick had a razor box that was carved by the Indian woman Sacagawea. It was in the family, but now it's in the museum at Fort Clatsop out in Oregon, where the expedition spent the winter of 1805/1806. My grandmother said he was friendly with Sacagawea, but his journal doesn't seem to pay a lot of attention to her. He also had a hatchet that he carried with him on the expedition that he brought back to Wellsburg and used to build houses. I don't know what happened to it. The museum here has a gun that they say was his, but who knows."

Across the parking lot came a tall fellow in his fifties. Katharine would later say he reminded her of her father, also a Gass descendent. Mr. Painter introduced him as his son Gene. Mr. Painter kept on talking as Gene stood there quietly with a twinkle in his eye. He said to Katharine aside, "I live on a farm that's been in the family 200 years and this history stuff can get old after a while." Soon Gene bode us goodbye. He had to go pick up a battery for his daughter's car.

Mr. Painter, whom I was now calling Eugene, pulled himself into the front seat of our car, and we began our tour. We drove up to the top of the ridge on the east side of Wellsburg to the cemetery. We parked and looked out over the town and the hillsides along the Ohio River. To the south on the river a power plant spewed steam

Photo by the author

high into the sky. Eugene pointed to a gravestone with a small American flag next to it, and we walked in that direction. The marker was inscribed: "GASS" and below, on one side, PATRICK W., SGT. LEWIS & CLARK EXP., 1771-1870; on the other side MARIA HAMILTON, HIS WIFE, 1812-1849.

Eugene said, "Patrick and Maria were married in 1832. She was twenty; he was sixty. My grandmother Rachel was their seventh child; one died. She was born in 1846, three years before her mother died. Patrick, faced with raising all these children, paid a family $60 to raise Rachel. When she was eighteen and he was ninety-three, he went to get her back. The family refunded him $16." He went on to say that Patrick and Maria hadn't originally been buried here, but out at Pierce Run where he would take us later. Through all this discussion I wondered how there could have been only two generations separating Patrick and Eugene. I finally figured out that Patrick had been seventy-five when Eugene's grandmother Rachel was born.

Katharine reminded me that, while we were at the Lewis & Clark Center in Great Falls, our granddaughters mentioned Patrick Gass and a guide said, "You girls come from solid stock." No doubt about that.

And I said to Eugene, "It's a bit clearer now how you could be Patrick's great-grandson and still be here with us."

We next stopped back downtown at a house on the river behind the library. Patrick, a carpenter by trade, had constructed it and several other buildings in Wellsburg. The house itself had siding but its stone foundation showed its age. It was these carpentry skills that Meriwether Lewis wanted for the expedition. Patrick directed the construction of the winter forts: Dubois near St. Louis in 1803, Mandan in North Dakota in 1804, and Clatsop at the mouth of the Columbia in Oregon in 1805.

Continuing on our tour, we enjoyed the bustling town with its many old buildings. From the waterfront park and wharf, flatboats had departed for New Orleans, beginning in 1790, hauling cargo down the Ohio. Patrick made a trip to New Orleans on one of those boats before the expedition west. The paddle wheeler, the *Delta Queen*, even now occasionally brings her passengers to Wellsburg. Eugene said a group promoting the coming two hundredth anniversary of the Lewis and Clark Expedition had come down the Ohio from Pittsburgh the month before in pirogues, large canoe-type boats, the kind Lewis and Clark used going up the Missouri. Eugene met them and gave them a tour.

Eugene next took us out the Bethany Pike, which follows Buffalo Creek. Four miles from downtown, the road cuts through a hillside. We stopped, and Eugene pointed down a side road. "Patrick lived here with his daughter Annie, my great aunt, in his old age. He used to walk to town to get the paper every day," said Eugene. "There were some old flour mills here on Buffalo Creek."

We walked down the side road and looked over an embankment. There we saw a stream and the stone foundation of the mill. "This road goes out to Bethany College, and in the late 1800s a trolley ran out from town to the school. It went through a tunnel right here, built in 1831, the first tunnel ever constructed west of the Alleghenies."

Back in the car, we drove a couple of miles farther out the pike and then turned up a one-lane road, following a small creek called Pierce Run. "Stop here," said Eugene. We got out, and he pointed to a field. "Maria and Patrick built a log house over there about 1835. At least I think it was over there. But it could have been on the other side of the road. We just don't know. I saw an old picture of the place before it was torn down and it's hard to tell where it was. Patrick became a farmer."

Eugene walked us over to a weed patch alongside the road. "This is a cemetery for a family that lived near here. Maria was thirty-seven when she died. She caught the measles from her children. Patrick buried her here, close, of course, to where they lived with the six children. When he died twenty years later, he was buried here beside her. But nobody ever kept this cemetery up, as you can see, so he and Maria's remains were moved to the place in town."

Back in the car, Eugene pulled a document from a folder. "Read this," he said. It seemed to be a research paper on the Gass family origins that I had thought were Scotch. It said that they had been Huguenots from France (like the Lewises) and had a fulling mill in the Netherlands; a fulling mill thickens cloth. The English king brought the Gasses to England because of their talents and then sent them to Ulster or Northern Ireland to set up a mill. Patrick's grandfather Benjamin immigrated to Pennsylvania about 1700, landing at Philadelphia. He moved out to Falling Springs near Chambersburg, the western edge of civilization at that time. They set up another fulling mill. His son Benjamin, Jr. was born there in 1751. He married an Irish girl, Mary McLene, and they had eight children. From Falling Springs Patrick's restless father moved his family repeatedly farther west to Fort Fredrick, Maryland, near Cumberland, on to Uniontown, and then to Catfish Camp, now Washington, Pennsylvania. Using three mules they climbed over the Alleghenies. Patrick's father led one mule packed with the household goods while his mother and baby brother rode another. Patrick and his sister followed on the third, sitting between two baskets hung on the mule's sides. At one spot his father exchanged a horse for two hundred acres, cleared some land, and built a cabin. They were following Braddock's Trail, which later became the National Road over the Alleghenies from Cumberland to Wheeling. They finally settled on Pierce's Run outside Wellsburg where Benjamin Gass established another fulling mill. This tracing of the Gass ancestry in America, we found out, had been done in the late 1800s by James R. Gass, my wife Katharine's great-great-grandfather, who was Patrick's nephew.

Patrick, as a boy, took packhorses by himself to Mercersburg, back into eastern Pennsylvania and south to Hagerstown, Maryland to get salt and iron for the family. Each horse could carry two hundred pounds of iron or two bushels of salt. Once during a dry spell, he went to Charles Town to get corn and have it ground at a mill there. There was little time for formal schooling.

The family, living on the frontier, did not seem bothered by the Revolutionary War, but afterwards in 1792, Patrick's father at age 41 was drafted to protect the frontier from the Indians. Patrick served for his father. Patrick never saw any Indians but met some interesting fellows while stationed at Wheeling Creek on the Ohio near his home at Wellsburg. At the Battle of Falling Timbers, General Anthony Wayne put an end to the Indian threat to the Ohio. In

1793, with his service over, Patrick joined a group of frontier scouts, floating a square bowed scow down the Ohio to the Mississippi and hauling trading goods to New Orleans. The trip took over a month. He came home on a ship by way of Cuba to Philadelphia.

Later, while in the Carlisle area, Patrick saw George Washington. The President was there to put down the Whiskey Rebellion. Backwoods Pennsylvanians were causing havoc over the federal tax on alcohol. The next year Patrick became a carpenter's apprentice in Mercersburg where he worked on a house for James Buchanan, Senior, who had a three-year-old boy, named Jimmy. "Little Jimmy Buchanan," as Patrick Gass would always call him, served as President of the United States just prior to Lincoln and was noted for his indecisiveness regarding the slave issue.

In 1799, fearing that the United States might be going to war with France, Patrick rejoined the army and served at the federal arsenal at Harpers Ferry, Virginia. The next year President John Adams and Napoleon, through their emissaries, reached an agreement that ended any further threat of war. Patrick was discharged. However, he was back in the army again when he joined the Lewis and Clark Expedition.

At noon, we went back into Wellsburg. Eugene said we should follow him to the interstate. His farm was just off the Washington Pike. We trailed him though wonderful, rolling farmland. He stopped and came back to our car. "I sure wish you had time to come see the farm. It's been in the family since 1790. My ancestor on the Manchester side bought up the warrants given to Revolutionary soldiers. The house we live in is over 180 years old. I dairy-farmed the place for a long time, but it finally got to be too much."

We thanked Eugene for his kindness but said that we had a long trip ahead of us back to Lewisburg.

Driving home, Katharine and I talked about how much we enjoyed Eugene Gass Painter. And the fun was that Katharine, the Californian, had now discovered her West Virginia relations. Patrick's brother William had moved from Wellsburg west into Ohio and Indiana and his descendants ended up in Missouri in the late 1800s. From there Katharine's grandmother, Grace Gass, continued westward to New Mexico and finally to California. It had taken six generations of her family 120 years to move across the country. Grace's great-granduncle, Patrick Gass, completed the trip in two years as part of the Lewis and Clark Expedition and helped pave the way for those that followed.[1]

10

VOYAGE OF DISCOVERY

On Monday the 14th of May 1804, we left our establishment at the mouth of the river du Bois . . . and having crossed the Mississippi proceeded up the Missouri on our intended voyage of discovery. . . . The corps consisted of forty-three men. . . . The best authenticated accounts informed us that we were to pass through a country possessed by numerous, powerful and warlike nations of savages, of gigantic stature, fierce, treacherous and cruel; and particularly hostile to white men. And fame had united with tradition in opposing mountains to our course, which human enterprise and exertion would attempt in vain to pass. . . .[1]

Thus wrote Patrick Gass as his first entry in his journal of the Lewis and Clark Expedition.

Patrick met Captain Meriwether Lewis at Kaskaskia, Illinois, south of St. Louis, in November 1803. Having reenlisted in the army three years earlier, he was stationed there with an artillery company on the Mississippi River, which had been up to that time the western border of the United States.

Captain Lewis stopped at Kaskaskia on his way to St. Louis to select men for the expedition directed by President Thomas Jefferson. He was to find a water route by way of what was called the Northwest Passage to the Pacific Ocean. Captain Lewis was raised in Albemarle County, Virginia, near Jefferson's home and had served as the President's secretary.

In May 1803, the United States purchased the Louisiana Territory from France, which covered all the land west of the Mississippi to the Rocky Mountains. In truth, no one really knew what the boundaries were. Jefferson believed that his purchase stretched to the headwaters of every river that flowed into the Missouri. This made Lewis' expedition all the more important. He and his men would follow the Missouri until it ended at the foot of the Rockies, then would cross over a mountain and find the Columbia River, which would carry them to the Pacific Ocean. They expected to go sufficiently far the first summer that they would reach the Pacific in the early summer of the following year and have time to return by fall. It didn't happen that way.

Meriwether Lewis left Pittsburgh September 1, 1803. He came down the Ohio in his keelboat while others traveled in pirogues, large dugout canoes rowed by several men. Captain William Clark, who was living in Indiana, joined Lewis and brought with him his slave York. Captain Clark, a former Virginian and an Army officer, had been Captain Lewis' commanding officer at one time. Lewis picked Clark to be his co-commander for the expedition. Lewis was the scientific observer; Clark was the surveyor, the waterman, and the mapmaker. Their skills complemented each other.

Lewis carried a directive from the secretary of war allowing him to recruit men from Patrick's detachment at Kaskaskia. With twenty other men, Patrick eagerly volunteered, but his commanding officer declared that Gass, the unit's best non-commissioned officer, could not be spared.

Captain Lewis saw in Patrick a short, stocky fellow with large shoulders, a thick chest, and muscular arms, as well as a man with strong features, alert eyes, energetic movements, and a quick mind. But what Captain Lewis needed was carpentry skills. Lewis carefully picked three men and then overrode the commander's objection to losing Patrick. Thus Patrick became the last military man chosen for the expedition. It didn't matter to him that he would be going as a private. At thirty-two, he was one of the three oldest men on the expedition.

The corps left Kaskaskia in the keelboat with the pirogues following. They proceeded up the Mississippi to St. Louis where they selected a campsite for the winter, across from the mouth of the Missouri. Patrick supervised the building of log huts surrounded by a palisade that was called Camp Dubois. Forty men stayed there during the winter of 1803/1804. In this encampment the captains tested the men's skills, determining who were the best hunters, the best marksmen, the best gun repairers, and who knew the most about the Missouri and Indian languages. The camp also became a test of character to see how the men got along together in close quarters. Captain Clark stayed mostly in camp, while Captain Lewis spent much of his time in St. Louis, procuring supplies and gathering knowledge on where they were going. At the time, St. Louis was a center for the fur trade with 1,500 residents, mainly French, Spanish, Indians, and slaves.

Spring came and Patrick and the expedition prepared to depart. The keelboat was loaded and tested in the river. She was fifty-five feet long with an eight-foot beam. She had twenty-two oars plus a sail. She carried two swivel-gun blunderbusses that fired buckshot as well as a cannon that shot one ball. Going against the current, she sometimes had to be poled rather than rowed. If the river bottom was too soft, Patrick and the men had to get out and walk along the shore pulling the keelboat with long elk-hide towropes. In addition to the keelboat there were two pirogues, forty-foot open boats with shallow drafts. All three boats were loaded with thousands of pounds of supplies, items to trade to the Indians, ammunition, and bags of food.

The party departed Fort Dubois on May 14, 1804, heading up the Missouri River. Eleven days into the voyage, they passed the last white settlement. Patrick had begun his journal, but his notations were brief. The country was pleasant, sometimes prairies, sometimes bluffs. Cottonwood, sycamore, hickory, and white walnut lined the bank. With Seaman, his dog, Captain Lewis frequently walked the bank, observing the vegetation and making notes. At times the wind blew so strongly against the boats that they were forced to stop for the day until it died down. Trees drifting down the river also gave them problems. Patrick reported that, "our boat turned in a ripple, and nearly upset." In early June "we broke our mast by steering too close to shore." On another day "going around some driftwood, the stern of the boat became fast, when she immediately swung around, and was in great danger, but we got her off without much injury." The men complained about the mosquitoes and ticks. Deer were plentiful and what wasn't eaten was dried or jerked.

On July 4, the swivel gun was fired at sunrise and the men received an extra ration of whiskey. As Patrick wrote, "passed a creek . . . which we called Independence." A private was caught sleeping on guard duty, a crime punishable by death, according to army regulations. However, the men voted that the private be given one hundred lashes four different times. And one of the men "got snake bitten, but not dangerously. After dinner we renewed our voyage. . . ."

The expedition made nine to twenty miles a day depending on

weather conditions. On July 21, Patrick noted, "We came to the great river Platte which at the mouth is three quarters of a mile broad. . . . We passed some beautiful hills and prairies. . . . Beaver appear plenty in this part of the country. . . . Two of our hunters went out and killed a prarow, about the size of a groundhog and nearly of the same color." It turned out to be a badger. Captain Lewis had it stuffed and later sent it to President Jefferson.

At Council Bluffs (Iowa) on August 2, after having traveled 640 miles, the expedition met its first Indians. Captain Lewis gave them a speech about President Jefferson, calling him their new father. He distributed gifts, including a U.S. flag. The Indians wanted ammunition and whiskey, which Captain Lewis reluctantly provided.

Six days later, north of the Little Sioux River, the men observed an unusual appearance. Floating down upon them, they saw a huge mass of white feathers, stretching the width of the river. Farther on, they arrived at a sandbar covered with hundreds of white pelicans. Patrick had seen brown pelicans on his journey from New Orleans to Cuba, but no one expected them to be found on the Missouri so far from the ocean.[2] He wrote, "In the bag under the bill and the neck of the pelican, which Capt. Lewis killed, we put five gallons of water."

Sergeant Floyd, one of the two sergeants on the expedition, became sick in mid-August with what Patrick described as, "a complaint somewhat like a violent colic." His blood was drained, and he was given purgative pills to clean out the bowels. But the treatment seemed to make Sergeant Floyd worse. On August 20, he died. The men buried him "on high prairie hills on the north side of the river." He was twenty-two years old. The bluff was named after him, and is near Sioux City, Iowa. From the perspective of today's medical knowledge, Sergeant Floyd probably died of an infection from a ruptured appendix. He would be the only person lost on the expedition.

Two days later, the men elected Patrick Gass to replace Floyd as sergeant. He received nineteen votes in the first American election west of the Mississippi. Captain Lewis issued an order, which he wrote in his journal, promoting Patrick to "Sergeant in the corps of volunteers for North Western Discovery." The order ended with, "the commanding officers are still further confirmed in the high opinion they had previously formed of the capacity, diligence and integrity of Sergeant. Gass, from the wish expressed by large a majority of his comrades for his appointment as Sergeant."[3] Displaying a degree of modesty, Patrick made no mention of his promotion in his journal.

While tasting arsenic and cobalt mineral samples during one of his scientific endeavors, Captain Lewis became sick. Captain Clark feared that, like Floyd, Lewis might die. Captain Lewis took the purgative pills or Rush pills that he had obtained from a Dr. Rush in Philadelphia. The pills containing mercury and chloride, were called "thunder Clappers" by the men, and were the standard remedy for all ills during the expedition. In this case the pills worked, and Captain Lewis was soon back to normal.

On August 29 sixty Yankton Sioux camped on the river across from the expedition. The Sioux presence concerned the men, but the Indians seemed peaceful. At a council the two sides exchanged gifts. Captain Lewis gave his "new father" speech referring to President Jefferson and called the Indians "children." The peace pipe was passed; the Sioux men danced. But the Sioux seemed more interested in setting up trading arrangements than going to Washington to meet their "new father," as Lewis had proposed.

The expedition moved into what is now South Dakota. Patrick observed that, "a person by going up on one of the hills may have a view as far as the eye can reach without any obstruction." Animal life was abundant. Some of the men came on a prairie-dog town. "They gathered kettles and other vessels for holding water; in order to drive the animals out of their holes by pouring in water." Only one prairie dog came out. In another encounter Patrick and one of the men killed a buffalo, and he wrote, "We left a hat to scare off the vermin and beasts of prey, but when we came to the place, we found the wolves had devoured the carcass and carried off the hat." A pronghorn, an antelope-like creature, was also killed. One of the men shot the first jack rabbit they had ever seen. Captain Lewis measured a twenty-one-foot leap by one rabbit. Captain Lewis, on another one of his walking excursions, spotted what he estimated to be a herd of 3,000 buffalo. At night the men could hear wolves and coyotes howling all around.

On September 24, the expedition came to the mouth of the Teton River. There an Indian stole a horse from one of the men while he was out hunting. The expedition camped and met with the Indians, and convinced them to return the horse. The next day fifty of the Lakota Sioux arrived. Captain Clark went ashore in a pirogue. The Indians wanted to keep the pirogue and would not let him return to the keelboat. Patrick described the action: "Captain Clark told them his soldiers were good, and that he had more medicine aboard his boat than would kill twenty such nations in one day." Captain Clark drew his sword and told his men to pick up their arms. The Sioux raised their bows and guns. On the keelboat the cannon and two swiveling blunderbusses were pointed toward the Indians. The chief released the rope to the pirogue.

The expedition proceeded a short distance. Patrick wrote, "The bank of the river was covered all the way with Indians. Captain Clark went on shore. When the Indians saw him coming, they met him with a buffalo robe, spread it out and made him get into it, and then eight of them carried him to the council house. Captain Lewis went ashore and was carried to the council house in the same manner. They killed several dogs for our people to feast on, and spent the greater part of the day in eating and smoking."

The next day, Patrick and some of the men went over to the Indian camp with Captain Lewis. "They are the most friendly people I ever saw but will pilfer if they have an opportunity. They are also very dirty.... About 15 days ago they had a battle with the Mahas, of whom they killed 75 men and took 25 women prisoners...." In the evening the Indians had a dance. "On one side the women, about 80 in number, formed in a solid column round the fire, with sticks in their hands, and the scalps of the Mahas they had killed, tied on them. They kept a continual noise singing and yelling.... They continued until one o'clock at night when we returned to the boat. "

In the morning "we went to shove off, some of the Indians took hold of the rope and would not let go.... Captain Lewis was near giving orders to cut the rope and to fire on them." The chiefs intervened and Captain Lewis agreed to give them some tobacco if they let go of the rope. Farther up the river an Indian approached, saying 300 more Indians wanted to meet with them. Captain Lewis declined.

By now it was the middle of October. Out hunting, Patrick "saw about 300 goats or antelope and some buffalo." The weather was getting cold. "We had a disagreeable night of sleet and hail. It snowed during the forenoon." And they "saw Indians . . . who not withstanding the coldness of the weather, had not an article of clothing except their breech-cloths."

On October 27, the expedition arrived at the villages of the Mandan Indians (near what is now Bismarck, North Dakota) and

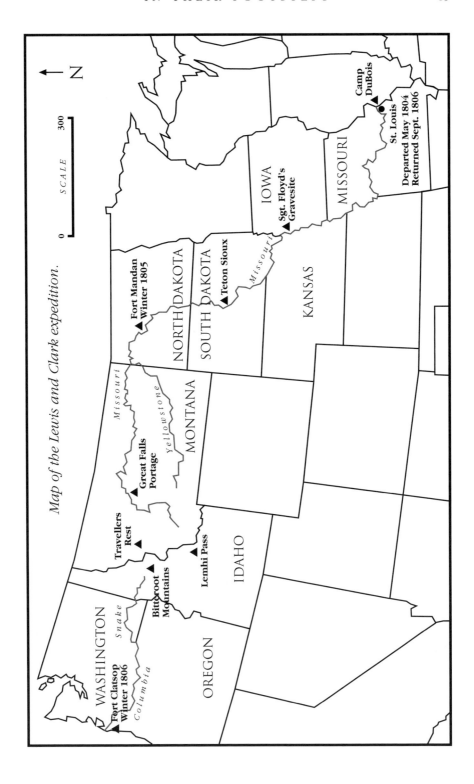

Map of the Lewis and Clark expedition.

camped in order to hold a council. They wanted to make sure that these Indians were friendly and that it would be safe to spend the winter there. Four thousand Indians lived in the area. After locating a suitable place for the winter quarters, Patrick supervised the construction. He noted, "We began to clear a place for a camp and fort. We pitched our tents and laid the foundation. . . . The huts were in two rows containing four rooms each. . . . The fort was enclosed by a picket wall eighteen feet high." With the bitter cold, ice on the river, and some snow, the expedition settled into Fort Mandan. Captain Clark calculated that they had come 1,610 miles up the Missouri from where they had embarked six months earlier. They had crossed the future state of Missouri, touched the corner of Kansas, followed the border between Nebraska and Iowa, spanned South Dakota, and ended up in west central North Dakota.

During December, the men concentrated on hunting to stock up for the winter. But soon "the buffaloe were gone from the river." The men lived off corn obtained from the Mandans in trade for sheet iron, made from anything iron the men could find. On Christmas Patrick wrote, "The morning was ushered in by two discharges of the swivel [gun], and a round of small arms by the whole corps. Captain Clarke then presented to each man a glass of brandy, and we hoisted the American flag in the garrison, and its first waving in Fort Mandan was celebrated with another glass." After dinner the men danced "without the presence of females."

Since Patrick's journal was brief by necessity so as to keep it "small and portable," he did not "give some account of the fair sex of the Missouri; and entertain . . . with narratives of love as well of arms. . . . It may be observed generally that chastity is not very highly esteemed by these people [the Indians]. . . . The fact is, that the women are generally considered an article of traffic and indulgences are sold at a very modest price. As proof of this I will mention, that for an old tobacco box, one of our men was granted the honor of passing a night with the daughter of the head chief of the Mandan nation." Patrick knew that young squaws were offered to the captains, but did not think they accepted. As to his own activity, nothing was said. Venereal disease was a problem and, like everything else, was treated with Dr. Rush's pills.

The winter passed without serious incident. Hunting parties provided some deer and elk. The Indians visited daily. It was so cold, forty-five below zero, that some of the men's feet froze. Capt. Lewis had to cut off one boy's toes. Captain Clark's slave York had frostbite on his penis.

During the winter stay a French Canadian trader Toussaint Charbonneau and his Indian wife Sacagawea, who had been staying with the Mandans, joined the expedition. Sacagawea was a Shoshone, a tribe that lived in the Rockies near the headwaters of the Missouri. "We expect she will be of service to us, when passing through that nation," wrote Patrick. She had been captured by the nearby Hidatsa and brought back to the plains. She was now fifteen, pregnant, and her baby was born that February. Sacagawea, her husband, and the baby, called Pomp by the captains, would accompany the men westward.

On April 7, 1805, Patrick noted the continuation of their journey; "We left Fort Mandans in good spirits. The expedition expected to reach the Pacific that summer and return to Fort Mandan by next winter. Thirty-one men and a women [and a baby on a cradle board] went up the river and thirteen returned down it" to St. Louis. The keelboat contained "boxes full of skins, buffalo robes, and horns of the Mountain ram, of a great size for the President." Capt. Lewis included the reports he had written and the maps that Capt. Clark had drawn.

Traveling in April, the expedition members fought headwinds much of the time as they paddled their pirogues. On some days the wind forced them to stay in camp, but on other days they made twenty to twenty-five miles. There were no trees because the Indians burned the prairie each spring. Patrick reported the expedition's arrival at the mouth of "the Yellow Stone River . . . 1888 miles from the mouth of the Missouri . . ." They had come 278 miles from Fort Mandan in eighteen days and had crossed into Montana from North Dakota. "Captain Lewis and one of the men traveled some distance by land and killed a white bear. The natives call them white but they are more of a brown gray. They are longer than the common black bear, and have much larger feet and talons." The wounded bear had chased the Captain, but there had been time to reload and shoot him. It was a grizzly.

Though it was May, Patrick reported that "snow and green grass on the prairies exhibited an appearance somewhat uncommon. . . . Banks of snow were seen lying on the hills. . . . The river [was] more crooked and the country mountainous." There were more bear stories: "Some of the men discovered a large brown bear, and six of them went out to kill it. They fired at it: but only having wounded it, it made battle and was near seizing some of them, but they all fortunately escaped, and at length succeeded in dispatching it." The Captain said he would rather fight two Indians than one bear. Patrick described the bears as "very bold and ferocious; and very large and powerful."

Farther on, they "passed through desert country "and "came to large rapids" where they forced their way through. All along the Missouri they saw Indian paths, "also roads and paths made by the buffaloe . . . . A buffaloe swimming the river happened to land at one of the pirogues, crossed over it and broke two guns. . . . He then went straight through the men where they were sleeping, but hurt none of them."

On June 2 the corps "encamped . . . at the mouth of a large river. . . . The commanding officers could not determine which of the rivers or branches, it was proper to take. . . . Captain Clarke, myself, and four others went up the South branch . . . about thirty miles and found the river still extending in a South West direction." Captain Lewis, having gone up the north branch sixty miles, returned two days later. He found it navigable, but "they saw no mountains ahead, but one" and "it was not covered with snow. . . . The officers concluded that the south branch was the most proper to ascend, which they think is the Missouri. The other they called Maria's river." Most of the men thought the captains had picked the wrong river, but, if Patrick disagreed, he never mentioned it in his journal.

Captain Lewis proceeded ahead on foot and discovered the Great Falls of the Missouri, which the Indians at Fort Mandan had described to him. Patrick wrote that Captain Lewis "had been up the falls 15 miles above the first shoot or pitch, and found the falls continue all that distance, in which there were 5 different shoots 40 or 50 foot perpendicular each, and very rapid water between them. . . . We engaged in making small wagons to haul the canoes and loading above the falls." By June 23 they had moved the first of their supplies around the falls. "Here the river is wide and the current gentle," he said. The country rises "in planes a considerable distance on both sides of the river; and far off [are] mountains covered with snow on both sides and ahead. Two of the men and myself remained with Captain Lewis here to assist him in putting together the iron boat," the frame for which had been made at Harpers Ferry. The rest returned for another load.

On the Fourth of July, Patrick and Captain Lewis worked on the framed boat. "The awful twenty mile portage around the falls, dragging the boats and supplies was completed, but we still needed a few days to finish the iron boat . . . and finally put her into the water. . . . The tallow and coal dust which was used to seal the seams and coat the skins as soon as dry, it cracked and scaled off, and the water came through the skins. . . . We had, after all our labour, to haul our new boat on shore, and leave it."

With the loss of the iron boat, the captains ordered the men to build two more canoes. Patrick and the men marched twenty miles to find the timber. From the time the expedition had reached the Marias River, decided which branch to take, and then portaged around the Great Falls, it had taken six weeks, and they had advanced only fifty miles. The men now knew that they would not return to Fort Mandan that year.

Over the next two weeks, the Missouri, as it passed through central Montana, turned south and then southeast, which was not the direction the expedition intended to go. It became narrow in spots with rapids as the pirogues passed through high mountains and a narrow valley that Captain Clark called the Gates of the Rocky Mountains. Patrick noted that the squaw, Sacagawea, began to recognize the country "and informed us she had been at this place when she was small." She assured the men that the Three Forks of the Missouri were not far ahead, and they reached them on July 27. The captains named the rivers the Jefferson, the Madison, and the Gallatin. The expedition continued up the Jefferson, the western-most river. "Our squaw informed us that it was at this place she had been taken prisoner [by the Hidatsas] 4 or 5 years earlier."

Captain Clark walked ahead, trying to make contact with the Indians. The first week in August, Patrick traveled with Captain Clark, looking for Sacagawea's tribe, the Shoshones. Over the next three days, they covered sixty miles but found no Indians. Captain Clark was becoming worried; the expedition needed the Indians to show them the way over the mountains. Meanwhile, stated Patrick, "The river passed through a mountain," and "became very crooked, narrow, and in some places so shallow, that we were obliged to get into the water and drag the canoes along." They passed a large rock formation that resembled a beaver head, which Sacagawea recognized from her childhood. The expedition was now 3,000 miles from the mouth of the Missouri.

On August 11, Captain Lewis caught sight of an Indian on horseback, but he galloped off. The captain followed the Indian's tracks up over Lemhi Pass, crossing into present-day Idaho at the Continental Divide, at an altitude of 7,300 feet. The next day he saw three Indians, a man and two women. They ran to warn their village. Sixty Shoshones came galloping toward Captain Lewis on horseback, ready to attack. He laid down his gun and held a flag to show that he meant peace. Together, he and the Indians returned to the village on the Lemhi River where food was offered to the first white man these people had ever seen.

On August 17, back on the other side of the pass, Patrick and the men saw Indians approaching. "There were about 20 of the natives with Captain Lewis." They had come back over the Lemhi Pass to join the rest of the group at what the expedition called Camp Fortunate. "Here we unloaded the canoes, and had a talk with the Indians: and agreed with them that they should lend us some of their horses to carry our baggage to the Columbia River." Sacagawea was pleased to see the people of her nation, and it turned out that the chief of the Shoshones was her brother.

The next day Patrick with "Captain Clarke and 11 more, including our interpreter and his wife, and all the Indians set out at eleven o'clock to go over to the Columbia River." They crossed the Lemhi Pass, leaving the rest of the men behind with Captain Lewis. Stopping at the Shoshone village, they made a disconcerting discovery. The Shoshones had never traveled west to the Columbia. "They gave us very unfavorable accounts with respect to the rivers, and expect [us] to perform the route by land." As a result, "we procured a guide and left our interpreters [Sacagawea and her husband] to go on with the natives and assist Captain Lewis and his party to bring on the luggage" over the pass.

Patrick, with Captain Clark, proceeded with the guide whom the Captains named Old Toby. Traveling northward, "we could not get through the narrows and had to cross a very high mountain." They came on the Salmon River and headed westward down it about twelve miles but had to return. "The water is so rapid and the bed of the river so rocky, that it seemed impossible to go along the river . . . . Our guide speaks of a way to sea by going up the (north) fork of this river, getting on to the mountains that way, and then turning southwest again."

After Patrick and Captain Clark's dead-end trip, they found

Captain Lewis and the rest of the party, who by now had come over the Lemhi Pass and were buying horses from the Shoshones. One of the Indians showed Patrick their method of producing fire: "They have two sticks . . . they lay down and rub the end of the other upon it in a perpendicular direction for a few minutes: and the friction raises a kind of dust, which in a short time takes fire."

On the last day of August, the whole corps gathered, and Patrick and the expedition "proceeded on with 27 horses and one mule. Old Toby, after consulting with the rest of the Indians, thought it was better to go along the north side of the Columbia, rather than on the south side" as they had first tried by way of the west fork of the Salmon River.

During the next ten days, they moved north and climbed over Lost Trail Pass back into Montana. Some days they made twenty miles, other days very few miles but all with great difficulty, as reported by Patrick. "Stones injured our horses feet . . . In going up ascents the horses would sometimes fall backwards, which injured them very much. . . . We pursued our journey up the creek, which still continued fatiguing almost beyond description." They ate "the last of our pork. . . . Our hunters had not killed anything. . . . To add to our misfortunes we had a cold evening with rain." Snow fell at night. They came upon "a band of the Flathead nation of Indians" and "recruited [from them] our horses to 40 and 3 colts. . . . They were a friendly people . . . but they have nothing to eat but berries, roots. . . . This band was on its way over to the Missouri or the Yellow-stone to hunt buffaloe. . . . They informed us that the Columbia River is 5 or 6 days journey distant." They were wrong.

The expedition continued northward, following the Bitterroot River. At Lolo, a few miles south of present-day Missoula, they turned westward, facing a dark range of mountains, the Bitterroots.

11

TO THE PACIFIC AND RETURN

"We reached the mountains, which are very steep; but the road over them pretty good, as it is much traveled by the natives, who come over to the Flathead [Bitterroot] river to gather cherries and berries," wrote Patrick. "We came to a most beautiful warm spring [Lolo Hot Springs], the water of which is considerably above blood-heat; and I could not bear my hand in it without uneasiness." The expedition, on September 12, 1805, passed back into Idaho, this time over Lolo Pass.

With no deer to be found, they became so hungry that "some of the men . . . agreed to kill a colt; which they immediately did, and set about roasting it; and which appeared to me to be good eating." They had followed the Lochsa River, but on September 15, with Old Toby guiding, they "again took to the mountains. In going up, one of the horses fell, and required eight to ten men to assist him in getting up again." They were at almost 7,000 feet, and the next day snow fell. They were proceeding along the top of a ridge, and as Patrick described, "over the most terrible mountains I ever beheld. . . . The snow fell so thick . . . that a person could not see to a distance of 200 yards. [Then] warm sunshine, which melted the snow very fast . . . made the traveling very fatiguing and very uncomfortable . . . one of our horses fell down the precipice about 100 feet [and] pitched into the water, without meeting with any intervening object, which could materially injure him. . . . The men are becoming lean and debilitated, on account of the scarcity and poor quality of the provisions on which we subsist."

Standing on the top of Mount Sherman at 6,650 feet, Patrick and the corps "discovered the appearance of a valley or level part of the country about 40 miles ahead . . . there was as much joy and rejoicing among the corps, as happens among passengers at sea . . . when they discover land on the long looked for coast. . . . We continued our march along a ridge. . . . We can see the valley ahead, but a great way off. . . . Our march [is] impeded by fallen timber. . . . We . . . killed a wolf and ate it. . . . On September 22 we proceeded . . . down the ridge along a very rough way: and in the evening arrived in a fine large valley, clear of these distant and horrible mountains."[1] The expedition had covered eighty miles of those "horrible mountains, " the Bitterroots, in ten days. This had not been the one-day trip over an Allegheny type mountain with the Columbia River just ahead as the group had originally anticipated.

The expedition descended into the Weippe Prairie, home to the Nez Perce Indians. "The Indians belonging to this band," Patrick wrote, "received us kindly . . . and gave us such provisions as they had . . . which consisted of roots, bread, and fish . . . and (the roots) resemble onions in shape, but are of a sweet taste. . . . [But] the men are generally unwell, owing to the change of diet. . . . Captain Clarke gave all the sick a dose of Rush Pills, to see what effect that would have. . . . Captain Lewis is very sick and taking medicine; and myself and two or three of the men are yet very unwell."

A few miles west of the Nez Perce camp lay the Clearwater River. Patrick wrote that the river " is about 200 yards wide: the water is clear as crystal, from 2 to 5 feet deep, and abounding with salmon . . . all hands that were able, [are] employed at the canoes" which were needed to continue the journey. "Hunters came in with 3 deer, a very welcome sight . . . " It was then October 1 and to save the men, "the greater number of them are still weak . . . we have adopted the Indian method of burning out the canoes."

Within a few days, "having got pretty well forward in our canoe making, we collected all our horses and branded them, in order to leave them with the Indians. . . . The morning of the seventh [of October] was pleasant and we . . . began our voyage down the [Clearwater] river, and found the rapids in some places very dangerous. . . . In passing through a rapid, I had my canoe stove and she sunk. Fortunately, the water was not more than waist deep, so our lives and baggage were saved." It took two days to repair the canoe. "Here our old snake guide [Toby] deserted. . . . I suspect he was afraid of being cast away passing the rapids. Meanwhile, some of the men "prefer dog-flesh to [dried] fish: and they here got two or three dogs from the Indians."

The corps stopped where the Clearwater joins the Snake on the Idaho/Washington border. Patrick "had a fit of the ague [malarial type fever]" and was "unable to steer my canoe." Going downstream, the men covered thirty miles in a day. On another day, riding the rapid current on the Snake, they made almost sixty miles. "We could get to the falls in four days which I presume are not very high as the salmon come above them in abundance. . . . The country . . . is high dry prairie plains without a stick of timber." The rapids continue "very bad, but we get over without injury." One of the canoes "hit a rock and part of her sunk . . . All the men got safe to shore."

On October 16, coming down the Snake, "we arrived at the great Columbia river" and they remained there for a day "for the purpose of taking an observation. . . . We got a number of dogs from the natives. Salmon are very plenty but poor and dying, and therefore not fit for provisions." At the junction of the two rivers there were many natives "of different nations here. . . . They are almost without clothing. . . . The women have scarce sufficient to cover their nakedness," Patrick noted.

Underway again with "white frost" in the morning "we passed . . . some bad rapids, but no accident happened. . . . The shores are lined with dead salmon, there are abundance of crows and ravens." The Indians have a "seine and some ash paddles which they did not make themselves. . . . White people have been here or not far distant during the summer." That day they went forty-two miles, the next day thirty-two miles despite passing "through two very rocky rapid parts of the river with great difficulty."

They then "came to the first falls or great falls; and had 1300 yards of portage over bad ground." They were in the Columbia River Gorge at the Cascades, near where the Bonneville Dam is today. Patrick stated that "in high water there is nothing but a rapid, and the salmon can pass up without difficulty." Below the falls we "came to other narrows . . . more confined and rocks higher. . . . We saw a great many sea otters swimming in the river and killed some, but could not get them as they sunk to the bottom. . . . We purchased from Indians a quantity of dried pounded fish, and then our hunters went out and killed six deer and some squirrels. . . . This is the first hunting ground we have had for a long time."

The wind "blew so hard ahead that we were unable to continue our voyage" for a time. On the last day of October "we had to unload our canoes and take them over the rapids . . . and over rocks 8 or 10 feet high." Still in the Columbia River Gorge, they laid down poles on the rocks and pushed the canoes over the rollers. "It was most fatiguing . . . the distance about a mile and the fall of the water about 25 feet in that distance. . . . The hills on both sides are very high, and a number of fine springs flowing out of them, some of which fall 200 feet perpendicular."

Near what is now Portland, Oregon "the river opened to the breadth of a mile, with a gentle current." That evening, "we could see the high point of a mountain covered with snow. . . . Our Commanding Officers are of the opinion that it is Mount Hood, discovered by a Lieutenant of Vancouver, who [thirteen years before] was up this river 75 miles." The next day "in the evening we saw Mount Rainy [Ranier] on the same side. It is a handsome point of mountain with little or no timber on it, very high, and a considerable distance off this place."

"We passed a great many Indian camps." The Indians were there for the fall salmon runs. "Here the tide rises and falls four feet. . . . The river is about three miles wide with a number of small islands.'" They "came to a bay 12 or 14 miles wide . . . the winds raised the waves so high, we had to coast around it." They reached a "point we called Cape Swell. . . . We found the waves so high . . . we can not proceed." They had to camp where "we scarcely had room to lie between the rocks and the water."

"Captain Lewis with four men started by land to see if any white people were to be found. . . ." There were none, and Lewis concluded that the white traders came in their ships to the mouth of the Columbia only during the summer.

On November 16, Patrick saw the Pacific. He said, "We could see the waves, like small mountains, rolling out in the ocean, and pretty bad in the bay.

"We are now at the end of our voyage, which has been completely accomplished according to the intention of the expedition, the object of which was to discover a passage by way of the Missouri and Columbia Rivers to the Pacific Ocean; not with standing the difficulties, privations, and dangers, which we had to encounter, endure, and surmount." The expedition had come 4,133 miles in nineteen months.

The men tried to find a campsite on the north side of the Columbia, but it was too steep and rocky. They stayed there a couple of weeks, while Captain Clark and some of the men explored north of the mouth along the ocean. Robert Gray had discovered the mouth of the river in 1792 and named it the Columbia. Another explorer came almost twenty years earlier, but somehow never found the mouth, and he named the place Cape Disappointment.

Patrick commented on Indian female fashion of which he obviously had an interest: "There were but a few Indians settled down about the seashore.... The women have a kind of fringe petticoats, made of filaments or tassels of the white cedar bark wrought with a string at the upper part, which is tied around the waste [sic]. These tassels or fringe are of some use as a covering, while the ladies are standing erect and the weather calm; but in any other position, or when the wind blows, their charms have but a precarious defense."

On December 7, they followed the river two miles and then "unloaded our canoes, and carried our baggage about 200 yards to a spring, where we encamped." They were seven miles inland from the ocean. Within a week Patrick, leading the construction of their winter quarters, reported, "we completed the building of our huts, seven in number."

In early January the expedition established an operation on the beach to make salt for the return trip. Beyond the salt works, they discovered "where a large fish had been driven on shore.... They found the skeleton of a whale that measured 105 feet in length. The natives had taken all the meat off its bones, by scalding and the other means for the purpose of trade."

Patrick wrote that the Indians were friendly. "The women are very much inclined to venery [gratification of sexual desire], and like those on the Missouri are sold to prostitution at an easy rate. An old Chin-ook squaw frequently visited our quarters with nine girls that she kept as prostitutes. To the honor of the Flatheads (Nez Perce), who live on the west side of the Rockies . . . we must mention them as an exception; they do not exhibit those loose feelings of carnal desire, nor appear addicted to the common customs of prostitution: and they are the only nation on the whole route where anything like chastity is regarded."

The men were ready to leave Fort Clatsop. The winter had certainly not been as cold as the previous one at Fort Mandan, but in the five months that they had been on the Pacific coast there had been only twelve days that it didn't rain and only six days with clear skies.[2] The Nez Perce had told the Captains that because of the snow the mountains could not be crossed until June. Departure from Fort Clatsop was set for March 23, 1806. The plan was to head back up the Columbia, over the Rockies, down the Missouri, and be home by the end of the summer.

As they went up the river, Patrick was still fascinated by Indian styles. "I took notice of a difference in the dress of the females from those below, about the coast. . . . Instead of the short petticoat, they have a piece of thin dressed skin tied tight around their loins, with a narrow slip coming up between their thighs."

By the second week of April, the corps had portaged around the Cascades of the Columbia. Indians were everywhere, waiting for the salmon run and always trying to steal something. They stole Captain Lewis' dog, Seaman, but the men got him back. Food was scarce; the salmon run hadn't started. "We had, however, a dog, which we bought from the Indians . . . but this was a scanty allowance for thirty odd hungry men." The men sat, eating a haunch of dog with Seaman looking them in the eyes.

In May the expedition returned to the village of the Nez Perce Indians to gather the horses that they had been kept for the corps over the winter. Patrick said that the natives "informed us we could not cross the mountains [the Bitterroots] for a moon and a half; as the snow was too deep, and no grass for our horses to subsist on. We have the mountains in view from this place, all covered white with snow." The Expedition stayed in the Weippe Prairie for five weeks waiting for the snow to melt. During that time Sacagawea's baby, which the Captains called Pomp, became ill and it took three weeks for him to get well. He was then fourteen months old.

On June 10, the expedition set out with 65 horses to cross the mountains. Seven days later they "turned back melancholy and disappointed." They had ascended a mountain where the snow "became deeper, until we reached the top, where it was twelve or fifteen feet deep; but it in general carried our horses. Here there was not the appearance of a green shrub, or anything for our horses to subsist on." It was no more than a four-day march over if they could just "find the road or course, which is almost impossible, without a guide perfectly acquainted with the mountains." They stored some baggage and went back down the mountain and camped in a glade where they found some Indians who would accompany them back over the mountains.

On June 26, the expedition set out again, proceeding early on a foggy morning. Patrick reported that they "found the banks of snow much decreased: at noon we arrived at the place where we had left our baggage and stores. . . . We proceeded over some very steep tops and deep snow . . . in the evening [we got] to the side of the hill where the snow was gone; and there was very good grass for our horses." The next day they proceeded "over some of the steepest mountains I have ever passed. The snow was so deep that we cannot wind along the sides of the steep slopes, but must slide straight down. The horses generally do not sink more than three inches in the snow; but some times they break through to their bellies." The third day they stopped "on the south side of this ridge [where] there is summer with grass and other herbages in abundance; and on the north side, winter with snow six to eight feet deep." On that day, June 28, they had gone over Lolo Pass. The next day "at ten o'clock we left the snow and in the evening we arrived at the warm spring (Lolo Hot Springs) and most of us bathed in its water." The following day "we halted for dinner at the same place where we had dined on the 12th of September 1805. . . ." This time their trip over the Bitterroots went much faster. They stayed on the ridge tops instead of dipping down along the Lochsa River, where Toby had misled them the previous fall.

Patrick wrote about the plans for the return: "Here the party is to be separated; some of us [with Captain Lewis] are to go straight across to the falls of the Missouri [Great Falls] and some [with Captain Clark] to the head waters of the Jefferson River [Camp Fortunate], where we left the canoes [last summer]." Captain Lewis, with Patrick as part of his group, headed directly east to Great Falls while Captain Clark swung south on a path somewhat similar to the one the expedition had followed the previous summer when they had first met the Shoshones. At Great Falls, Captain Lewis' group was to split into two groups, one to go up the Marias River with Captain Lewis, the other with Sergeant Gass to "remain at the falls to prepare harness and other things necessary for hauling our canoes and baggage over the portage." Captain Clark's group split where the three forks, the Jefferson, the Madison and the Gallatin form the Missouri. Some in canoes were to go down the Missouri and join Patrick's group at the falls; others led by Captain Clark were to go east to the Yellowstone River and follow it to the Missouri where everyone would meet in about six weeks.

On July 7, Captain Lewis' group "came to the dividing ridge between the waters of the Missouri and the Columbia; passed over the ridge and came to a fine spring, the waters of which run into the Missouri." They had crossed back over the Continental Divide. A week later they were at Great Falls. Captain Lewis took three hunters and proceeded north to explore the Marias. Patrick remained with four men to prepare the portage and to wait for the men from Captain Clark's group, coming in the canoes from the Three Forks. "When Captain Lewis left us, he gave orders that we should wait at the Marias River to the 1st of September, at which time, should he not arrive, we were to proceed on and join Capt. Clark at the mouth of the Yellow-stone river, and then to return home." Captain Lewis had given himself almost a month's leeway but expected to meet Patrick at the Marias River on August 5.

Sergeant Ordway "and nine men arrived at our camp with canoes and some baggage" on July 19. He said that "Capt. Clarke with ten men had left them (on July 13) . . . in order to cross over to the . . . Yellow-stone river."

Patrick's and Ordway's men completed the portage of the falls in a week and by July 28, were at the mouth of the Marias. Unexpectedly, they met Captain Lewis and the three men who had gone with him. Patrick described the action as reported by Captain Lewis. They had ridden "one hundred and twenty miles since the previous morning, when they had a skirmish with the . . . Bigbellied Indians . . . of which they gave the following account . . . . Captain Lewis and his party met with eight of those Indians who seemed very friendly . . . ." They exchanged gifts "and they all continued together during the night; but after break of day the next morning, the Indians snatched up three of our men's guns and ran off with them. One Indian had the guns of two (of our) men, who pursued and caught him, and one [of our men] killed him with his knife; and they got back the guns. Another had Captain Lewis' gun, but immediately gave it up. The Party then went to catch the horses, and found the Indians driving them off; when Captain Lewis shot one of them, and gave him a mortal wound. . . . The Indians, as they ran off in confusion . . . left everything they had. Our men then saddled their horses, and made towards the Missouri as fast as possible. . . . Captain Lewis has satisfied himself with respect to the geography of the country up Marias river," but was disappointed that the head waters did not go above the 50th parallel which would have expanded the area of the Louisiana Purchase northward into what is now Canada.

"We commenced our voyage from the mouth of Maria's river," wrote Patrick, "and the current of the Missouri being very swift, we went down rapidly." On August 3 they covered seventy-three miles."

[Four days later], "we arrived at the mouth of the Yellow Stone River. We found that Captain Clarke had been encamped on the point some time ago and had left it. We discovered a few words . . . traced in the sand which were 'W.C. a few miles further down on the right hand side.'"

They proceeded on. Stopping to hunt, Captain Lewis and one of the men went out after a herd of elk. "In a short time Captain Lewis returned wounded . . . ordered us to our arms, supposing he had been shot at by Indians. Having prepared for an attack, I went out with three men to reconnoiter . . . and could see no Indians; but after some time met with the man who went out with Captain Lewis, and found on inquiry that he had shot him [Lewis] by accident through the hips and without knowing it pursued the game . . . we returned to the pirogue; examined and dressed Captain Lewis' wounds; and found the ball which had lodged in his overalls."

"This morning . . . Captain Lewis was in good spirits; but his wound stiff and sore." On that day, August 12, they "overtook Captain Clarke and his party, all in good health." Captain Clark and his men had run into a grizzly which, smelling meat, had swum out into the river after then, but they were able to kill it. Indians stole the whole of their horses and the party was obliged to descend the river in skin canoes" which they had to build. "They . . . found the Yellow-Stone river a pleasant and navigable stream, with a rich soil along it; but timber scarce."

By August 14 "we arrived near to our old friends the Mandans and fixed our encampment" near where they had spent the winter of 1804/1805. The corps stayed with the Indians three days. The Captains persuaded the chief to accompany them to Washington to meet President Jefferson. The chief agreed only if he could take his wife, son, and the interpreter with him.

The squaw, Sacagawea, her husband, and her son, "Pompy" left the expedition at the Mandan camp. They were paid, as agreed, $500. Captain Clark offered to raise their son, who was then nineteen months old, and they said they would send him after he spent another year with his mother.

Continuing on, the expedition was making "fifty or sixty miles a day. Captain Clark from the top of a small hill saw what he estimated was 20,000 buffalo feeding on the plain. It was the most he had ever seen at one time. Captain Lewis is getting much better (from his wound) and we are all in good spirits." On August 30 we "met a band of Teton Sioux, fifty or sixty in number. . . . We halted on the opposite side of the river . . . and waited for three (of our) hunters who were behind; and . . . eight or nine of the Indians swam to a sand bar about sixty yards from us, and we found that they were the same rascals, who had given us trouble as we went up. . . . We let them know . . . that if they troubled us, we would kill everyone of them. They then withdrew, and the whole party left the river and went off to the hills."

On "the 19th [of September, 1806] . . . we saw several turkeys on the shores, but did not delay a moment to hunt; being so anxious to reach St. Louis, where, without any important occurrence, we arrived on the 23rd and were received with great kindness and marks of friendship by the inhabitants, after an absence of two years, four months and ten days."

And so ended Patrick's journal and the expedition's Journey of Discovery.

Portrait of Patrick Gass *Courtesy Edith Wade*

12

JOURNEY'S END

Patrick's words, in the winter of his life, echo down through the years.[1]

I still have a couple of years left in me. I no longer walk the four miles down the Bethany Pike into town from the farm every day to get the Wellsburg paper. I had my cane and chewing tobacco, and sometimes I'd stay in town and have a couple of beers.

Today, there's some snow covering the fields, but I hear rain falling on the roof so it will soon melt. I'm glad to be sitting here in this old log house feeling some warmth from the fire. My daughter Annie takes care of me, does the housekeeping. She and her seven-year-old son, James, live with me. I can't see well enough to read the paper anymore, so I do a bit of thinking about things past. Sometimes, I just fall asleep. In my lifetime I have done a lot and seen a lot, but I guess the most important thing I ever did was go with Captain Lewis and Captain Clark up the Missouri and out to the Pacific Ocean. I remember those days well and even some of the other things that happened many years ago.

In my ninety years, the country has grown from the thirteen colonies to thirty-eight states, and there have been eighteen presidents, so my daughter Annie tells me. I saw George Washington over in Pennsylvania one day when I was in my twenties. I knew James Buchanan when he was a child because I worked on his father's house. And to seek better pensions, I went to Washington with a group of old veterans to meet with President Pierce. We saw him at his house, and most of the cabinet was there, too. In Washington I received a brass spread eagle, which I afterwards wore on the front of my hat. I lived through four wars: the Revolution, the War of 1812 (when I lost my eye), the Mexican War, and the Civil War. Some of us old timers were honored at a dinner about three years ago. A patriotic toast was given and I responded, "May the American Eagle never lose a feather." One of my friends gave another toast to me. He said something like this: "Ate horse, ate dog, killed Indian, and played the devil generally." He was about half right. I can remember this because it was printed in the Wellsburg paper.

I know about being a soldier. I was in the War of 1812 and lost my left eye. I forget, sort of, where that happened. However, my petition for the pension said I lost the eye in the Battle of Lundy's Lane up there on the Canadian border near Niagara Falls, where my unit had moved in 1814. There were almost 3,000 Americans facing 3,000 British soldiers. Our commander directed us to charge; I felt some "bashfulness" but I replied, "I'll try, Sir." I thank the good Lord that I am a short fellow because a ball went right through the top of my hat. I'm not sure if either side could put claim to winning that day. Some said it was the most ferocious battle of the War of 1812. We got in another battle right by the Falls at the rim of the cataract. The British had an artillery battery on a hill. We charged the hill with bayonets and put those fellows to flight. It was all over before we knew it, but I do remember seeing one of those British cannons tumbling over the falls, maybe pushed by the British so we wouldn't capture it. As we were outnumbered, our commander thought the British would counterattack, overrun us, and get their cannons back. He ordered me to spike the cannons so they couldn't be fired. I did the job with a hammer and some rat-tail files. The following year the war was over.

The fellow who wrote that book about me was the one who said that my eye injury was from a splinter from a falling tree when I was building a fort out on the Illinois River. Damn it, I don't know where he got that idea. It was in the War of 1812. There was also this story about me being court-martialed for being drunk and having my whiskey removed for a while. I suppose that was true, but as I recall that was after I lost my eye. Anyway, the government gave me a pension of $96 per year, which I have lived off about all my life. But I had to fight for that pension. I even wrote directly to the Secretary of War so I could get out of having medical checkups twice a year. A few years ago I got some of the local dignitaries in Wellsburg to support a petition to increase my pension. I was eighty-three then and had six children. More recently, I have become a Christian and joined the Campbellite Church. All of Wellsburg gathered on the edge of the Ohio one sunny Sunday afternoon, and I was dunked in the river and baptized. It's never too late.

After the War of 1812, I came here to Wellsburg and lived as best I could. I tended a ferry, tended brewery, and helped build the old

Baptist Meeting House. At one point I was living in "Judge" Hamilton's boarding house. He had a daughter, Maria, who was "blooming into womanhood." She and I got married. The "Judge" and I tied on a good one before that wedding. I was forty-some years older than her. Maria and I had seven children, one of whom died as a baby. Maria loved chocolates, which I bought for her when I could. The children got measles and gave 'em to Maria. She died. She was thirty-seven, leaving me, an old man, with all those children to care for. Rachel, the youngest, was only a year old. I finally had to place all of them in other homes to be raised. I cared for all my children as best I could. That's when I tried to get the pension increased. I wanted to make sure they had some schooling.

I didn't live entirely on my pension. The government gave me 320 acres for the expedition with Captains Lewis and Clark and another 160 acres for my service in the War of 1812. The government was generous and gave me another double bounty about ten years ago. I also had my father's land. I sold off all this land over time. I also did some carpentry work around town. And living on a farm most of the time, I did produce some crops. A lot of the Gass family, that is the part that descended from my brother William, moved on into Ohio and Indiana. I have a great nephew John Gass who crossed the country like I did. But it wasn't until 1851; he was part of the buckeye camp from Ohio that went out to settle Oregon.

My journal on the Corps of Discovery was the first published by any member of the expedition. It was 262 pages long. A fellow by the name of David McKeehan, a schoolmaster in Wellsburg here, edited it and got it published in Pittsburgh. He said it was in sort of a "raw state." But, as it turned out my book was "very slightly altered in verbiage or arrangement from the original." The following year it was published in England and even translated into French.

Captain Lewis was upset that my journal had come out first. I heard he said that it was unauthorized, whatever that meant. But then he seemed to have lost himself after we got back to St. Louis and, I guess, just kept putting off completing his journal. His was published along with Captain Clark's and some of the other men's in 1814. By then he was dead, having killed himself on the Memphis Trace, traveling from St. Louis back to Virginia. And he had been appointed the governor of the Territory of Louisiana. His death was an awful loss. He was as fine a commander as there ever was. And so was Captain Clark.

I'm the oldest living member of the expedition. And I was the first member of the corps to have a biographical book written about me. It was called the Life and Times of Patrick Gass and was written by J.G. Jacobs, the editor of the "Wellsburg Herald." I thought he did a pretty good job, but my journal is what I care about. I never knew what happened to the original. I sure don't have it. Maybe that publisher lost it. But I have the book, which I look at every once in a while. I like the title page that says:

A Journal of the Voyages and Travels of a Corps of Discovery, from the mouth of the River Missouri through the interior parts of North America to the Pacific Ocean, during the years 1804, 1805 & 1806, containing An authentic relation of the most interesting transactions during the expedition, -A description of the country, -And an account of its inhabitants, soil, climate, curiosities and vegetable and animal productions. By Patrick Gass, one of the persons employed in the expedition.

PART III

Captain John Avis, John Brown's Jailer (1818-1883)

CHRONOLOGY

1679 Robert Avis arrives in Maryland from England.
1740 Francis Avis moves to the Charles Town area.
1776 David Avis serves in the Revolutionary War.
1800 John Brown is born.
1812 John Avis, Sr. serves in the War of 1812.
1818 Johns Avis, Jr. is born at Charles Town.
1847 The Charles Town militia with Lieutenant John Avis marches off to the Mexican War.
1857 John Brown and his men murder five Southern sympathizers at Pottawatomie Creek in Kansas.
1859 John Brown attacks Harpers Ferry and is hanged at Charles Town.
1861 Virginia secedes from the Union. Captain John Avis joins the Fifth Virginia Infantry.
The Fifth Infantry fights under Stonewall Jackson at Manassas.
1862 Stonewall Jackson loses at Kernsville near Winchester. Captain Avis becomes the provost marshal of Staunton, Virginia.

1863   Stonewall Jackson is killed at Chancellorsville.
        The Confederate Army is defeated at Gettysburg.
1864   Federal General Hunter burns Staunton.
1865   Robert E. Lee surrenders to General Grant at Appomattox.
        John Avis returns to Charles Town.
1871   The Supreme Court rules that Charles Town is to remain part of West Virginia.
1875   John Avis prepares an affidavit defending his treatment of John Brown.
1883   John Avis dies at Charles Town.

13

CHARLES TOWN AND HARPERS FERRY

I didn't know John Avis existed, but when I found out about him and his relationship to John Brown I wanted to go to Harpers Ferry where Brown's raid took place and to Charles Town where John Avis had lived.

It all started when I began searching for information on Braxton Davenport Avis, my great grandfather. My grandmother, Florence Atkinson Avis, had said that he was "the youngest drummer boy in the Confederate Army."

Some weeks before the trip to Charles Town and Harpers Ferry, I had visited the Rockingham County Historical Museum near Harrisonburg, Virginia. Braxton had supposedly lived in that area. In the small, well-organized museum, I flipped through tidbits from old newspapers. I discovered an announcement of Braxton's marriage to Hattie E. Wilson.[1] I also found a wedding announcement for a James Avis, who it appeared might be Braxton's older brother. There was nothing else.

In desperation, I thumbed through slim volumes about various Virginia army regiments in the Civil War. At the back of *5th Virginia Infantry*, I discovered brief biographies of the unit's members, and a John Avis was listed. The biography stated that he served in the Mexican War and later in the Confederate Army. Born in 1818 near Charles Town, he died there in 1883. But what really interested me was the statement: "Deputy Sheriff and Jailer at Charlestown [old spelling] during John Brown crisis, 1859."[2]

His son, James Avis, was also listed, and he served in the same regiment as his father. But there was no mention of Braxton. It took a handwritten, four-generation genealogy tree, sent to me by an Avis cousin, to confirm the father-son relationship. The tree showed that Braxton's father was, indeed, John Avis. My Grandmother Florence had never mentioned him. I would not have expected her to keep John Avis a secret since it enhanced the southern background she portrayed. Maybe she didn't know, but wouldn't her husband, Samuel Brashear Avis or her father-in-law, Braxton, have told her? It was fairly common knowledge. I would find that most books about John Brown mentioned John Avis. Could it have been that my grandmother considered his being a jailer a social stigma? Whatever the reason, the answer died with her in 1958. My prime interest now became finding out about John Brown and his jailer.

We entered Charles Town, and it looked like a busy farm town. On the main street stood an impressive old brick courthouse that dates back to 1837. According to a historical marker, Confederate artillery fire gutted the building during the Civil War. John Brown's trial took place there.

Near the courthouse stood the library and in its basement was the Jefferson County Museum. Katharine decided to explore antique shops; I entered the museum. Inside, I asked the two ladies at the desk for information on John Avis. Immediately, one of them led me to a display counter. Under the glass in a single frame were two pictures, one of John Brown and the other of John Avis. The picture of the man with bushy hair and the thick, long beard that hung down to his chest left no doubt who he was. The other picture showed a clean-shaven man with a thin mouth, narrow, piercing eyes, and neatly cut hair. John Avis wore a white shirt, a bow tie of the sort worn in those days, and a dark coat. He looked more like an attorney or a judge than a jailer. His military dossier, which I found later, gave his physical description: "Height 5' 7", eyes blue, hair light, complexion fair."[3]

My guide next showed me the cot on which the wounded John Brown lay in the courthouse while being tried and the wagon on which he rode through the streets of Charles Town to his execution. One of the ladies mentioned a Jim Avis of Washington, D.C., who recently had visited the museum. He had done research on the genealogy of the Avis family. Also, I was informed that there was an Avis Street in town.

I would later contact Jim Avis. He sent me a booklet, stating that a Robert Avis arrived in the Maryland Colony on the Patuxent River shore in 1679. He came from London as an indentured servant. His granddaughter Dorcas married Sir Walter Shirley, a fugitive from the British Crown, who in a rage tried to murder a member of Parliament. Staying one step ahead of the Crown, Shirley with Dorcas and her younger brother, Francis Avis, left Maryland in 1740 and moved into Virginia. Shirley bought 800 acres near the Potomac River from Lord Fairfax. (Thomas Lewis, son of John, shortly thereafter surveyed the southern boundary of the Fairfax lands.) Francis, as an assistant surveyor and chain carrier, worked for eighteen-year-old George Washington. Washington was laying out the Shirley property and acquiring land in what would be the Charles Town area.[4] (Thus, George Washington surveyed with an Avis, knew the Lewises, and had been seen by Patrick Gass. In those days, the United States was indeed a small country. Everyone seemed to know George or, at least, claimed they did.)

Five generations of Avises lived in Charles Town during the next 140 years. Four of these generations participated in the nation's first four wars. Francis Avis' son David fought in the Revolutionary War and his grandson, John, Sr., fought in the War of 1812. John Avis, Jr., John Brown's jailer, participated in the Mexican War and in the Civil War. John's sons, James and Braxton, served in the Civil War also.[5] This era ended in the late 1800s with John Avis' death. James and Braxton, for reasons I have yet to discover, moved to Harrisonburg.

While Charles Town is noted for its old homes, not one seemed to have an Avis connection. On the other hand, many of George Washington's relatives and their descendants lived in the area, inhabiting the grander, more historic houses. Thus, the main street is Washington Street. Two blocks south, we found Avis Street, an area of modest homes. In the museum a picture entitled "Capt. Avis' House" showed what looked like two single-story houses attached - one log, the other frame.

During our explorations, we came on a marker two blocks south of Avis Street. It read, "John Brown Scaffold," stating that just to the east, in what was once a field and now is someone's back yard, "is the site of the scaffold on which John Brown, leader of the Harpers Ferry Raid, was executed December the second, 1859."

We left Charles Town and drove the few miles to Harpers Ferry. When George Washington was President, the town was built around the old armory. Meriwether Lewis came there in 1803 to procure rifles for the Lewis and Clark Expedition. On an October day in 1859, John Brown attacked Harpers Ferry.

Tourists packed the town. Traffic was stop and go. I finally found a parking spot at the commuter train station and squeezed in. We left the car and walked a half block to John Brown's fort, the rather small, brick fire engine house with a cupola and three arched doorways. There, Brown and some of his men with their hostages fortified themselves after attacking the Harpers Ferry Armory. I would learn that a block away, down Shenandoah Street, Captain John Avis and his men of the Charles Town militia had positioned themselves in storefronts during the assault on John Brown's fort. At that time, the engine house was located inside the gate to the armory, but at present it is situated across the street in a park-like setting.

The stores and museums on Shenandoah Street have been restored to look like Civil War times. Katharine and I entered the John Brown Museum. There, we saw a video depicting the entire escapade. An illustration in the video showed John Brown in the courtroom. Beside him stood John Avis, looking like his picture in the Jefferson County Museum. Enlarged illustrations from magazines of the time decorated the walls. They showed John Brown riding to his execution in the wagon that we had seen at the museum and standing on the scaffold where he was hanged. John Avis stood beside him in the wagon and on the scaffold.

Several months after the trip to Charles Town and Harpers Ferry, I solved the Braxton Davenport Avis mystery through an Internet source that included Staunton-related Confederate military records.[6] Braxton, only eleven years old at the time, was listed as a musician in the Provost Marshall Company in Staunton. His father commanded this company during the latter part of the Civil War. Being in a non-combat unit, Braxton was not a drummer boy like those older boys serving on the front lines. But he played in the company band and would have worn the uniform, which my mother once showed me. So, with an official military record, Braxton possibly was the youngest boy to serve in the Civil War.[7] The real story, however, was not about Braxton, but about his father and his association with John Brown.

14

JOHN BROWN'S RAID

Shouting and a banging on the jail door woke John Avis. He sat up in bed then reached for the ring of keys lying on the nightstand. His wife, Imogene, groaned and turned over in her sleep.[1] His bare feet hit the cold floor, and in his nightshirt he headed for the door. His sons, James, Braxton, and Edward, lay asleep in the next room.

The Jefferson County Jail was a two-story brick building with a corniced roofline. It didn't look like a jail. The front windows had shutters; only the back windows had bars. The jailer's apartment opened onto a narrow front porch with a latticework railing and steps at either end. Just to the side, a separate door with a small porch led into the jail receiving area. The cells lined the back of the building, and a high brick fence surrounded the exercise area in the rear.[2]

John Avis opened the front door of the jail apartment. In the gray light he saw one of the men in the Jefferson Guards, the local militia unit, standing on the porch. Rain had fallen during the night, and it was still drizzling.

The man told him that the militia had been ordered to assemble. John Avis first thought that maybe the Union had invaded the South. There had been talk of succession, but he didn't think it had gone that far. He tried to understand what the militiaman was saying: "There's trouble in Harpers Ferry. A fellow by the name of John Brown, with a bunch of men and slaves, has taken over the armory. They're killing people. Doc Starry sent a message over during the night. The town needs help."

Where had he heard of John Brown? John Avis couldn't remember. Was he the man who had killed people out in Kansas?

Avis told the militiaman he would be ready as soon as he could get someone to watch the jail. He got dressed, woke his son James, who sometimes pulled guard duty, and left him in charge.

The previous night, Sunday, October 16, 1859, John Brown and seventeen of his men left a leased farm in Maryland and sneaked across the Baltimore and Ohio railroad bridge into Harpers Ferry. Three men stayed behind to encourage and support a slave uprising. Brown's "army" entered the town, grabbed three watchmen, and captured the armory without a fight. John Brown announced, "I come from Kansas, and this is a slave state; I want to free all the Negroes in this state: I have possession now of the United States Armory, and if the citizens interfere with me I must only burn the town and have blood."[3]

Brown dispatched a group of his men to the home of Colonel Lewis Washington, a grandnephew of George Washington. They took him hostage and brought him to the arsenal. Brown wanted the pistol and sword that the colonel had inherited from his famous ancestor. The raiders then held up the 1:25 A.M. B&O passenger train from Wheeling to Baltimore. Ironically, they killed Howard Sheppard, a black porter who was a freed slave. At the railroad station he had disobeyed their orders to halt.

Doctor John Starry, a Harpers Ferry physician, realizing that his town was under siege, sent word to Charles Town for help.

At dawn, Brown let the B&O train leave, and at the first telegraph station the conductor alerted his superiors and officials in Washington. John B. Floyd, Secretary of War in President James Buchanan's cabinet, received the message.[4] Floyd, a recent governor of Virginia, consulted the President. He and Buchanan decided to send the only nearby military unit, a small detachment of Marines from the Washington Navy Yard. To take overall command, they chose Lieutenant Colonel Robert E. Lee.

While Buchanan and Floyd made decisions in Washington, Brown had gathered his men and forty hostages, including Colonel Washington, and established a fort in the fire engine house just inside the armory gate. He awaited the arrival of slaves that were to be armed by some of his men left behind in Maryland under the command of his son, Owen.[5] The slave uprising never occurred. Brown had picked an area where there were few slaves.

By mid-morning, Captain Avis and Captain Lawson Botts, another militia officer, recruited a volunteer unit and assembled them in front of the courthouse with the regular militia, the Jefferson Guards commanded by Captain J.W. Rowan. The men wore a mix of uniforms. Their firearms included squirrel rifles, flintlocks and shotguns. Church bells tolled. They marched to the railroad station where a Winchester and Potomac train stood on the siding, its engine sending a plume of smoke into the gray sky. The men boarded the train. Spectators stood around, watching the commotion. With a blast of the whistle, the train began to move, heading for Harpers Ferry, seven miles away. Avis might have stood in the aisle of the railway car surrounded by men with their guns, thinking about his first military experience in the Mexican War.

In January 1847, to the accompaniment of a band and speeches, Lieutenant John Avis and the Jefferson Guards, sixty-seven strong, mounted a train for Norfolk. There, with other Virginia militia units, they boarded a ship for Texas.[6] The lieutenant was 28 years old and left behind a wife and a young son.

President James Polk had already sent the U.S. Army under the command of General Zachary Taylor to the Mexican border to prevent an "invasion" of the new state of Texas. To reinforce the army the President called state militias into action. The Virginia units, after a three-week trip around Florida and across the rough seas of the Gulf of Mexico, arrived in Texas and were stationed along the border. Meanwhile, General Taylor had moved south to capture the Mexican port of Vera Cruz. It became clear to Lieutenant Avis and the militia that they were replacements to protect the border. They saw little action other than an occasional skirmish while on scouting trips. It was hot, boring duty.

In September 1847, Taylor captured Mexico City and initiated peace negotiations. As President Buchanan intended, the United States gained California, New Mexico and Arizona. Lieutenant Avis and the Jefferson Guards did not return home to Charles Town until the following summer. Fourteen years later the Civil War began, and many of its participants, including Lieutenant Avis, had gained military experience during the Mexican War. The most notable were Captains Robert E. Lee, George B. McClellan, Lieutenant Ulysses Grant, and Colonel Jefferson Davis.[7]

On the high ground just west of Harpers Ferry, the train loaded with the Charles Town militia stopped, and the men disembarked. Colonel John Gibson, commanding the Charles Town units, gave orders to his officers, Captain Rowan, Captain Avis and Captain Botts.

Rowan and the Jefferson Guards waded the Potomac into Maryland a mile north of Harpers Ferry, proceeded down the Chesapeake and Ohio Canal towpath, and took control of the B&O Bridge from the east. At the bridge they shot one of Brown's men, Dangerfield Newby, an ex-slave.

Avis and Botts marched their volunteers down the hill into town to take up positions facing the arsenal. Botts and his men occupied the area around the Galt House Saloon, next to the railroad station and the Wager Hotel. From there, they looked down Potomac Street at the entrance to the armory grounds and the fire engine house just inside the gates where Brown, his men, and the hostages had retreated. Captain Avis placed his men in stores and houses along Shenandoah Street, looking into the arsenal where guns from the armory were stored. Avis could also see the approaches to the toll bridge going across the Shenandoah River.[8] Chaos reigned. Drunken men ran up and down, hollering and firing shots into the air. A body lay in the street in front of the arsenal.

At this point, John Avis knew little of John Brown. In the next few weeks he would come to know him well. Brown was born in Connecticut in 1800, but as a child, he and his family moved to the Ohio frontier. His mother died shortly after they arrived. Brown grew up with a father who taught him to fear God and obey the Commandments. During the War of 1812, at age twelve, John Brown, by himself, drove a herd of cattle to sell to Army posts in Michigan. He wanted to be a minister but married instead. When he was twenty-nine, his wife died giving birth to their seventh child. He quickly remarried, choosing the daughter of the family maid. Always restless, he became a tanner, a surveyor, and a farmer. He raised sheep, speculated in land, and sold wool. An associate gave him funds to buy sheep, but he never delivered, kept the money, and then declared bankruptcy.[9]

Brown once hid a runaway slave, and the experience triggered his obsession against slavery. In the mid 1850s, he left his wife and the younger children on a scrubby mountain farm in North Elba, New York, and went to Kansas to join his sons in the fight against slavery. The territory stood ready to enter the Union, and Southerners, mostly from Missouri, battled with northern extremists to make it a slave state. Brown and his sons yanked five southern sympathizers from their houses one night along Pottawatomie Creek and murdered them. Brown believed that he was doing God's will. Shortly afterwards, Southerners killed his son Fred in a battle at a town called Osawatomie.

After Kansas, Brown began to implement his long-standing idea of starting an uprising among the slaves. He would conduct the revolt from a fortress in the Appalachian Mountains. Hoping that in time a northern convention would overthrow the pro-slavery government in Washington, he prepared his own constitution that outlawed slavery. As part of his plan, he raised money from rich, northern abolitionists to finance the attack on the U.S. Government Arsenal at Harpers Ferry.

With the B&O Bridge captured, the Galt House secured, and the approaches to the Shenandoah toll bridge covered, the Charles Town militia had surrounded Brown and cut off his primary escape routes. No one had any idea how many raiders were in the engine house, or how many might be hiding in the armory or on the arsenal grounds.

In the early afternoon, Captain Avis saw a man at the end of Shenandoah Street. He was waving a white flag. Avis couldn't see the engine house, but the man must have come from there. Brown, realizing that he was surrounded, had made his first effort to secure a truce. But some men grabbed the flag waver and hauled him off toward the Galt House. Meanwhile, the town became more crowded and more rowdy as militia units arrived from Virginia and Maryland.

Three more men came out into the street with a white flag. One appeared to be a hostage. Shots rang out from the vicinity of the Galt House where Captain Botts was located. Two men fell; the other ran into the hotel. One of the men on the ground started crawling back toward the engine house. A figure ran out and carried the other man into the hotel. Avis had no idea what was going on.

The man who crawled back to the engine house was Brown's son Watson. He would die of his wounds by morning.

Suddenly, a shot rang out. George Turner, who had come to Harpers Ferry on business, fell dead. He was a wealthy slave owner and a friend of Captain Avis'. Avis spotted a mulatto across the street, positioned between two buildings, who he thought fired the shot. He selected Dick Washington to return the fire. Washington was a renowned squirrel shooter and a cousin to Colonel Lewis Washington, one of the hostages held by Brown in the engine house. While Avis and his men diverted the attention of the mulatto from their ground-floor position, Dick Washington shot him from an upstairs window.[10]

In the meantime, a raider tried to escape from the armory. He set out across the Potomac and hid on an island in the middle. A townsman waded out after him, put a gun to his head, and shot him. The town's mayor, trying to see what was going on, stuck his head out from behind a tree and was shot.

Rumors spread about more people being killed. Smoke hung over the street. The smell of gunpowder filled the air. The town was in full panic. Dr. Starry, who had spread the word of the attack to Charles Town, and several other men crossed Shenandoah Street and entered the arsenal. Avis would have seen them and probably figured that, since the militia wasn't doing anything, these men were taking things into their own hands. Shortly afterwards, shots rang out down by the Shenandoah River. Starry's men had killed two of the raiders and captured another, a Negro. Starry prevented the men from killing the Negro.

Captain Avis heard a barrage of shots from the vicinity of the engine house. The shots stopped as quickly as they started. A militia unit arrived by train from Martinsburg and immediately attacked the engine house. Brown's men poured out of the building, firing their guns, wounding eight of the volunteers. The militia called off the attack.

With darkness, the town quieted down except for an occasional gun firing in the vicinity of the hotel and the Galt House.

About eleven o'clock, Avis and his men heard a train approaching from the east. It rumbled across the B&O Bridge, and its brakes screeched as it pulled up in front of the station. Within an hour, rumors spread that a Colonel Robert E. Lee and a group of Marines had arrived from Washington. Avis could only hope that, at last, somebody was taking charge. But nothing happened the rest of the night.

Dawn arrived. The sun was still behind the Blue Ridge. The town lay in shadow. Suddenly, shots shattered the air by the engine house.

When Colonel Lee had arrived the night before with ninety Marines, he offered the honor of attacking Brown's fort to a couple of the militia units—he thought the situation was a state, rather than a federal, matter. The militia declined. They had families. Let the Marines do it; they were getting paid.

At daylight, Lee sent Army Lieutenant J.E.B. Stuart, later a famous Confederate general, to the engine house to persuade Brown to surrender. Stuart tried to negotiate through a crack in one of the doors. Brown demanded that his raiders and the hostages be allowed to cross the bridge into Maryland. Once there he promised he would free the hostages. Stuart said Brown's only option was for immediate surrender. Finally, Stuart gave up. He raised his hand. Twelve Marines, some with fixed bayonets and some with sledgehammers, led by Lieutenant Israel Green, rushed the door. The sledgehammers struck the door but had no effect. Two Marines picked up a fire ladder, lying on the ground nearby, and rammed the door. It splintered. The Marines stormed into the engine house with Green first. One of the hostages, Colonel Washington, pointed at Brown who held a Sharp's rifle. Green attacked Brown with his saber. Brown's men shot two of the Marines as they came through the door. The Marines killed two of Brown's men, one with a bayonet, and the other with a saber. The hostages escaped injury. The attack lasted only three minutes.

If later Captain Avis had walked down Shenandoah Street to inspect what was happening, he would have seen the engine house door open, the Marines holding two raiders at bayonet point, and bodies lying on the grass. One was a man with a flowing beard who seemed still to have some life left in him. This was John Brown. The hostages stood to one side. The Marines circled the area, holding off the surging crowd. Yells of "Lynch'em, lynch'em" filled the air.

By noon Avis had gathered his men and returned to Charles Town. He was informed that Brown and the other captured raiders would be brought to Charles Town and placed in his jail.

15

BE QUICK

During the afternoon following the attack, Virginia Governor Henry A. Wise arrived in Harpers Ferry. He attempted to question the wounded John Brown about his intentions and his supporters. Brown talked freely, admitting that he had intended to free the slaves but said that only he and his God were responsible for his actions. Cries for a lynching continued. Wise faced the crowd and told them that a lynching would be cowardly.

John Brown and his remaining followers, Aaron Stevens, Negroes Shields Green and John Copeland, and Edwin Coppoc were escorted by troops to the railroad station to ride by train to Charles Town. Stevens was the one who had come out with the second truce flag the day before and had been wounded and captured. Green and Coppoc had survived the attack on the engine house. Copeland had been saved from a lynch mob by Dr. Starry after trying to escape across the Shenandoah. These five were the only raiders left. Ten had been killed, including Brown's son Watson and Brown's two sons-in-law, the Thompson brothers. Seven of the raiders escaped, including Brown's son, Owen.

Brown and Stevens arrived at the jail in Charles Town on a stretcher. John Avis could see that Brown was still suffering from the saber wounds inflicted by the Marine lieutenant. The jailer led the stretcher-bearers, surrounded by guards, across a hallway in back of his family apartment and into a cell at the rear corner of the building. The room contained two cots, a stove in the middle, and a table. Brown and Stevens were carried into the cell and placed on the cots. The two Negroes, Green and Copeland, were put in an adjacent cell. Coppoc was in a cell by himself. With the raiders secure inside, troops rimmed the outside of the jail. Rumors spread of an attempt by northern sympathizers to break the prisoners out.

John Avis and his wife, Imogene, probably discussed whether she and the boys should move out of the jail apartment into a friend's house. Since John had to be there most of the time, especially in the current situation, and son James was one of the jail guards, they decided to stay. With all the troops surrounding the jail, they were in the safest place they could be.[1]

Six days later on October 25, the raiders were arraigned at the Jefferson County Courthouse across the street from the jail. Avis arranged for Stevens to be carried over on a cot, but Brown walked with the others. Inside the packed courtroom the stench of tobacco and men's bodies filled the air. Avis placed Brown and Stevens on cots in front of the judge's bench.

Heading the Examining Court was Braxton Davenport, who had served with John Avis's father in the War of 1812. John had named his second son after Braxton Davenport.[2] The Examining Court asked Brown if he had counsel. Brown ignored the question and made a statement that there was no way that he could have a fair trial. The court "might just spare itself the trouble. I am ready for my fate . . . I beg for no mockery of a trial."[3] The court designated two local men to defend Brown: the Mayor of Charles Town, Thomas Green, and Lawson Botts, a local lawyer. Botts, along with Avis, had led the volunteers at Harpers Ferry the week before.

The Grand Jury met the next day at noon. John Avis tried to get Brown up off his cot, but he refused to stir. Avis reported that Brown said he was too sick to attend. The judge said to bring him over anyway. Avis took some men to the jail, picked up Brown's cot with him on it, and hauled him over to the courthouse. Brown told the judge that he was in poor health and that the trial should be delayed. The judge had Avis sworn in and asked him if he thought Brown was able to stand trial. Avis said that Brown had told him that his mind was confused and that he had difficulty hearing.

Doc Mason, the jail doctor, was called to the courthouse. He said Brown could stand trial. That was what the judge and the prosecutor wanted to hear. Fearing that an attempt would be made to rescue Brown, they wanted to get the trial over as soon as possible.

The Grand Jury handed down three indictments: treason against the state, inciting slaves to rebel, and murder. The judge demanded that the prisoners stand; Stevens required help. Each man pled not guilty. Each requested a separate trial, which the judge allowed. A jury was finally selected after Botts and Green had rejected the first eight candidates, all locals. Some participants thought that Botts and Green should have asked that the trial be moved elsewhere. When the day ended, Brown surprised John Avis and everyone else by rising from the cot and walking out of the court with the other prisoners.

On Friday, Brown's trial began. The prosecutors were the Commonwealth Attorney for Jefferson County, Charles Harding and Lawyer Andrew Hunter. County Circuit Judge Richard Parker presided. Avis knew these men well. Harding liked the bottle, plus he was a braggart. Andrew Hunter handled himself in an impressive manner, understood the law, and spoke seriously. Judge Parker was a small man, mild mannered, but dignified. He had a reputation for being firm but fair. Not many people argued with the way he handled things.[4]

Almost immediately after the trial opened, Lawson Botts read a telegram received the night before from a man in Ohio. The telegram stated that insanity was hereditary in Brown's family. It listed family members, particularly on his mother's side, who had died from insanity or had spent time in an asylum. Botts was attempting to save Brown's life with an insanity plea. Brown would have no part of it. He lifted his head from his cot and said," I look upon it as a miserable artifice . . . I am perfectly unconscious of insanity and I reject any attempt to interfere in behalf on that score."[5] John Avis might have thought Brown a fanatic but not crazy.

The judge rejected the insanity plea, saying that the evidence was sketchy. He also rejected Botts' request that the trial be delayed so that Brown could select his own lawyers from Ohio. During the day, a young lawyer, George Hoyt, from Boston, arrived. Hoyt seemed inexperienced or as John Avis might have said "still wet behind the ears." Some speculated that Hoyt was really a spy who planned to provide information to those plotting Brown's escape. He certainly didn't know anything about courtroom procedure or about Virginia law. In the meantime, Brown became fed up with Botts and Green and demanded that they no longer represent him. Before the day ended, two veteran lawyers, Samuel Chilton of Washington, D.C. and Hiram Griswold from Cleveland, Ohio, arrived to represent Brown.

The trial proceeded. The prosecution witnesses told the story of the attack, the attempted arming of slaves, the kidnapping of hostages, and the killing of the black baggage man, the mayor, and two other men. A witness, Harry Hunter, son of the prosecutor, said that he felt it was his duty, and he had no regrets, when he put a gun to a captured raider's head and pulled the trigger. The defense, Brown's new lawyers, took the position that Brown was leading an army and, therefore, should be judged by the rules of war.

At 1:45 P.M. on Monday, October 31, after closing arguments, Brown's case went to the jury. They returned forty-five minutes later with a verdict of guilty. The crowd listened in absolute silence. Brown said nothing, turned around, and lay down on his cot.

Two days later, the judge read the sentence. Brown's wounds had sufficiently healed so that he could stand. His was handcuffed, and John Avis stood by his side. The judge declared that Brown would hang in thirty days. Avis led him out of the courtroom and back to his jail cell. Troops lined the way. Again, Brown showed no emotion.

In the next few days, the number of prisoners in John Avis's jail increased. Two of the seven men who had escaped into Maryland, John Cook and Albert Hazlett, had been caught and were returned to Charles Town. Their trials and those of the other prisoners proceeded one after another, with each man found guilty and sentenced to hang.

The fear of a raid by Brown's sympathizers hung over the town. The troops remained to ensure that nothing happened. Governor Wise issued a proclamation that strangers found within Jefferson County—having no apparent business there, would be arrested. Wise became obsessed with the idea that Brown would escape. He wrote letters to Prosecuting Attorney Andrew Hunter, to the militia leaders, and to Jailer John Avis, encouraging them all to be alert to a possible escape. The citizens of the county were emphatically warned to remain in their homes armed and to guard their own property.

During his trial, John Brown wrote a letter to his family in New York stating: "I am in charge of a jailer like the one who took charge of 'Paul and Silas' & you may rest assured that both kind hearts & kind faces are more or less about me; whilst thousands are thirsting for my blood."[6]

As his jailer, John Avis had a unique relationship with John Brown, and became acquainted with the man awaiting his hanging.

In the thirty days waiting for John Brown to be hanged, I, John Avis, got to know him about as well as a jailer can know his prisoner. He had no desire to escape. I think he felt that he would serve his cause if indeed he were hanged. I think some of his sympathizers realized this also. Perhaps this is why there was never a concerted rescue attempt. Anyway, it would have taken an army to break him out with all the militia and federal troops that were in town.

Captain Brown, as I had begun to call him, and I had some serious conversations. I certainly did not agree with what he had done, but I understood his purpose, and I indeed had some admiration for the man. He believed that he was at war and, as he said, it was a righteous war so therefore "robbery became confiscation and murder became execution."[7] But in my mind that didn't justify the five men he killed that one night in Kansas, or for that matter, the people killed at Harpers Ferry.

Brown said he had written in his Provincial Constitution: "Slavery is none other than the most barbarous, unprovoked and unjustifiable war of one portion of its citizens upon another portion. It was hard to disagree with this. I knew about slavery. I had no slaves myself, of course, but I had been a slave dealer in Winchester just before the war.[8] It had been a way to make a living.

A Negro woman who had been freed asked my wife if she would take her in. Freed slaves could not stay in the state unless they were re-bonded to a white family.[9] There weren't many slaves around Charles Town except for house servants to people like the Washingtons, but it was the way of life farther south on tobacco and cotton plantations. I don't think that part of the South could have survived without slaves. When the slave issue split the Union, my feelings stood with Virginia, and when the state seceded, I certainly was with them.

Captain Brown said, "If God be for us, who can be against us."[10] But he also said, quoting from the Bible," Those that live by the sword will die by the sword." And he told me that once he had said to his followers, "Take more care to end life well than to live life long. I feel

Captain John Avis, John Brown's jailer (1818-1883) *Courtesy Stan Cohen*

no conscience of guilt. My will and God's will are one."¹¹ He was ready to die.

Captain Brown's wife arrived from their home in Elba, New York the night before he was hanged. He said he didn't want her to come, but I think he was glad that she did. She visited with him in his cell.

I invited Captain Brown and his wife to take supper with me and my family at our table at our residence in the jail."¹² It was the least I could do. Mrs. Brown was a small, serious woman, who had obviously been through a lot, but she was strong. I cannot remember the conversation of that evening, but we all got through it. After dinner Captain Brown asked that his wife be allowed to stay in his cell with him for the night. I could not allow that. Tears came to his eyes. I returned him to his cell and left Mrs. Brown with the soldiers who would escort her to her hotel. She waited in Harpers Ferry for the delivery of her husband's body the next day.

Captain Brown took many occasions to thank me for my kindness to him, and he spoke of it to many persons, including his wife. In further proof of the kindness he received from me, Captain Brown bequeathed to me his Sharp's rifle and a pistol in his last will and testament."¹³

At 11 A.M. the next morning, Dec. 2, 1859, I walked Captain Brown down the steps of the jail. I had tied his arms together behind his back at the elbows. Before we stepped outside, Brown slipped a folded note to me. I held the paper to the window and read:

> I John Brown am now quite certain that the crimes of this guilty land: will never be purged away; but with blood. I had as I now think: vainly flattered myself that without very much bloodshed; it might be done.¹⁴

John Brown knew that a war was coming, as did John Avis. The two men walked out into the sunshine. A wagon with two white farm horses stood waiting. Brown, Jefferson County Sheriff James Campbell, and Avis climbed into the wagon by way of the tailgate. A pine coffin lay inside. Brown sat on the coffin. John Avis and the sheriff stood. A mass of soldiers surrounded the wagon. Brown looked around and said, "I had no idea that Governor Wise considered my execution so important."¹⁵

The wagon began to roll, heading to the field on the edge of

John Brown in May 1859, taken in Boston by J.W. Black *Courtesy West Virginia State Archives*

town where the scaffold stood. Soldiers lined the road as the two horses clomped along. It was a warm day for December. Gazing out at the distant Blue Ridge Mountains as the wagon arrived at the hanging site, John Brown said, "This is a beautiful country. I never had the pleasure of seeing it before."[16] Neither John Avis nor the sheriff responded. Fifteen hundred troops circled the field with the scaffold in the middle. Among them were Virginia Military Institute cadets led by Professor Thomas Jackson, later known as Stonewall Jackson. Also present was John Wilkes Booth, a member of a Richmond militia unit, who would assassinate Abraham Lincoln near the end of the Civil War.

The troops looked on as Sheriff Campbell and John Avis led Brown up the steps of the scaffold. The sheriff put a white linen hood over Brown's head and adjusted the noose around his neck. "I can't see gentlemen; you must lead me," he said. John Avis asked Brown to step forward on to the trap door, hinged on one side and held by a rope on the other. "If only you would not keep me waiting," said Brown. John Avis made a final adjustment to the noose while Brown said, "Be quick." [17]

With a chop of the hatchet the sheriff cut the rope, springing the trap door. Out of the silence of a thousand men, a militia colonel's voice rang out, "So perish all such enemies of Virginia. All such enemies of the Union. All such enemies of the human race."[18]

16

WAR AND ITS AFTERMATH

The hanging of John Brown gave little rest to John Avis. He still had a jail filled with Brown's accomplices, plus a recently hired guard who was a spy. Charles Lenhart, a troublemaker from the Kansas battles, had sneaked into town and, unwittingly, been added to the expanded guard detail when Governor Wise demanded more protection for the jail. Lenhart had approached Brown about escaping, but the abolitionist declined, having accepted his fate. After Brown's hanging, Lenhart slipped knives to John Cook and Edwin Coppoc. They scraped the mortar from between the bricks of their cell wall, loosened the bricks, and made a hole that faced the jail yard. At night they slipped out. With the aid of timbers stored in the yard for the gallows, they reached the top of the fourteen-foot wall, expecting Lenhart to be there waiting for them. His shift had been changed, however, and instead, they faced the bayonet of a replacement guard. They scurried back down the wall and surrendered to a surprised John Avis. The next day, they were hanged.

Another rescue attempt was made.[1] Silas Soulé, also a Kansas veteran, had himself thrown into the jail for drunken behavior. He approached Stevens and Hazlett to plan their escape. They told him that with over eighty guards there was little chance. Besides, Jailer Avis was absolutely fearless, and they would have to kill him to get away. They didn't want to do that; he had been kind to them. The next morning Soulé was discharged, and he slipped out of town. Within the month the remaining prisoners were hanged.

On April 22, 1861, Captain Avis and the Charles Town militia returned to Harpers Ferry. On that day Governor John Letcher announced that Virginia had seceded from the Union. Militia units from all over the Shenandoah Valley were instructed to assemble at Harpers Ferry. The few Union soldiers there tried to burn the Federal armory, but the Virginians extinguished the fires and captured

1,500 guns. As more militia units poured into the town, the scene was reminiscent of the John Brown episode eighteen months earlier with rough, undisciplined troops milling about.

A week later General Robert E. Lee, commanding the Virginia forces, sent Colonel Thomas Jackson to take charge of the rowdy troops at Harpers Ferry. Jackson had been teaching at Virginia Military Institute, and like John Avis, was a veteran of the Mexican War.

Colonel Jackson did not make a particularly impressive first impression: his clothes were sloppy, and he had a brown beard that needed trimming. For the first month, the colonel subjected his troops to excruciating training. Some of the younger men who had joined on a lark began to realize what they faced. When Jackson found one of the units had stashed whiskey in town, he had it thrown over the bluff into the Potomac. He was stern, but he did everything he required of his men. He was also a religious man who often could be seen praying in his tent, and at church services he served as an usher for his men.[2]

John Avis was assigned to the Continental Morgan Guards, a unit from the Staunton area. The sixty-man company chose him as their captain. The Guards were designated Company K of the 5th Virginia Infantry Regiment, a part of Colonel Jackson's brigade. Unlike many of the other units, the Guards had been in existence for some time, and were well equipped. The men wore buff and blue uniforms and three-cornered cocked hats like those used in the Revolutionary Army. Perhaps, because they looked sharp, Jackson assigned Captain Avis and his men as drillmasters for the other troops.[3]

In June 1861, Colonel Jackson's brigade, consisting of four infantry regiments with 3,000 men, moved to a camp just north of Martinsburg. A Union Army camped across the Maryland border ready to move south into Virginia and the Shenandoah Valley. Both sides waited.

During that time, Captain Avis' son, James, who was sixteen, joined his father's company as a private. Company K's initial activity was dismantling the railroad facilities at Martinsburg so they could not be used, if captured by the Federals.

In the early morning of July 2, 1861, Captain Avis' company, as part of the Fifth Infantry, marched up a road on a scouting expedition across the Maryland line. Colonel Jackson rode alongside. As Avis and his men came over a rise, they saw, less than a mile away, hundreds of troops in blue uniforms approaching. The Federals' battle line spread across the road and the fields. Flags snapped in the breeze and bayonets glistened in the sun. The Confederate troops stared in a state of shock, seeing the enemy for the first time. A buzz went through the ranks. Then the sound of shots rang across the open space, as bullets whizzed past the startled men. Colonel Jackson in a calm voice directed his men to move into the woods alongside a field that stood between them and the Federals.[4]

As the Fifth Infantry positioned itself, lines of blue troops entered the field, firing their rifles. Jackson ordered his men to retreat a short distance. Badly under-manned, he feared his troops would be outflanked. The Yankees rushed forward. A Confederate six-pounder fired on them from the woods. The enemy stopped, turned and ran, but rallied as they countered with their artillery. Jackson called up his reserves and held the line. By then the enemy had had enough and fell back. The battle, which occurred near a place called Falling Waters, lasted less than two hours. One man was killed and seven wounded.

Young James Avis was one of the wounded. He and some of the men had been firing at the Federals from behind a woodpile on the edge of the road. A cannon ball hit the woodpile, throwing James out into the open. He was hauled off by a courier. Later, James was taken to the hospital in Winchester, where the doctors determined that his wounds made him unfit for further service. After healing, he stayed on at the hospital as an apothecary.[5]

The Fifth Virginia remained in camp near Winchester for a couple of weeks, expecting at any time that the Federals would again try to move into the Shenandoah Valley. Then Jackson's Brigade received orders to cross the Blue Ridge to Manassas to reinforce the troops there. General McDowell's Union Army had marched out from Washington to north of Manassas, hoping to move south on Richmond and end the war quickly. The Confederates were lined up along Bull Run to stop them.

Jackson's brigade marched thirty miles eastward, wading across the Shenandoah, and climbing over the Blue Ridge through Ashby's Gap. At 2:00 A.M. they stopped. Avis and his men were exhausted. In the morning they boarded railroad freight cars to ride the remaining thirty miles to Manassas Junction. It was July 21, 1861.

Cannon fire woke the men. General Jackson formed the brigade and led it northward toward Henry House Hill. He placed the Fifth Infantry on the east side of the brigade's flank. Bull Run lay a half-mile farther east. By early afternoon, Captain Avis' Company had dug in below the crest of Henry House Hill with the rest of the brigade closer to the top. The Henry House sat on the brigade's west flank. The Union Army attacked. Confederate General Bee tried to rally his men, who were retreating through the brigade's lines. Jackson, mounted on horseback at the top of the hill, commanded his men to hold their positions. Bee asked Colonel Harper, Avis immediate commander, "What Troops are these?"

Harper replied, "Fifth Virginia Regiment, Jackson's Brigade."

General Bee yelled, "Rally, men, rally! Look! These Virginians stand like a stone wall."[6] Whether the statement was meant for the brigade or for General Jackson, it didn't matter. The name was his.

The Federals had artillery and fired away as their infantry swarmed across a creek and up Henry House Hill. Jackson's Brigade charged, screaming the rebel yell, and broke the enemy ranks. Reserves poured forward, routing the Yankees.

The Fifth had been in the rear, but its men, including Captain Avis' Company K, overran the artillery pieces on the opposite hill, swept right, and chased the enemy across the Stone Bridge over Bull Run. The Federals fled up the Warrenton Pike back to Washington, "their tails between their legs," as Avis might say.

The Brigade remained near Manassas through the fall. Robert E. Lee promoted Jackson to major general in command of all the Shenandoah Valley with headquarters in Winchester. In early November, the Fifth Infantry returned to Winchester as part of Jackson's army. They looked forward to going into winter quarters, but Jackson had other plans. He sent the brigade over to the Potomac to destroy a dam and to block barge traffic on the Chesapeake & Ohio Canal.

Captain Avis and his men experienced a miserable Christmas–a day so cold their water turned to ice. They were sleeping on piles of hay and leaves, so it took several blankets, if they could find them, to stay warm. They awoke in the morning to frost covering their tents.

And it got worse. On New Year's Day, 1862, Jackson led his army into the Allegheny Mountains of northwestern Virginia to capture the town of Romney. He planned to split the Federal forces. He believed that armies could fight in winter, and that they did not have to stay in camp until spring. Sleet, snow and a full blizzard descended. The supply wagons bogged down in the rear, and there was no food. The army of 8,500, trying to plow through drifting snow, covered ten miles in a day. Still Jackson kept them moving.

One morning, after a terrible snowstorm, Captain Avis and his men climbed out from under their blankets to find snow that lay a foot deep. The men slipped and slid on the ice. The horses were useless. The men had to push the wheels on the wagons and artillery. General Jackson was right there in the snow, pushing side by side with his men.

On January 14, the Confederates arrived in a deserted Romney. The brigade found houses where they could sleep. Jackson anticipated going on to Cumberland, twenty miles north, but he realized that his troops were too tired to march any farther. So the brigade moved back to Winchester, much to the men's relief. The Federal Army stayed in camp at Frederick, across the border, but remained a constant threat to head south again.

The rest of the winter stayed quiet as the brigade recovered. When March came, so did the expectation of returning to action. General N. P. Banks, with his 25,000 Federal troops, left Frederick and moved into the Valley. The enemy arrived just north of Winchester and halted, waiting for reinforcements. Jackson had 4,000 men, and wanted to attack immediately, before enemy reinforcements could arrive. Orders became confused, and, much to Jackson's disgust, the attack did not occur. The Confederates retreated south with the Federals following close behind.

Neither army seemed to know what the other was doing. Jackson, however, achieved his strategic goal of keeping the Federals tied down in the Valley and away from Lee's forces over the Blue Ridge in Manassas.

The Federals moved north again, and Jackson's forces followed. On the afternoon of March 23, 1862, they reached Kernsville, four miles south of Winchester. The Brigade had marched thirty-six miles that day, and the men were exhausted. Jackson was ready for battle but wanted to bivouac, then attack the next morning. But the situation changed. As the men stacked their guns, orders came to go into battle. The regiment lined up behind a stone fence to the left of the Winchester Road. The Cavalry was to make a diversion on the right across the road. Then the Brigade would attack the enemy's right flank. The Federals came; John Avis helped to turn back the Federals.

We turned them back a couple of times but could never gain the initiative. More Federal reserves entered the battle, attacking to our left. Artillery fire was everywhere. Smoke covered the field. The noise was awful. Our ammunition was about gone. We were so tired we could hardly move. At one point, General Jackson took one of the drummer boys to the high ground and had him try to rally the troops, but the noise was so loud no one could hear the drum. We did get inspired when our regimental color bearer leapt over the stonewall and waved his flag, taunting the Federals, daring them to advance. The enemy was so amazed they didn't even shoot. We held on as the rest of our lines cracked and our army fell back into the woods. The sun was setting and the Federals didn't follow. We were lucky. Had they continued their attack, we would have been destroyed. As it was, we retreated five miles back down the road to where our supply wagons were. We had been defeated, outnumbered ten to one. It was our first loss.

Through the rest of the spring of 1862, Jackson's army moved back and forth within the Shenandoah Valley to keep the Federals guessing.

When General Jackson moved his army through Staunton, Captain John Avis received a new assignment. He became the provost marshal for the town. Avis, at 43 years old must have felt relieved and grateful. During the first year of the Civil War, he had led his company up and down the Shenandoah Valley and across the Blue Ridge, fighting the elements as well as the enemy, and he must have been worn out. Certainly, the higher-ranking officers were his age and older, but they weren't leading an infantry company. They rode their horses; he marched with his men.

Staunton was the supply base for Jackson's army. Ammunition, cannons and other arms, quartermaster and commissary items, and 10,000 uniforms were stored there. With a company of fifty men, Captain Avis became responsible for the security of the town. His family joined him since Staunton was presumed safer than Charles Town, which changed hands frequently.

Excerpts from a Staunton resident's diary portrayed the situation in the town:

> Soldiers are constantly going from house to house applying for something to eat . . . . We heard heavy cannonading, indicating a conflict near Richmond . . . . Yesterday a poor woman who lives in town heard that her husband had been killed. Her wailings, which kept up for an hour or two, were most

distressing. . . . All the wounded men who can walk have been creeping up from Winchester, trying to get to their homes. Staunton is full of them. Many look very forlorn, hands and arms hurt, faces bound up, badly clad, barefoot and dirty. . . . Several wagons went through town today on their way to Kanawha county for salt. . . . We have more to fear from the scarcity of sustenance and clothing than from the Federal armies. . . . I learned that the sentinels had last night halted citizens on the streets, and ordered them not to pass unless they were going to their homes . . . the Provost Marshall [Captain Avis] was present at one of the street corners, and required the sentinel to use [a] gun when necessary to arrest passers-by. . . . It was almost appalling to see the rows of graves recently dug waiting with gapping mouths for the still living victims . . . flour has gone up to $25 a barrel, bacon $1 a pound, indicating "either a time of famine or an utterly ruinous depreciation of the currency.[7]

Son James Avis left the hospital at Winchester and joined his father's unit as a first lieutenant in September 1862. James remained with the Provost Guard until the fall of 1864, when he enrolled in the Medical College of Virginia in Richmond to study pharmacy. Avis' eleven-year-old son Braxton also joined the Provost Guard and was a musician with the unit for three years. In this position he gained his reputation as the youngest man in the Confederate Army. Eight-year-old Edward became the only family casualty at Staunton. The local newspaper reported that Captain Avis' youngest son had fallen out of an old apple tree on the hill in front of the American Hotel because a limb split. He broke his leg above the knee. The article stated: "He is doing well at present."[8]

General Jackson's maneuvering in the spring of 1862 finally paid off. He outflanked the Federals at Front Royal and chased them over the Potomac back into Maryland. With the Valley safe for the time being, his army crossed the Blue Ridge to help protect Richmond from General McClellan. His men fought bravely at Second Manassas and repelled the Federals. In May 1863, Jackson's army joined the battle at Chancellorsville on the turnpike that runs from Orange to Fredericksburg. As General Jackson returned in darkness on horseback from scouting the front lines, North Carolina troops shot him by mistake. He died from his wounds.

Jackson's death left his men in shock. They loved him. Afterwards, Captain Avis' old unit was officially named the Stonewall Brigade. From that time on, the Confederacy won only one more significant battle.[9]

That summer the Confederates attempted to rally and advanced into Pennsylvania to Gettysburg. The Federals forced them back into Virginia. The Stonewall Brigade lost half its men They spent the winter of 1864 near Orange, Virginia and in May 1864 were overwhelmed by Grant at the Wilderness Campaign and at Spotsylvania.[10]

That June, Federal General David Hunter burned the Valley, including Staunton. He stayed for four days tearing up the Virginia Central Railroad tracks, destroying military supplies, and burning houses. With only fifty men, Avis could not defend against him. There were no other Confederate forces around to protect the town. General Hunter was a first cousin of Andrew Hunter, the man John Avis admired as John Brown's prosecutor. When General Hunter later marched through Charles Town, he burned the house of Andrew Hunter, his own cousin.

After Staunton, Hunter burned Lexington and headed for Lynchburg. The Stonewall Brigade, now under General J. A. Early, had recovered from the Wilderness Campaign and they drove Hunter out of Lynchburg and into the mountains of southern West Virginia. At Sweet Springs, Leticia Floyd Lewis, wife of a William Lewis descendant, talked Hunter's men out of burning her home and the resort. She was the sister of John B. Floyd, secretary of war during John Brown's raid on Harpers Ferry.

General Early's army, after chasing Hunter into the mountains, tried to take the pressure off the Confederate forces to the east. He marched up the Valley to the outskirts of Washington unopposed. Some thought that he could have taken the capital. Fearful to attack, he decided to back off and returned south. Afterwards, the brigade moved to Petersburg and spent the winter and spring there. In April 1865, Lee surrendered to Grant at Appomattox Courthouse.

John Avis' old unit, the 5th Virginia Infantry, surrendered with Lee. Only 100 men remained out of the 600 with whom Captain Avis had served three years earlier.

The Civil War was over, and John Avis and his family returned to Charles Town in 1865. The fields were overgrown, fences gone, farmhouses burned, and the trees bare from the battles. Only the walls remained of the courthouse where John Brown had been sentenced to hang. Ex-slaves milled around town but wouldn't work. There wasn't enough labor to cultivate the farms or rebuild the town. Farmland sold for as little as $25 an acre. A radical group had taken over all the political positions, and Charles Town now resided in West Virginia, no longer Virginia.

During the war in 1863, Jefferson County—which included Charles Town and Harpers Ferry—separated from Virginia and became part of the new state of West Virginia. The Union wanted Jefferson County and the eastern panhandle because it was important to have the B&O railroad, which ran from Baltimore to Wheeling, in northern territory.

It probably didn't make sense to John Avis that he was now a resident of West Virginia. Jefferson County was tied to Virginia, to the Shenandoah Valley, not to some wilderness west of the Allegheny Mountains. Elections in the county had taken place while it was occupied by Federal troops. Only a small part of the eligible voters, mostly Union sympathizers favorable to West Virginia, voted.

After the war, Jefferson County and the State of Virginia appealed the separation to the United States Supreme Court. John Avis friend Andrew Hunter represented the county. The appeal occurred during a time of national political turmoil. Congress attempted to impeach Lincoln's predecessor, Andrew Johnson. Ulysses S. Grant followed Johnson as President. Congress expanded the Supreme Court from seven to nine, allowing Grant to appoint two new judges. The expanded court ruled in 1871 that the 1863 Jefferson County election making the county part of West Virginia was valid.[11]

Things finally settled down in Charles Town, where John Avis served his community well.

During the years after the war, I served as town sergeant, mayor, justice of the peace, and finally, as superintendent of the Jefferson County Alms House.

My two oldest sons, James and Braxton, moved to Harrisonburg. At least they were back in Virginia.

When James was wounded during the war, he was carrying that Sharp's rifle that John Brown willed me. Brown also gave me his pistol, which James kept at his house in Harrisonburg. James later gave the pistol to my youngest son, Edward, then a lieutenant in the regular army. While Edward was traveling on the Mississippi, the steamship foundered, and the pistol was lost. That was too bad. Both that Sharp's rifle and the pistol would be worth something today.[12]

After my return from the Civil War, I had to be careful because I had some notoriety from the John Brown incident. Some of the carpetbaggers who came to town just might have wanted to get even. A Yankee nitwit, Thomas Hughes, wrote a book about Captain Brown and made up lies. He said Sheriff Campbell and myself allowed Brown to lie in his bloody clothes in my jail from the time he was captured until we hanged him. He claimed that Captain Brown kissed a Negro baby. Brown said his mother brought him up not to suffer from fear, and he walked cheerfully to the scaffold.

This was all poppycock. But I believed that the truth should be told. And I wrote a document to set the record straight about my association with Captain Brown. As justice of the peace of Charles Town, I prepared and notarized an affidavit for the record so that the truth would be known for all time. I stated that, "I did not think his bearing on the scaffold was conspicuous for its heroism, yet not cowardly." I concluded my affidavit by stating that when I adjusted the noose, the only thing he said was: "Be Quick."[13]

PART IV

John D. and C.C. Lewis, Capitalists (1800-1917)

CHRONOLOGY

1755 Indian captive Mary Draper Ingles makes salt at Campbells Creek.
1774 Andrew Lewis' army marches through the Kanawha Valley to Point Pleasant.
1785 Colonel John Dickinson acquires the salt land at Campbells Creek.
1789 George Washington is elected President. Kanawha County is formed.
1797 The first commercial salt is produced at Campbells Creek.
1800 John D. Lewis is born at Fort Lewis in Bath County, Virginia.
1810 John D.'s family moves from Point Pleasant to the Clendenin fort at Charleston.
1815 James Wilson, John D.'s stepfather, strikes gas drilling a salt well.
1817 First coal used in salt production.
1822 John D. goes to work for Shrewsbury and Dickinson Salt Company.
1839 C.C. Lewis is born in Kanawha County.
1840 Coal is shipped down the Kanawha River.

1846   Kanawha Valley salt production peaks.
1851   John D. acquires Skyles Survey land.
1862   C.C. participates in the Battle of Scary Creek.
1863   West Virginia becomes a state.
1872   C.C. is appointed president of Kanawha Valley Bank.
1873   The C&O Railroad reaches Charleston.
1882   John D. dies at Charleston.
1889   Kanawha County coal production reaches one million tons.
1890   C.C. develops Kelly's Creek coal land.
1903   C.C.'s son Cam purchases the Old Sweet Springs resort.
1918   C.C. Lewis dies in Charleston.
1920   The Lewis family sells Old Sweet Springs.

17

KANAWHA VALLEY

They still worked on in this way until they got down some little Distance above the mouth of the great Kanawha. They came to a little salt spring in the Bank of the river the Indians stopped there and rested for a day or two there & with what kittles they Had with them boiled & and made some salt.[1]

Thus began the first recorded history of the Kanawha Valley, as described by a son of Mary Draper Ingles. In 1755, the Indians forced her, as a captive, to make salt at Campbells Creek where it flowed into the Kanawha River.

Thirty years later, Colonel John Dickinson saw the salt springs as he marched with Charles Lewis to the Battle of Point Pleasant. He acquired the land, and from it his grandson, John Dickinson Lewis, or John D. as I will call him, made a fortune. Charles Lewis was John D.'s other grandfather.

I wanted to find Campbells Creek. My great-grandfather, Charles Cameron Lewis, described the area in a 1904 article about his father in the *West Virginia Historical Magazine*:

The greater part of his [John D.'s] life was spent at the old homestead five miles above Charleston on the bank of the Kanawha River, just above the mouth of Campbells Creek, on the 502 acres tract of land patented to John Dickinson in 1785 and by him sold to Joseph Ruffner in 1793 and by his heirs in part to my father. . . . On this 502-acre tract was the celebrated Salt Spring located near the edge of the river about 1,000 feet below a point opposite the Thoroughfare Gap. My father once told me that when he was quite young the old settlers told him that when they first came to Kanawha the elk and deer came down Campbells Creek to this spring to get salt, and that they would go there and see hundreds of them waiting their time to get to the spring. And to this day the path made by the elk, deer, and Buffalo in places is distinctly traceable for several miles up this creek.²

On a gray November morning, I exited I-77 just after it crosses the Kanawha River before going into Charleston. I had looked at a copy of an 1862 map showing Campbells Creek where it entered the Kanawha. The road from Charleston to Malden crossed the creek. The map showed the J.D. Lewis salt furnace alongside the river. Several buildings, marked J.D. Lewis, were close by; one of these must have been his home. Beyond the Lewis salt furnace the map depicted a line of salt wells and furnaces, stretching along the riverbank to Malden. They bore the names of Ruffner, Shrewsbury, and Dickinson.³

Off I-77, I entered Port Amherst, an industrial wasteland of old buildings, railroad spurs, and junkyards. Coal came by rail down the Campbells Creek hollow from the mines upstream to be loaded on barges for shipment downriver to the Ohio. It took me a while to find the creek. I drove into the parking lot of a dilapidated drive-in with a sign showing a hot dog. Behind it, I found the stream, running through a gully lined with bare trees. It began to drizzle. I stood on the bank; rain running down my neck, amazed at how clear the stream still ran. I imagined that Great-grandfather C.C., as a boy, might have hunted deer along these banks in the mid-1800s.

Back in my car, I followed Campbells Creek, as best I could, until it took a curve and flowed into the Kanawha under the I-77 overpass. After referring to the old map, I turned around and headed upriver. There, I found a subdivision of small homes along the river. A fence separated it from a coal loading dock. I figured that this must have been the approximate location of J.D. Lewis salt furnace and his home.

Eighteen file boxes of items on the Lewis family are in the archives of West Virginia University at Morgantown. One item in particular pertained to Campbells Creek—a 1906 survey that traced John D.'s ownership back to Colonel John Dickinson's original acquisition. Two other files contained letters written to and by family members. The recurring names (besides Lewis) were Ruffner, Dickinson, and Wilson. Topics included coming to the Kanawha Valley in 1835 and the decline of the salt business in the 1840s. With the Civil War came letters about the selling of Negroes, the fate of

Richmond, and a prison camp where Confederate soldiers were starving. There was news from a sister-in-law who was a missionary in South America in 1875, a receipt for coal royalties in 1887, a four legal-page handwritten appraisal of property for the John D. Lewis estate, a wife's grand trip to Europe in 1905, and letters reflecting the problems and family sale of Old Sweet Springs in 1920. Many other items seemed nothing more than the contents of an old desk dumped into file boxes: newspaper obituaries of family members, a C&O timetable, a grandson's grades from a prep school in Virginia, a wedding invitation list of twenty-five pages, a dress chart for men, post cards, receipts, and checkbook stubs.

In essence, these files at West Virginia University represented a time-capsule description of the life of a well-to-do nineteenth century American family. Underlying these things, however, I found clues to other unspoken family matters: the murder of an in-law by cousins, intermarriages, the death of a child, a sister-in-law in prison, tiffs over estates, a mother-in-law's obituary that ignores her wayward husband, a hint of a sister's insanity, and a son's poor investment. Some of these things I would learn more about; others I would not.

Up to this time, I knew my great-grandfather, C. C., as he was called, as the owner of coal land that supplied royalties to four generations of an ever-increasing number of his descendants. I came to know him more intimately when my aunt sent us his portrait. He had posed formally, wearing a full gray beard. The children called him Uncle Wooly. But we could see Uncle Wooly was not happy in a Florida house. He just didn't fit. We decided to contribute his portrait to the Kanawha Banking and Trust in Charleston, a bank he had founded. Today Uncle Wooly hangs in the trust department in what is now, through merger, the United Bank. I'm sure he watches what goes on with a keen eye.

Approaching downtown on Kanawha Boulevard, I spotted a historical marker and pulled over. It said that across the street stood the site of Fort Clendenin, "a western frontier outpost, guarding settlers against the Indians." The fort had been built by the Clendenin family in 1788. It had faced the river and originally consisted of a two-story log house surrounded by a log stockade.

Another marker nearby said: "First Gas Well." Here, in 1815, Captain James Wilson vowed he would "drill to Hades, if necessary," to find salt. He succeeded with the Hades part as the well burst into a ball of flame. He had hit natural gas. He capped the well, and it would be years later before it was recognized that gas, like salt, had an economic value. Captain Wilson was John D.'s stepfather.

The first Charles Cameron Lewis, John D.'s real father, was a baby when Indians killed his father, Charles Lewis, at Point Pleasant. Charles Cameron also fought the Indians, serving as a lieutenant at the Battle of Falling Timbers in Ohio. He returned home from that battle to marry Jane Dickinson, daughter of Colonel John Dickinson. The Dickinsons and the Lewises had been neighbors, both with large land holdings along the Cowpasture River in what is now Bath County, Virginia. Colonel Dickinson's father, Adam Dickinson, and Charles' father, John Lewis, had been contemporaries. Adam was born in Scotland, moved to Ireland, settled in America in New Jersey, and then obtained a patent for 2,500 acres on the Cowpasture. In the mid 1700s, he established a settlement and built Fort Dickinson on his property, located just south of present-day Millboro Springs, only about fifteen miles, downstream from Charles Lewis' home.

After their marriage, Charles Cameron and Jane moved from Fort Lewis to the Lewis property at Point Pleasant, in search of better farmland. Charles Cameron died when John D. was a small boy. Jane married Captain Wilson, who took the family to Charleston to the Clendenin fort.

There on the site of that fort, C.C. built his home in 1876. From a picture I saw, the house was three stories with a large encircling porch and a smaller porch on the top floor front. C.C. chose the spot because his father had grown up living in the fort.

C.C. built another grand home, next door to his in 1900, this one for his daughter and son-in-law, Anne Lewis Johnson and Howard Johnson. Their son and my father, Kit Johnson, grew up there. At age four, I visited my grandmother there just before she died. I can remember the huge columns on the front. My mother told me that as a boy, my father dug in the dirt floor of the basement of his Grandfather C.C.'s house, searching for arrowheads and other relics from the old fort.

I looked across Kanawha Boulevard from the two markers and tried to imagine a fort. Suddenly, it dawned on me that five generations of Lewis descendants, including my father, had lived on that property. When my grandmother died, her house passed out of the family. None of her three sons had wanted it. My two uncles had their own homes in Charleston, and my father had moved to Florida for health reasons. John D.'s house passed on to his son Cam's family, lasting until it was torn down in the 1960s. In two hundred years the place had changed from a frontier fort to two homes to an apartment building. Had the homes survived, they would be on the National Historical Register. A "Now Leasing" sign was stuck in the ground out front near a rock marker commemorating the site of the fort. C.C. gave the Daughters of the American Revolution permission to place that rock in front of his house in 1915. Except for those historical signs, progress had covered up a lot of local history.

Did it bother me that the family had lived there for all that time and then moved on? Not particularly. I was a child when it happened. Even the two-hundred-year-old Lewis farm in Point Pleasant is now out of the family. But it would have been wonderful if either C.C.'s or my grandparents' house had been preserved like the Hubbard House and some of the other old houses on Kanawha Boulevard. Does it bother me that my mother and father broke tradition and moved to Florida? No. In reality, I have enjoyed living there and the move probably broadened my horizons. Yet, I was sufficiently exposed to the family traditions, because in time I returned to West Virginia.

Before John D. and his salt-making associates spurred the development of the Kanawha Valley in the 1800s, its settlement had progressed slowly. Twenty years after Mary Draper Ingles passed though, Walter Kelly built a cabin on a stream a few miles upriver from Campbells Creek. Indians quickly scalped Mr. Kelly and burned his cabin. The Morris and the Clendenin families arrived next. Their sons joined Andrew Lewis' army as it marched to battle at Point Pleasant. With Cornstalk defeated, the Kanawha Valley was safe for a time. Some of the men from that battle saw opportunities there and returned.

The Clendenins became the first to settle where Charleston is today. The five brothers liked the land where the Elk River ran into the Kanawha. They bought 1,000 acres from Mr. Thomas Bullitt. This was the same Mr. Bullitt who had developed Hot Springs with Andrew Lewis some years before. Bullitt had explored the Kanawha Valley and marked trees with his tomahawk to claim the property. The brothers built the Clendenin fort. Thus, began Charleston, named after their father Charles.

In the early days, turkey, bear, deer, elk, and buffalo were plentiful within what is now the city limits. When the bears migrated northward in the spring, they swam the river, passing right by the fort. In fall the bears became so thick, rooting around in the mast from the beech trees, that a hunter could walk up to the fattest and shoot it without disturbing the others. The bear would then be cleaned and salted down for winter.[4]

Attracted by the game, Daniel Boone lived in the Valley for several years. Daniel and Andrew Lewis' son, Thomas, participated in the formation of Kanawha County in 1789; the year George Washington became President. Thomas Lewis served as a colonel in the Kanawha County militia. Daniel Boone represented the county in the legislature in Richmond before moving on to Kentucky where he gained his fame. Maybe he thought Charleston had become too crowded. By 1800, the town had twelve houses and sixty-five people.

There was another spot I wanted to visit, another creek. It lay west of Charleston, after I-64 crosses the Kanawha, on the way to Huntington. At the first exit over the river, I turned off the Interstate and headed toward St. Albans. Seeing a small bridge ahead, I pulled into a parking lot in front of a restaurant, which overlooked the river and the old Nitro munitions plant. A muddy stream flowed into the Kanawha next to the restaurant. This was Scary Creek. I found a marker almost hidden by weeds. It said: "Battle of Scary. First Confederate victory in the Kanawha Valley fought here July 17, 1861." C.C. Lewis participated in this battle as a member of the Kanawha Riflemen, his only battle of the Civil War. When the fighting moved out of the Valley, he resigned, leaving his Riflemen companions to join his father in the salt business. I would have to search further to understand this.

I drove back into Charleston and up the road to the Spring Hill Cemetery. It contains 200 acres straddling a series of ridges overlooking Charleston and the Kanawha Valley. The cemetery plots are laid out in intricate, intersecting curves and circles. The monuments and obelisks reflect the architecture of the late nineteenth and early twentieth centuries—Gothic Art Deco, Romanesque, and Neo-Classical Revival. The cemetery dates back to 1818. Many of my ancestors, the Lewises, the Dickinsons, the Ruffners, the Wilsons, the Atkinsons, the Avises, and the Johnsons are buried there.

I found my way up to the Lewis plot. The centerpiece is a cement replica of a tree trunk, inscribed with LEWIS. Around the stump, mounted flat on the ground, are smaller markers: C.C.'s grandmother,

Jane Dickinson Lewis (1777-1835): his father, John D. (1800-1882); himself (1839-1917); his wife, Bettie Wilson Lewis (1840-1923); and his daughter, my grandmother, Anne Lewis Johnson (1875-1937). C.C.'s grandmother and his father were probably buried in Malden, but C.C. had them moved to Spring Hill Cemetery. I found no marker for C.C.'s mother, Anne Dickinson Lewis, who died when he was a child. The cause of her death is unknown. Plaques for my uncles, Charles and Howard Johnson, are also there. Breaking tradition, my own father is buried in Florida.

As I stood on that cemetery hill in the damp, penetrating cold, I looked through the bare trees to the river and the tall buildings of downtown Charleston below. Heavy gray clouds hung over the valley. I thought about how C.C. Lewis and his father John D. had played a role in the industrial development of this area in the 1800s. The salt marsh that John D.'s grandfather, Colonel Dickinson, acquired at the mouth of Campbells Creek begins the story.

18

SALT KINGS

Rising smoke from a hundred salt furnaces filled the valley. The sun looked like an orange ball in the gray sky. Eleven-year-old C.C. Lewis stood on the riverbank of the Kanawha, watching a flatboat loaded with barrels of salt move down river. The water looked oily and iridescent from the salt-well seepage as it swirled in the boat's wake. A man stood in the rear of the boat steering with a long oar. C.C. figured the salt was headed for the meat packers in Cincinnati. In summer the water dropped so low that the steamboats couldn't come this far upstream to pick up the salt.

C.C. turned and walked the short distance to his father's salt furnace. The family's house was close by and he had come to call his father for dinner. The boy approached a small log building where his father conducted business. Nearby stood a long shed with evaporating tables. At one end a stack spewed smoke into the air. A wooden frame tower sat over the wellhead next to the river. Several slaves, their bodies shiny with sweat, loaded barrels with the finished salt. C.C. waved at the white foreman who was supervising. The foreman said that John D. had ridden by horseback up to Malden where C.C.'s grandfather and his uncles, the Dickinsons, had wells. His father frequently visited with the Dickinsons, the Ruffners, and the Shrewsburys to talk salt prices. C.C. walked back to the house to tell his stepmother that his father was away. The shade of the trees by the house felt cool. It was good to get away from the stench of brine and smoke along the river. It was 1850.

The land at Campbells Creek had passed from C.C.'s great-grandfather, Colonel John Dickinson, to pioneer salt maker Joseph Ruffner and then eventually back into the family to C.C.'s father, John D. Lewis.

Colonel Dickinson had decided that the Virginia legislature, even then, was never going to support the development of western Virginia. While visiting Richmond one day, he ran into Joseph Ruffner. He described the Campbells Creek property to Ruffner, who bought it on the spot. Colonel Dickinson worked out a deal where Ruffner paid 500 pounds for the land with the price increasing to 10,000 pounds based on the amount of salt produced.[1] Ruffner went home, saddled his horse, and rode to the Kanawha Valley to inspect his purchase."[2] Colonel Dickinson's great grandson, C.C., would one day marry Joseph Ruffner's great granddaughter.

Initially salt makers drove hollowed-out logs to a depth where the brine from the springs could be ladled by hand to the surface. They then boiled the brine in kettles to produce salt crystals. Later, Joseph Ruffner's sons, David and Daniel, developed a metal drill that penetrated rock, deepening the wells, thus transforming Campbells Creek into one of the best salt-producing spots in the Valley.

The Ruffners, like the Lewises, had settled in the Shenandoah Valley. The Ruffners then moved to the Kanawha Valley, acquiring both the Campbells Creek property and the Clendenins' 1,000 acres, including the fort. Joseph Ruffner in essence bought most of what is now Charleston from Elk River to the present Kanawha City Bridge, and from the Kanawha to the hill."[3]

Two other families, the Shrewsburys and the Dickinsons, arrived in 1820. They quit growing tobacco in the Shenandoah Valley to come to the Kanawha Valley to produce salt. These Dickinsons were no relation to Colonel John Dickinson. But it didn't take long for the new Dickinsons to get mixed up with the Lewises.

At age twenty-two, John D. Lewis sold his interest in the Lewis land at Point Pleasant to his brother and went to work for Shrewsbury and Dickinson. Shortly thereafter, he married Joel Shrewsbury's daughter Sally Lee, solidifying his position in the business. Sally Lee died in 1830, giving birth to a son, Joel Lewis. John D. later married Anne Dickinson, the daughter of the other partner, William Dickinson, Sr.

John D. decided to leave Shrewsbury and Dickinson to go into the salt business on his own. He acquired interest in three salt furnaces, two of which lay just upriver from the mouth of Campbells Creek.[4] The Ruffners owned three furnaces nearby. All these furnaces must have been on the land that the Ruffners originally purchased from Colonel Dickinson. The 1906 survey, prepared for John D.'s heirs, defined the Campbells Creek property that he bought from the Ruffners, probably in the 1830s.[5]

Another furnace, named the J.D. Lewis, sat farther upriver just beyond Burning Springs, the very springs that George Washington and Andrew Lewis once owned. Apparently, it was leased from John D. All the furnaces seemed to have interlocking, multiple owners. As the Kanawha Valley salt business hit its peak in the 1840s, John D. had placed himself in an advantageous position. He was one of the first to use coal in the manufacture of salt. Also he was an early user of natural gas.[6] Coal from mines located in the nearby hills along the river was initially hauled to the salt furnaces in baskets and then later by small wagons pushed, in some cases, by slaves. This was the beginning of the coal industry in the Kanawha Valley.

Wells and furnaces lined both sides of the river from just east of Charleston, for twenty miles upriver past Campbells Creek, Malden, and beyond Burning Springs. People needed salt to preserve meat and vegetables and to make butter. The Kanawha "red salt," discolored by iron impurities and with its penetrating qualities, was particularly good for curing meat.[7] Barrels of salt carried by flatboat were floated downstream with the current to the Ohio River and on westward. Workers would go up the creek, cut down poplars, build the boats, and then float them down to the river where they were loaded. After the salt was delivered, the boatmen would either walk or buy a horse and ride back to the Kanawha Valley.[8] Cincinnati, the meat-curing center of the West, became the Kanawha Valley's prime market. And since money was scarce in the early 1800s, salt became a common method of exchange in Charleston and Malden stores.

The Kanawha Valley quickly became the second largest salt-producing area in the United States, surpassed only by the brine springs in Onondaga, New York. In the early 1800s, the New Yorkers possessed no means to transport their salt over the Appalachians except by mule. England, the major supplier of salt to the East Coast of the United States, faced the same problems, plus its imports had been interrupted by the War of 1812.

Kanawha salt initially monopolized western markets. The Ruffners, Shrewsburys, Dickinsons, and John D. Lewis schemed to maintain that monopoly, forming a cartel, the Kanawha Salt Company. When overproduction occurred on the Kanawha, the cartel tried to either buy the small producers or cut prices to drive them out of business. At other times they joined together to manage production and keep prices high. This was all considered a part of doing business. However, with so many wells on the Kanawha, it was difficult to keep all the producers in line.[9]

Senator Thomas Hart of Missouri in a speech in the Senate at the time attacked artificially high salt prices. He said, "The American monopolizers operate by the moneyed power and with the aid of banks. They borrow money and rent the salt wells to lie idle; they pay owners of the wells not to work them; they pay other owners not to open new wells. Thus, among us, they suppress the production, by preventing the manufacturing of salt."[10] Senator Hart's attack was aimed at John D. and his associates.

An old story tells about a professor from Harvard College, riding through the Valley in a stagecoach. A salt well belonging to William Dickinson, Jr., John D.'s brother-in-law, blew. The stage stopped so the passengers could watch. The drillers had hit gas and all the piping came out of the hole as someone said "like an arrow shot out of a cross-bow." Water and gas spurted a hundred feet into the air. The professor, being of an inquisitive nature, got out of the coach and lit a match to see if the gas would burn. A great blaze ensued. The heat singed the professor's hair and eyebrows, and he leaped into the Kanawha to save his life. The well frame and the engine house burned. The professor remounted the stage and rode on into Charleston to find a doctor. William Dickinson was not pleased and had the man apprehended. But the sheriff let the professor go when he admitted he was "a god dam [sic] fool and didn't know any better."[11]

Incidents like this led to the use of natural gas and coal to replace wood as fuel for the salt furnaces. The hillsides along the river had been stripped bare when wood was used. In C.C.'s time the trees started growing back.

England had similar competitive advantages to the Kanawha Valley: a combination of salt, nearby coal and gas for fuel, and cheap water transportation. Its biggest disadvantage was distance. However, ships carrying goods to Europe seldom had loads coming back so carried salt almost as ballast to New Orleans and other ports. But the Kanawha Valley had the additional advantage of cheap labor—slaves brought in from the plantations of eastern Virginia.

The Reverend Henry Dana Ward, rector of St. John's Episcopal Church in Charleston, demanded that John D. stop making salt on Sundays. The Rector said there was "a duty to the laboring class, the slaves." John D. chose not to pay attention to the rector. John D. had been an Episcopalian but switched over to the Presbyterian Church in Malden. Whether the Reverend's comments were the cause is not known. John D. did, however, contribute 100 bushels of salt to Reverend Ward to help pay off the church debt.[12] Salt, as a basis of exchange in the Kanawha Valley, could be converted to cash at the opportune time. The price of salt, however, like the stock market, fluctuated greatly. The Ruffners began selling salt at $2 a bushel, but with increased production and competition, the price soon fell below a dollar. At one point, the price was as low as twelve cents a bushel.[13] At that rate, John D.'s gift amounted to $12.

The local government proposed taxing salt, a common practice in other areas, to finance much-needed public schools. John D. and his friends fought the tax and won. It wasn't up to them to support schools.

While business prospered, John D. and Anne Dickinson had three children. Each received a family name: Sally from John D.'s first wife; Charles Cameron or C.C. from John D.'s father; and Margaret from Margaret Lynn, the wife of the original John Lewis. When C.C. was four years old, his mother, Anne, died, perhaps during the birth of his younger sister Margaret. John D. and Anne had been married eight years.

John D.'s business was demanding and time consuming. Having been left with a son from his first wife and three younger children from Anne, John D. needed help with his family, so he married his third wife, Elizabeth Darneal. She was his cousin by way of her mother who was a Shrewsbury whose father had married one of Colonel John Dickinson's daughters. Like John D.'s previous wives, Elizabeth, of course, had ties to the salt business. The Darneal name was linked to furnaces operated by the Shrewsburys and by John D. himself. And C.C. soon had a stepsister and a baby stepbrother. It was 1850 and John D. was fifty. He would outlive Elizabeth Darneal and marry for the fourth time.

Those making their fortunes in salt, some with incomes as high as $50,000 a year were called Salt Kings.[14] John D. fit into this group, but probably didn't appreciate the title or the notoriety that went with it. The Salt Kings built brick mansions with spacious grounds along the river in Charleston on Kanawha Street. They wanted to live away from their salt furnaces and the riffraff in Malden, which at the time had forty wells and more people than Charleston. C.C. probably wondered why his family didn't have a big home in Charleston. It would have been fun for him to live near the old fort where his father was raised. John D., perhaps being of a humbler nature than his fellow Salt Kings, insisted that his family stay in their home at Campbells Creek. He probably considered it quite adequate despite the addition of two more children after his third marriage.

Despite his growing wealth, John D. would have told C.C., if he had asked, that the Lewises were not part of the *nouveau riche* salt fortune society in Charleston. Yes, they had made lots of money, but they had come from old families that had owned land. That was the distinction.

Growing up on Campbells Creek, C.C. must have been further amazed at the extravagance of some of his father's business acquaintances. They built houses in Lewisburg, a hundred miles away, to escape the summer heat in the Kanawha Valley.

It is likely that C.C. had been to Lewisburg, having passed through on the way to Old Sweet Springs. A stagecoach, called the Cannon Ball, made the run from Charleston to Lewisburg to Sweet Springs. It sped along at six miles an hour, and its riders referred to it as the "Shake Guts." The trip took three days, going by way of the Kanawha Turnpike, now U.S. 60. The exciting part of the journey occurred when the stage passed within a few feet of the edge of the New River Gorge with its 600-foot drop to the river below.[15] Lewis family members probably traveled to Sweet Springs in their own carriage. They liked to visit there and soak in the spring waters. After all, Lewis cousins did own the place. C.C. probably had never seen a building as big as the Jefferson Hotel.

By 1858, C.C., would be attending, with his father and stepmother, his sister Margaret, and his half-sister Julia, performances in Brooks Hall by either Madame Parker's Opera Troupe or the talented ladies of Charleston.

The lanterns in the theater shone brightly. They were lit with cannel coal oil, recently discovered in the Valley. Mrs. Jeffries and Mrs. Shrewsbury entertained with a duet. Miss Caldwell, a debutante, played the piano. C.C.'s father wore a frocked coat and a top hat, his stepmother a hoop skirt. The ladies wore so much crinoline that John D. had trouble placing his top hat under the seats. C.C. saw members of the Dickinson and Ruffner families in the audience. His older sister, Sally, sat a few rows away with her new husband, Henry Clay Dickinson.

Sally had married her first cousin on her mother's side. Henry's father was William Dickinson, Jr., who was Sally's mother's brother—the Lewis' children's uncle. Charleston, being so isolated by the mountains and so small, apparently didn't offer many attractive matches between unrelated old families. So some people married their first cousins.[16] But it didn't end there. C.C.'s younger sister, Margaret, would later marry first cousin John Q. Dickinson, Henry's brother. Thus, two Lewis sisters and their husbands, the two Dickinson brothers, all had the same grandfather, the first William Dickinson.

A few miles downstream from Charleston, another branch of the Kanawha Valley Lewises had more serious problems. C.C.'s Cousin Margery, whose family owned property on Coal River that went back four generations to ancestor Andrew Lewis, had married John Kenna. A lawyer from Cincinnati, Kenna was involved in mining up Coal River. The couple had three small children, but their marriage had become so disagreeable that divorce, a rare thing in those days, appeared imminent.

According to the *Kanawha Valley Star*: "Mr. Kenna was in "the sitting rooms at the Kanawha House, between the bar and the dining room, [which] was crowded by guests assembling for dinner. Mr. Kenna was in a legal discussion, and one party called him a liar, and struck him with his fist. A scuffle ensued. . . . At this instant three or four discharges from a pistol or pistols sounded. Kenna fell, and expired instantly, a pistol ball striking him in the back . . . passing through his chest and lodging under the skin below his right nipple. . . . No one could tell who fired the shots; such was the suddenness of the affray and the consequent confusion in the room.

"Coroner Newton called a jury, and . . . promptly commenced a thorough investigation . . . the jury came to the conclusion that Mr. Kenna came to his death by wounds [sic] inflected by a pistol or pistols in the hands of James and Andrew D. Lewis, brothers in law of the deceased." One report stated that they had greeted Kenna in a friendly manner, then one of the brothers pulled out a revolver and shot him. Kenna fell to the floor. The killer then fired another shot into Kenna's prone body. It happened so quickly that the bystanders had no time to react.

After the fracas, C.C.'s Cousin James, or maybe Cousin Andrew, left the Kanawha House, went over to the courthouse, and returned with the sheriff. They sat down together and ate dinner. Afterwards, the Lewis boys headed for Missouri. Cousin Margery and her three children soon moved there to live with one of her brothers who later became a sheriff. After the Civil War the family returned to Charleston. Margery had remarried. Her son, John Kenna, Jr., later became a United States Senator from West Virginia. His statue stands in the Capitol in Washington.[17]

After C.C.'s night at the opera house with his family, he stepped outside and admired the highly polished carriages and surreys, lining the street waiting for the theater goers. C.C. and his family found their coach. He assisted his stepmother in and they proceeded to the Kanawha House. Since it is was late, John D. had arranged for the family to stay there overnight rather than ride home to Campbells Creek. In the hotel C.C., with some curiosity, looked into the sitting room where his cousins had allegedly murdered Mr. Kenna.

The best days of the salt business on the Kanawha soon passed. New York salt was now being moved by way of the Erie Canal across the Great Lakes to the Midwest. The Kanawha's transportation advantage of the early 1800s, floating flatboats loaded with salt downstream to the Ohio, disappeared with the coming of the steamboat. They made it easier to haul salt, but at times low water kept the steamboats from reaching the area upstream from Charleston. Also, they hauled imported salt from the port of New Orleans up the Mississippi to the Midwest. Salt deposits discovered in Michigan further expanded the supply. The coming of railroads made salt less dependent on river transportation. The Kanawha had no railroad access. Thus, a market that the Kanawha Valley once had all to itself became saturated with salt from New York, foreign sources, and newly discovered Midwestern locations. And the government dropped protective tariffs on English salt due to the demands of disgruntled western consumers, who thought they were paying too much.

In 1846 and 1847, a series of letters from John D. Lewis to his brother-in-law, John J. Dickinson, depicted the state of the Kanawha salt business. John D. wrote of the gloomy prospects for salt, including the competition from New Orleans. He mentioned the possibility of shipping salt to Memphis and trying to open new markets on the lower Mississippi. Then there were the general operating problems: the scarcity of boats, claims for bad debts, wages to be paid to Negroes on the boats, paying off debt, and a shipment of salt that was sunk.[18]

To maintain any kind of competitive edge, the Kanawha needed to be navigable year-round so that steamboats could reach the salt wells. The Kanawha River Board was formed with John D. as a member. This group wished to independently finance river improvements and pay back the cost with tolls. Since the Virginia legislature would never invest in river improvements, the salt manufacturers sued every time one of their boats sank. Mr. Tompkins sued the Kanawha Board for negligence in not removing a snag that sank one of his salt barges. A defense witness said a Negro, but used a more disparaging word, had removed it. Mr. Tompkins' lawyer demanded that the Negro, again using the disparaging word, be produced as a witness. The defense attorney explained in a droll manner that he was referring to a nigger head, a nautical term for a small winch.[19]

George Washington had concocted the original plan for a continuous water route linking the Atlantic Ocean and the Ohio over the Alleghenies by means of the James and Kanawha Rivers. Andrew Lewis even did some initial surveying for the project. But the future of those in the Alleghenies was tied to the rivers that flowed westward rather than the tidewater rivers like the James that flowed into the Chesapeake and the Atlantic. The Virginia legislature typically funded improvements to the eastern rivers. The number of whites in the West almost equaled those in the East, but the counting of slaves added to the population and the legislative representation in eastern Virginia. Western Virginians felt shortchanged. Talk of splitting off from eastern Virginia began well before the Civil War.

John D. stayed in the salt business but was beginning to think that the future lay in coal and gas. He bought a part of the Skyles Survey, an original patent covering 40,000 acres that had been under litigation for years and only recently settled. Western Virginia land had been granted to favored speculators (like John Lewis) since colonial times when it was divided into large grants by the Ohio, Greenbrier, and Loyal Companies. The Virginia system of land registration was complex and chaotic, thus allowing local land lawyers to make fortunes resolving ownership disputes. Skyles may have obtained his land by receiving a warrant for his service in the French and Indian or Revolutionary War, then expanding it by buying up the warrants of other soldiers. He had surveyed it by "metes and bounds," a form of measurement accomplished by walking a certain distance for a certain time.[20] This type of activity led to multiple claims against the land. These old Skyles patents lay north of the Kanawha River between the Gauley River on the east and the Elk River on the west and covered the headwaters of Kelly's Creek and Campbells Creek. A part of this land would be the basis for C.C.'s future wealth.

Meanwhile, C.C. completed Mercer Academy where he studied English, Latin, Greek, mathematics, bookkeeping and surveying. David L. Ruffner, grandson of the Ruffners who developed the salt business at Campbells Creek and cousin to C.C.'s future wife, served as principal of the academy. David gave his students, including possibly C.C., practical experience in surveying by laying out the road up the hill to what eventually would be Spring Hill Cemetery.[21] But as C.C.'s career would show, he shared the enthusiasm of his Lewis ancestors for land, but he didn't need to do the surveying to gain it. Instead, he put his bookkeeping training to immediate use by going to work as a clerk for his grandfather, William Dickinson, Sr., in the salt business.

But war was coming.

19

SLAVES, SECESSION, AND SCARY CREEK

On a bright fall afternoon in 1860, C.C., age twenty-two, finished drilling with the Kanawha Riflemen at Mercer Academy. Across the parade field, he saw Bettie Wilson standing with some friends. Looking lovely, holding her parasol, she waved. Her mother was a Ruffner. As far as C.C. knew, she wasn't even a cousin. He walked over to talk with her, carrying his rifle across his chest.

"Good afternoon, Miss Wilson."

"Good afternoon, Mr. Lewis. You look very smart in your uniform."

"Thank you. It's a bit warm for October," he said, holding his rifle with one hand and removing his plumed hat and wiping his brow with his other hand.

"If Mr. Lincoln is elected president, will the states divide?" she asked, twirling her parasol.

"My father hopes not, as do I."

"Will you all protect the Kanawha Valley if the Yankees invade?

"I suppose we will. Please excuse me, Miss Wilson, I have to go do some work for my Grandfather Dickinson."

"Goodbye, Mr. Lewis."

It was very much the thing for prominent young men to belong to the Kanawha Riflemen. Many, like C.C., were sons of salt families. Twenty members were attorneys. The young ladies of Charleston came out to watch the drills. The men wore white gloves, splendid uniforms of olive broadcloth, matching overcoats with wide gold stripes down the pantaloons and a hat with ostrich feathers and a wide brim. The Riflemen were invited to many social events and holiday affairs to display their drilling movements. Someone said that they were good at guarding the lemonade and chicken and were probably better dancers than fighters.[1]

Captain George Patton, a graduate of the Virginia Military Institute, commanded the Kanawha Riflemen. (His grandson by the same name would be both a heroic and controversial general in World War II.) George Patton, who was not much older than C.C., was a dashing fellow with a goatee. A lawyer, he recently moved to Charleston from Richmond where he had been associated with the Light Infantry Blues.

The previous year the Kanawha Riflemen almost embarked to Harpers Ferry to help put down John Brown's insurrection. However, much to the disappointment of the men, the conflict ended quickly, and there was no need to go.

Following John Brown's raid, the local community held a mass meeting at the Kanawha County courthouse to discuss "the present critical state of the Union," as the newspaper said. A local committee was selected to address the issue. C.C.'s father, John D., was a member. The committee made a resolution "approving the dignity and decorum, and at the same time the irresistible power and stern justice, in the trial, conviction and execution of the desperadoes who had invaded the soil of Virginia." The committee also resolved "that it was the duty of the Virginia General Assembly to put the entire Commonwealth in a complete state of defense."[2]

An incident did occur that had an impact on the Riflemen.[3] The unit was invited to march at a fair in Point Pleasant. Two Riflemen visited friends across the Ohio in Gallipolis. The pro-Union townspeople hooted and hassled them. A detachment of the Riflemen entered Gallipolis and retrieved the two men. Captain Patton kept the situation in hand; otherwise, the War Between the States might have started right there.

As in much of the country, people in Charleston and western Virginia were of different opinions concerning the slave issue. Slaves had been leased from the plantations in eastern Virginia to work at the salt furnaces. The census showed 3,000 slaves in Kanawha County. Yet many people thought slavery was wrong. In 1847, Henry Ruffner, father of C.C.'s principal at Mercer Academy, issued the "Ruffner Pamphlet" proposing the gradual emancipation of the slaves in western Virginia. This made a lot of people angry. His family used slaves in their salt business.

John D., undoubtedly, objected as well. He kept slaves. Using leased slaves was cheaper than hiring white men even with the cost of food, housing, and the small incentive wages they earned. John D.

might have been against slavery, but as long as it existed, he would take advantage of the situation to maintain a competitive edge.

John D. would read in a local paper that a Negro boy, nineteen years old, had been sold in Charleston for $1,500. This was an amazing price compared to the assessed tax value of $300 for slaves over twelve years old. Another notice stated that the Donnallys, who had been in the salt business since its beginning, were auctioning off twenty slaves to satisfy a claim. The notice said that the slaves were of different sexes and included children. They were described as some being first-rate hands such as are usually employed in the manufacture of salt. The auction took place at the Ruffner and Hale Store House in Malden.

The Methodist Episcopal Church had already split over slavery and in Charleston the southern faction moved its services to the courthouse. The Southern Methodists deleted from their Book of Discipline all reference to the buying and selling of slaves. It was revised to say, "The Church had no right to meddle, except to enforce the duties of master and servant as set forth in the Holy Scriptures."[4]

Despite the feelings for and against slavery in the Kanawha Valley, things remained amazingly calm. Whether a person was a Whig (most of the prominent people were), a Democrat, or one of those new Republicans (of which there were probably few), the Lewises and the other families continued to attend church, the opera house, and socials together just as they always had.

Slavery and the continued dissatisfaction with the eastern Virginia controlled legislature put western Virginia in a unique position. John D. often discussed with the Dickinsons and the Ruffners what would happen if West broke away from East. Would western Virginia be proslavery or antislavery? This could have national implications, like the battles in Kansas, in which John Brown had participated. The proslavery supporters fought to keep the number of slave states equal to the free states so neither side would have a majority in the U.S. Senate. In 1857, the Dred Scott decision in the Supreme Court said that a state, not Congress, had the right to permit or prohibit slavery. So if the threat of western Virginia separating from Virginia ever materialized, there would be a battle over which direction western Virginia would lean.

With the feeling for separation growing stronger in the West, Virginia Governor Henry Wise took a conciliatory step. He pushed the Virginia legislature into approving funds to extend the railroad over the mountains to Charleston and to make the Kanawha navigable year-round. John D. and his fellow Salt Kings had been fighting to improve the river for years. They felt that funds for the river were far more important to their salt-shipping interests than funding the railroad. But the Civil War intervened, and the railroad reached only as far as Covington.

The nation's two major political parties had been the Democrats and the Whigs, but they broke into pro and antislavery factions. Then came the Republican Party and its presidential candidate Abraham Lincoln. Eastern Virginians were mostly pro-slavery Democrats. Along the Kanawha, many people were Whigs and they were not ready to affiliate with the new antislavery Republican Party and its candidate nor the more radical pro-slavery Democrats who were for secession. Kanawha County, and probably John D., voted for John Bell of Tennessee, who took a vague middle-of-the-road position that appealed to some elements of the Whigs. Bell carried Tennessee, Kentucky, and by a slim margin, Virginia. The few Virginia votes for Lincoln came from the Wheeling area.

With Lincoln's election in November 1860, South Carolina led the southern states in seceding from the Union. In April 1861, Virginia held a convention in Richmond. Kanawha Valley's representative, George Summers, fought secession in frequent clashes with former Virginia Governor Henry Wise. The final vote was 88 to 55 to secede.[5] Western Virginia representatives voted 32 to 15 against. At that same time, John D. spoke at Malden "against the ordinance of secession before a threatening and angry mob."[6] C.C. said it was the only speech he ever made.

That same month South Carolina forces fired on Fort Sumter and the Civil War began. Richmond became the capital of the Confederacy in May, with the Kanawha Valley standing between it and Union forces in Ohio.

The 1st Kanawha Regiment was organized to protect the Valley. On May 8, 1861, the Kanawha Riflemen, with Captain Patton in command, joined the regiment. C.C., his half brother Joel, and his cousin James Lewis, from the William side of the family, all became members of the new unit. The regiment went into immediate training outside of Charleston. At the end of May, scouts reported that Union forces stood at Gallipolis, preparing to invade.

Henry Wise, recently the governor of Virginia but now an instant Confederate general, arrived from Richmond with additional troops. He was appreciated along the Kanawha for having pushed the legislature into funding the railroad across the Alleghenies and dredging the river. Wise was an erratic leader who had little experience in military matters. He trusted no one, had no faith in his troops, and attempted to jail people he thought were traitors. He impulsively marched 800 men 40 miles north to Ripley only to find the enemy not there. Meanwhile, the Kanawha Riflemen became part of the 22nd Virginia Infantry. Wise's Army of the Kanawha had grown to almost 3,000 men. They were mostly unequipped, untrained, and generally led by incompetent officers with the exception of a few men like Captain Patton.

Skirmishes with the Federals occurred to the north of Charleston, but neither side seemed eager to initiate combat. In July, the Federals under General Cox started a full invasion of the Kanawha Valley, moving men from Point Pleasant up the Kanawha in four steamboats and then putting them ashore west of Charleston. Patton, quickly promoted to colonel, positioned the Kanawha Riflemen as skirmishers on the left flank along the east bank of Scary Creek (by what is now St. Albans).[7] The major part of Patton's force lay behind the creek in timber and underbrush near the Kanawha River. The Federals approached down the Winfield road along the river and by way of the Teays Road.

C.C. would have seen a church and a house and then what seemed like a thousand men in blue uniforms advancing in a long line across an open field. Most of the Riflemen were probably afraid and wanted to get up and run, but they stood their ground. The battle began about 2 P.M. and lasted for what seemed hours. Rifle shots ricocheted about, artillery boomed, smoke bellowed from the field, men hollered, and the wounded screamed. Most of the fighting remained close to the river. The Union cavalry charged the Riflemen's line and almost caused a panic. Captain Patton, on horseback, rallied the troops. He ordered two field artillery pieces to fire on the cavalry and force it back. Suddenly, C.C. and the men lost sight of their commander. Captain Patton had been shot in the shoulder and carried from the battlefield. By dark the Federals, unable to advance, ceased their attack and withdrew.

The Virginians had won. They held their position along Scary Creek all that night and the next day. Some of the men helped bury the Yankee dead. The next morning, after nineteen hours without food, C.C. and the men marched back to their camp near Coal River.

Orders arrived directing Wise's army to retreat out of the Kanawha Valley. C.C. and the men were shocked. They had held the enemy in their first encounter. Weren't they there to protect Charleston? But another Federal army led by General McClellan was advancing across the northern part of western Virginia. General Wise feared that his army would be trapped in the Kanawha Valley, caught between McClellan and Cox. The Virginians proceeded upriver toward Charleston with the Federals close behind.

When John D. found out about the situation, he undoubtedly wanted to find his son and talk with him. And C.C. probably went to the house on Campbells Creek, seeking his father's advice. Sitting in John D.'s parlor, they talked.

"Father, I don't know what to do. My unit is leaving the Valley. Most of the men are going, even though I don't think they want to. I should go with them. They're my friends. I thought we joined the Kanawha Riflemen to defend the Valley, if that day ever came. Now I'm supposed to leave."

"Wise has no concern for the Valley," said John D. "He may have tried to help us when he was governor, but he was playing politics. He'd just as soon give Charleston to the Federals, and go off and defend some other part of Virginia. I don't think he knows what he's doing. You don't want to follow a man like that."

"But, Father. . . . "

"Your ancestors fought to make this country and you will have no part in destroying it."[8]

"I feel awful, letting my friends down. What are they going to think?"

"C.C., you didn't sign up to go off and fight someone else's war. I don't believe in this secession thing. Virginia is wrong. Yes, I had slaves. I had to for business reasons. But that's over."

"I have to go."

"No, you don't. I need you here. The years ahead are going to be rough ones. There are people who are going to want to split us off from Virginia. So be it. We've been complaining for years about what goes on in Richmond. The Federals are going to take over this valley, and we're going to have to figure out how to live with that. We have to survive. We have to keep the business going."

"But, Father, isn't my duty. . . ?"

"Your duty is to stay here and help me with the business. The

slaves are gone. I've lost most all my men to this damn war. Your duty is here. Staying here and keeping things going. That's the best thing for this Valley."

"I could be charged with desertion."

"No, you won't. Your commitment was to defend the Valley. You did that at Scary Creek. Thank God you survived. I'll talk to some people and your resignation will be accepted."

"You could do that?"

"Yes, and I will. Now go get some rest."

A week after the Battle of Scary Creek, C.C. was furloughed. A month later he was honorably discharged. Officers he knew must have made the arrangements. However, some of the men, who did not have the opportunity he did, deserted. On the other hand, men from Charleston, including his stepbrother and some of his cousins, so believed in the Confederate cause that they stayed with the 22nd Virginia Infantry throughout the war.

As the Army of the Kanawha retreated eastward over the mountains, General Cox's army arrived to occupy Charleston. Many people greeted the Federal troops with cheers. Many didn't. C.C. had begun his business career, joining his father in the salt enterprises, and probably thought it best to remain quietly at Campbells Creek. The future would be traumatic. In that first fall of the Civil War, the Kanawha flooded, wiping out many of the wells and furnaces.

The 22nd Virginia Infantry moved eastward and lost a battle at Carnifex Ferry on the Gauley River. In the meantime, another former Virginia governor, John B. Floyd, was placed in charge over Governor Wise. Confederate headquarters in Richmond considered Floyd the senior man. He had been secretary of war under former President Buchanan and involved in the decision to send the Marines to Harpers Ferry when John Brown had attacked. Floyd turned out to be a worse leader than Wise. All the two generals did was squabble. Eventually, General Robert E. Lee himself arrived at Sewell Mountain (between Charleston and Lewisburg) to intercede, but with little result. Floyd did nothing but retreat. Some believed he was in constant fear that he would be captured by the Federals and shot for perceived, previous misdeeds when he was secretary of war.

John D. and C.C. would probably not admit that there was a Lewis family connection to General Floyd. His sister, Leticia, had married a cousin on the William Lewis side of the family. They lived at Sweet Springs in a grand house called Lynnside, which William had built before the war. Floyd's father also had served as a governor of Virginia. He was buried on a hill in the Lewis Cemetery, overlooking his daughter's house and the Old Sweet Springs resort.

In the winter of 1861-62, Colonel Patton became the commanding officer of the 22nd Infantry. He rejoined the regiment in its winter quarters at Lewisburg. In the first action under his command there, the regiment lost a battle to the Federals in May of '62.

In August, many of the Federal troops moved out of Charleston to reinforce the Union army in the Shenandoah Valley where General Stonewall Jackson was defeating them. A Rebel army under General W.W. Loring, which included the 22nd, took advantage of the situation and attacked the Kanawha Valley to obtain much needed salt for the Confederacy. It is assumed that John D. and his compatriots supplied salt to whichever army occupied the Valley at the time.

The 22nd arrived on the south side of the river opposite Charleston in the early morning of September 13, 1862, and began to bombard the city. The Federals fired back from an artillery piece located by a barn on the Ruffner estate (the location of the present Capitol). People ran into the streets. Some moved up on Cox Hill to watch the battle. The 22nd crossed the river. Family and friends greeted them enthusiastically, interfering with their ability to shoot at the retreating Federals. By noon, the Federals abandoned the town, followed by northern sympathizers who boarded boats and headed downriver toward the Ohio.

John D. and C.C. must have heard the shelling from Campbells Creek and watched the smoke rising from the city down the valley.

Old Mrs. Goshorn, who lived on the corner of Broad Street and Kanawha Street in Charleston, had the foresight to take the family cow up to the second floor of her house. Her plan was to protect the bovine from the marauding soldiers on both sides, who were raiding the neighbors' chicken yards and cow stables.[9]

The next day, if C.C. had ridden his horse into Charleston, he would have found the place in ruins. Many stores, Mercer Academy where he had been a student, the Bank of Virginia, the Kanawha House Hotel, and the Methodist Church were burned to the ground by the Federals. The Elk River Bridge lay in the water. Federal troops had cut the suspension cables as they fled. Dead bodies littered the street.

Loring's army did not pursue the Federals. Instead, he put some of his men to work at Malden gathering salt. The general attempted to punish Union sympathizers left in Charleston by making them swear an oath to the Confederacy. After only two weeks, Loring and his army departed, and headed back to Lewisburg. Nobody knew why he had not marched on north to Wheeling as General Lee had apparently ordered. There, the Reorganized Government of West Virginia was meeting to plan western Virginia's separation from Virginia and the Confederacy. Loring was immediately relieved of his command for disobeying orders. By the end of October, Union forces reoccupied Charleston.

The 22nd Virginia Infantry remained in Lewisburg for the winter of '62-'63. Their objective was to protect the passes through the Alleghenies. They whipped the Federals in the battle of White Sulphur Springs in May 1863, but in November were routed at Droop Mountain, north of Lewisburg.

Two of C.C.'s Charleston cousins were killed fighting in the Shenandoah Valley in the summer of 1864. Columbus Lewis, a descendant of Andrew died at New Market. John Lewis, a descendant of William, died in the defeat at Winchester. C.C.'s former commanding officer, Colonel George Patton, was also lost at Winchester. Wounded in the leg and captured, he refused to have his leg amputated and died from his wounds.

Federals captured C.C.'s two brothers-in-law (and first cousins), Henry Clay Dickinson and John Q. Dickinson. They had fought with the 2nd Virginia Cavalry, were captured, and placed in Federal prison camps. Henry Clay spent a great deal of the war in a camp for Confederate officers. There the men were given the same treatment as the Federals believed their men were receiving at the notorious Confederate prison at Andersonville. Two-thirds of the men in the Federal camp died of pneumonia, starvation, and scurvy. Henry Clay's health was so damaged by the experience that he died soon after the war.[10]

In the summer of 1864, Union General David Hunter, who had burned everything that stood in his way in the Shenandoah Valley, was finally forced to retreat into the mountains. His army passed through the Sweet Springs Valley. He ordered the Old Sweet Springs resort burned to the ground. He also ordered the magnificent Lewis home, Lynnside, to be burned. Leticia Floyd Lewis, wife of Cousin William Lynn Lewis, stood up to Hunter's adjutant and begged him to burn neither her home nor the hotel.[11]

The following spring, General Lee's forces surrendered at Appomattox Court House. When the news reached Charleston, a celebration erupted. C.C. surely attended the ensuing parade and watched as a hearse with "Secession" painted on its side moved by. Another wagon had Jefferson Davis hanging in effigy from a sour apple tree. The parade proceeded up to Cox's Hill, where a couple of leftover Union artillery pieces were fired, followed by prayer and eloquent speeches.

Like everyone else, John D. and C.C. were glad that the war was over. For four years C.C. must have had conflicting thoughts. He was undoubtedly concerned about cousins and friends who were off fighting but glad that he had stayed at home. Had he done the right thing? There was so much mixed feeling about secession in the Valley that people didn't hold it against a person, at least not outwardly, whether the person had fought for the Confederacy or had not. There were just too many who did and too many who didn't.

Now West Virginia had become a state in its own right, a part of the Union. This began with the Wheeling Convention in 1861. The convention declared itself the lawful government of Virginia. The U.S. Constitution allowed a state to divide itself. After all, Kentucky had split off from Virginia many years earlier. There was, however, certainly a question whether the Wheeling Convention constituted the lawful government of Virginia. The convention arbitrarily drew a boundary along county lines between western and eastern Virginia. The original plan included the Blue Ridge, but it was thought that the population in the Shenandoah Valley might be too southern in sentiment to be governed effectively. Elections were held in thirty-nine western Virginia counties. The boundary ran down the crest of the Alleghenies but included the Eastern Panhandle because of the location of the Baltimore & Ohio Railroad. The vote was light. In Greenbrier County people didn't vote. In Jefferson County (Charles Town), occupied by Federals, only northern sympathizers voted. There was no secret ballot in those days, only a voice vote. In some counties only one polling place was opened. The "election" went eight to one for formation of the new state. A constitution was written, and application was made to Congress for admission to the Union. Congress demanded that the state constitution include the abolition of slavery. Congress had many lengthy discussions about the legality of adding a state under a different set of circumstances than other states.¹² But Congress voted for the split, and on April 20, 1863, Abraham Lincoln proclaimed West Virginia a new state.

Just prior to the war's end, C.C. married Elizabeth Josephine Wilson, called Bettie. The wedding day occurred on October 19, 1864. She was the daughter of Nathaniel Venable Wilson and Elizabeth Ruffner. The Wilsons lived in a house on Ruffner property opposite Wilson Hollow, where the present Kanawha City Bridge crosses the river. C.C.'s father-in-law, Nathaniel, was the tallest man he had ever seen—six feet nine. Nathaniel was a farmer and a marginal salt maker, who had arrived in the Kanawha Valley from Farmville, Virginia in 1834. His grandfather, Nathaniel Venable, had been one of the founders of Hampton Sydney College in Farmville.

C.C.'s wedding continued the tradition of the intermarriages within the families of the four salt kings. John D. first married a Shrewsbury; after her death, a Dickinson, C.C.'s mother; and then Elizabeth Darneal, a Shrewsbury descendant. C.C.'s two sisters married Dickinsons; and CC. married Bettie, whose mother was a Ruffner.

Bettie's grandfather, Daniel Ruffner, having been a pioneer salt maker, built Holly Grove in 1815, now the oldest house in Charleston. A pamphlet stated that Holly Grove was "a house of private entertainment at his [Ruffner's] commodious residence. . . . Every effort will be made to render the lodging of the traveler comfortable, and his diet palatable." Over the years Daniel Boone, Henry Clay, Sam Houston, and President Andrew Jackson visited there.¹³

Bettie's mother's first cousins, Mr. Henry Ruffner and General Lewis Ruffner (John D.'s Latin and mathematics teacher) were distinguished men. Henry Ruffner had published a pamphlet condemning slavery in western Virginia. General Lewis Ruffner participated in the Wheeling Convention as a representative of Kanawha to form the new state of West Virginia. Bettie's two brothers had different sentiments. They had joined the 22nd Virginia Infantry with C.C., but they stayed on and fought for the Confederacy.

With the war finally over, Bettie and C.C. looked forward to raising children and enjoying the opportunities that the Valley and their families—the Lewises, the Ruffners, and the Dickinsons—offered.

20

KELLYS CREEK AND OLD SWEET

Late on an April day in 1876, C.C. Lewis, his wife, Bettie, and their five children, ages one to eleven, stood on the porch of their new home, looking out on the Kanawha River. C.C. had summoned the family to see a paddle wheeler pushing a barge piled with coal downriver. The children, with the exception of baby Anne in her mother's arms, waved at the boat. The toot of its horn echoed across the water. On the other side of the river, a coal train moved along the westbound tracks, its stack sending a plume of smoke into the sky. A C&O passenger train, heading east for Richmond, pulled out of the Charleston station. The eastbound and westbound trains sent a rumble across the valley as they passed each other on adjacent tracks.

C.C. smiled, turned to his family and said, "Let's go inside and have dinner."

C.C. had just moved his family into a large, three-story brick home, which he had built on the corner of Brooks and Kanawha Streets, a couple of blocks from downtown Charleston. The house sat on the site of the old Fort Clendenin, where his father, John D., lived as a boy. In the sixty years since, the property had several owners and the old log house had been removed.

Meanwhile, Charleston boomed. The railroad arrived in 1873, finally completing its route over the Allegheny Mountains, along the Greenbrier River, through the New River Gorge, and down the Kanawha Valley to the Ohio. The first Chesapeake and Ohio train rolled into Charleston to much celebration and a fireworks display. At long last the railroad connected the Kanawha Valley with the East Coast and the Midwest. Construction took so long that the transcontinental railroad, linking the Atlantic and the Pacific, had been completed four years earlier.

A dream that had started a hundred years earlier was becoming a reality. The Corps of Engineers was constructing the Kanawha locks, which John D. had supported before the Civil War and which more recently John Kenna, Jr. had promoted in Congress. Coal shipments would soon go downriver year-round. Investors poured money into the area as more and more coal companies began mining operations in the Valley. Soon, a million tons of coal a year would be shipped out of the area. With the salt business in decline, the improvements and expansion of the railroad, the river, and the coal fields came at the right time.

C.C. was prospering. His Uncle William Dickinson and C.C.'s Dickinson cousins, his brothers-in-law, Henry Clay and John Q., formed the Kanawha Valley Bank in 1867. Uncle William became the first president, followed by his son Henry Clay Dickinson. Henry Clay, the husband of C.C.'s sister Sally, died from poor health attributed to his Civil War imprisonment. William, who thought highly of his nephew, asked thirty-three-year-old C.C. to become president and cashier. At the time, a financial crisis fed by rampant speculation, over production, and inflation hit the nation. Brokerages and banks failed. The stock market shut down for ten days; 5,000 businesses went broke. The Kanawha Valley Bank survived, however, eventually becoming the oldest existing institution of its kind in Charleston. After seven years as president, C.C. resigned with the comment that the "the Dickinsons will never pay a man a living wage."[1] He was referring to his $1,200 a year salary. However, C.C. wanted to try other endeavors. Despite his comment, his relations with his Dickinson in-laws and cousins remained good. For several years, he retained his cashier position and the same salary that he had as president.

In the 1870s, C.C. witnessed many changes in Charleston. Brick streets replaced dirt streets. Gas lights lit the town. Children attended public schools. Charlestonians could telegraph Wheeling. Campbell Creek Coal Company hung a six-mile telephone line from its office in Charleston to its store near its mine upriver. The city laid pipes for a water system and built a pumping station. A streetcar system with mules pulling the cars spread across the city. The Kanawha Electric Light Company provided service from dark to midnight, but most people thought the rate, based on the number of light bulbs in a house, too expensive. A bridge again crossed the Elk River, replacing the one destroyed during the Civil War. But ice flows damaged it, and it had to be rebuilt. C&O passengers still had to take a ferry across the Kanawha to the railroad station.

Charleston became the temporary capital. When West Virginia became a state in 1863, the capital was in Wheeling. Its location lay far to the north of where most people in the state lived. Agitation began for a more central location. Local citizens raised $100,000 to support the move, with the state legislature approving the change in 1869. Five years later the legislature reversed itself and returned the Capital to Wheeling.

The Kanawha Valley had recovered finally from the turmoil of Reconstruction. The disenfranchisement ban had been lifted. Lawyers like Cousin Henry Clay Dickinson, black-listed because they had fought for the South, could again practice law. Confederate veterans could vote. Democrats now outnumbered Republicans. Control of the state government swung to the Democrats. The state Constitution was revised from the one prepared in 1863 to one that resembled the old Virginia Constitution. Prominent families, the so-called "local gentry elites," again were represented in the legislature.[2] Even John D. became a legislator, presumably for the public good, but also to ensure that his business interests were protected. C.C. tended to stay out of politics and concentrate solely on business even though the citizens of Charleston repeatedly elected him city treasurer.[3]

With a population of almost 5,000, modern improvements, and the politics again under control, John D. and C.C. could be proud of Charleston's progress.

John Dickinson Lewis died in 1883. A portrait shows him as an old man in a suit, white shirt and bolo tie, sitting by a table with a cane in one hand and a piece of paper in the other. He is clean-shaven, has short but thick white hair, and a straight, serious mouth.[4] He had left the salt business, bought land, and spent his later years with his fourth wife, Sally Spears, farming. The list of personal property for his estate appraisal showed: household and kitchen property worth $236 in his well-furnished, ten-room house; farm equipment valued at $1,170; corn in the crib and wheat worth $1,322; and live stock worth $3,064. The latter included 89 cows, steers, calves, bulls, mules, and horses. Mules and horses were the most highly valued at $100 each. One of the appraised mules was named Jenny. John D.'s estate totaled almost $6,000, excluding the house and his lands, which were not listed.[5]

On a cold December day, the Reverend John C. Brown of the

John D. Lewis. *West Virginia Historical Magazine*

Presbyterian Church in Malden delivered the funeral sermon. With the front pews packed with family, C.C. listened to the Reverend Brown speak of his father: "His name connects with a noble family, and the history of the Virginias. . . . He has been one of the most active of the men who have lived in the stirring events which marked the beginning of enterprise in Kanawha County. . . . Active in general and local issues, he never sought place or preferment for himself at the hands of his fellow-citizens. . . . He pursued with his far seeing judgment a course, that, in the end, gave him a princely domain. . . . Denying himself and his family, he lived in the plainest style, that everything might go to his creditors . . . the poor will miss Mr. Lewis. . . . Was he a Christian? I answer yes. . . . With no arrogance born of pride or presumption, he showed . . . one strong characteristic of the Savior himself - humility." [6]

Later C.C. told a story about John D.:

> My father, like most of the Scotch-Irish, was a man of more than ordinary determination and will power. I remember when I was a boy he used to tell me when I complained that I could not do something that he had told me to do "that there ought not to be such a word as 'can't' in our language; that we could do most anything if we would go at it the right way and with the right determination." As an illustration of this fact I will mention one instance that occurred when he was nearly eighty years of age. One evening I received a letter from my stepmother asking me to come up at once. I drove up and asked what she wanted. She said my father had been confined to his bed for ten days and that he had that day requested her to put the necessary clothing in his saddle pockets, that he was going to his farm in Nicholas County, (a distance of 75 miles) on Monday morning, this was Friday. I said to her if he has made up his mind to go he would go, and it was useless for me to speak to him. The next day she sent for the family physician, Dr. Ewing. When the doctor arrived she asked him to go and persuade Mr. Lewis not to attempt the trip. When the doctor went to his room and said to him that he was too weak to make the trip, and if he attempted it, it would be at the risk of his life. My father looked up and asked the doctor if that was all he came for. He said yes. Then, said my father, you can go back. On Monday morning he arose, dressed himself, had two men to help him down the steps and

on the horse, rode fifty miles the same day and the next day by noon the other twenty-five miles, and wrote back to his wife that he felt pretty well and that if he had had seventy-five miles further [sic] to ride he would have been entirely well.[7]

John D. left to his children his Skyles Survey property, which he had purchased in the 1850s. Joel, the son of John D.'s first wife, sold his portion to the remaining children. To divide the property, the other heirs, CC., his two sisters and his half sister and half brother, devised a method where each one submitted a bid for a certain acreage with the lowest bidder getting the first selection. C.C. bid the lowest, so he received his choice, a 4,475-acre parcel up Kelly's Creek. His half sister, Julia, with the next lowest bid, and with some assistance from C.C., picked the adjoining 4,500 acres.

It was a time when large coal landholdings were being consolidated all over the state. The land had passed from the warrants given to Revolutionary soldiers to large purchased patents, many of which reverted to the state due to uncollected taxes during the Civil War. The state then sold the land cheaply, much of it to out-of-state capitalists who waited for the railroad to come and then developed the mines. The small mines that supplied the salt furnaces forty years earlier and had been started with a minimum of capital were no more. Unlike the salt business, controlled by local entrepreneurs like John D. Dickinson, the coal industry, with its high capital demands to develop the railroads and the large mines, was being run from Philadelphia and New York. Some described West Virginia as a "colonial economy," thus comparing it to the way Europeans had stripped their resource rich-colonies.

With the inheritance settled, C.C. began to develop the Kelly's Creek land. Several seams of coal lay under it, and transportation was nearby. The Kanawha and Michigan Railroad constructed a track along the north side of the Kanawha passing the mouth of Kelly's Creek on its route east to a connection with the C&O. The Corps of Engineers had almost completed the locks on the Kanawha, so coal could be shipped downriver year-round. The Kelly's Creek coal land, like the Campbells Creek salt property, was well placed.[8]

C.C. initiated leases with three coal companies. He ran a five-mile spur, the Kelly's Creek Railroad, up to the mines from the Kanawha and Michigan tracks so that coal could be loaded directly at the mine. He received some financial backing from C.P. Huntington, the noted railroad tycoon who built the Central Pacific and then acquired the C&O.

An unfortunate event occurred on the Kelly's Creek Railroad tracks, which must have distressed C.C. A train ran over and killed Henry Tompkins, whom C.C. and his father knew well. A member of one of the original salt families, Mr. Tompkins also owned coal land on the lower part of Kelly's Creek. He had been walking down the tracks in the dark toward the Tompkins home in Cedar Grove at the mouth of the creek. There was some talk of suicide, but the family claimed it was an accident, and the train didn't have its headlight on.[9]

On his coal property, C.C. operated a sawmill that provided the lumber for tipples and houses. C.C. also erected a central power plant up the hollow that fed electricity to the three mines for undercutting the coal, probably the first operation of its type in the country. It took five years to develop the property, but by 1895 coal began flowing out of the mines. Unions hadn't established a foothold in southern West Virginia yet, so Kanawha Valley coal held a price advantage over the competition in Ohio.

While C.C. was developing the property, Bettie and the children came up during the summers and camped in the woods along the creek. Bettie brought along her cook, Lucy, so the men working on the site enjoyed wonderful meals.

In the meantime, C.C. became involved with Lewis, Hubbard and Company, in conjunction with his brother-in-law, P.H. Noyes. P.H. also had married a Ruffner granddaughter, joined the Kanawha Riflemen, and served the Confederacy for two years. Lewis, Hubbard became the largest wholesale grocery business of its kind in the Virginias (some said the nation) with a "commodious storehouse" seven stories high.

Charleston continued to grow. At long last a bridge spanned the Kanawha providing easy access to the C&O station. The Capitol was back in Charleston for good after a ten-year absence. An 85-room building with a 200-foot bell tower was built on Capitol Street. The Hale Hotel burned in 1885, but was soon replaced by the splendid Ruffner Hotel with its seven stories and 175 rooms. Electricity powered the streetcars instead of mules. The tracks extended from one end of town to the other. On weekends C.C. and his family could ride the streetcar up to Edgewood Park that by 1898 would become Edgewood Country Club. Telephones were available. The

Kanawha City Company was developing land just to the east of Charleston under the direction of Its general manager, Braxton Davenport Avis, son of John Brown's jailer, Captain John Avis.

Much to the chagrin of the Democrats, including the Lewises, West Virginia elected George W. Atkinson, the first Republican governor to lead the state since reconstruction. (C.C. would later sit on the Board of Directors of the Charleston YMCA with Atkinson.) The United States easily won a war with Spain, and Teddy Roosevelt became President of the United States.

The first automobile had arrived in Charleston. A local dentist bought a steam buggy from the John Wannamaker store in Philadelphia. It cruised at 15 miles per hour. Cars with gasoline engines soon followed. A 1905 picture shows C.C.'s daughter and son-in-law, Anne and Howard Johnson, in a "Merry" Oldsmobile on a muddy street. Sitting on the back seat is a nurse holding their son Charles. This is a true "horseless carriage," totally open with thin wheels. From the engine under the seat a bicycle chain drives the rear axle. Howard grips the steering stick. He wears a straw hat and a suit. Anne is dressed in white with a flowered hat. Baby Charles looks like he is in a christening dress. A perplexed dog, sitting on the brick sidewalk, looks at the stationary automobile. [10]

With the coal business flourishing and his property developed and producing, C.C. decided to go back into the banking business in 1901. He formed the Kanawha Banking and Trust Company and became its first president. Cousin Henry Lewis, from the William side of the family, participated. Harrison Smith, the son of Isaac Noyes Smith, who had been in the Kanawha Riflemen with C.C., became a board member.[11] Of course, the Dickinson cousins were still running the Kanawha Valley Bank.[12] C.C.'s brother-in-law, John Q. Dickinson, was president. Despite the fact that C.C. had been the president thirty years earlier, the competition among cousins remained friendly. There was plenty of business for everyone. The population of Charleston had doubled in ten years. The 1910 census counted 23,000 people.

Nat Wilson, C.C.'s father-in-law, died in 1910 at age ninety-six. The best his obituary could say was that "he was a man of remarkable physique" –referring to his height–and that "No man in Kanawha County was better known."[13] His wife, Elizabeth, had preceded him to the grave a few years earlier. In her later years, she lived with her daughter Bettie and C.C. Her obituary never

C.C. Lewis as President of the Kanawha Banking and Trust. *Author's collection*

mentioned Nat. They had eight children. However, Nat considered his wife a shrew, left her and moved up Elk River, where he started a "new" family. Only the immediate members of his family attended his burial in the family plot at Spring Hill Cemetery. There is no marker, but his grave is listed in the same location as his "shrew" wife.[14] She's probably not too happy about sharing her grave plot with him.

An offspring of Nat's "new" family was a "blond bombshell," as one family member put it. C.C. and Bettie took her in and raised her. Technically, this child was Bettie's stepsister. To give her some culture, C.C. and Bettie sent her off to New York City to visit relatives. While there, a maid found the "bombshell's" boyfriend's underwear in her bed. This undoubtedly caused some consternation in the family. Fortunately, she married the boyfriend. It helped that he was from a distinguished, old family in St. Louis, one that had been there since the days of Lewis and Clark.[15]

A family photograph of twenty-two people, taken on the front porch of the Lewis home on Kanawha Street, shows the Lewis children with their spouses standing in a row in back. C.C. and Bettie are sitting on chairs in the middle, and the grandchildren are lined up in front sitting on the steps. The picture was taken Christmas Day, 1904. A baby in Bettie's lap is Charles Lewis Johnson. Bettie, her hair in a bun, looks down at the baby. C.C. with his Vandyke beard shows a restrained sense of pride with his family all about him. Sitting on the arm of her father's chair and a bit out of line with her two brothers and two sisters is Anne, C.C.'s youngest daughter and presumably his favorite. Behind Anne, is her husband, Howard Johnson, handsome and looking somewhat distracted. An engineering graduate of Yale from Brooklyn, New York, he came to Charleston, selling electrical equipment. In an earlier time, he might have been considered a carpetbagger. C.C. built for Anne and Howard a grand home next to his own. He assisted Howard in establishing the Charleston Electrical Supply Company, which sold equipment to the mines. At the far right end of the picture, standing straight and tall is C.C.'s oldest son, Cam. He had purchased the Old Sweet Springs resort, and began incurring financial problems.[16]

C.C.'s final venture encompassed a new field, the resort business. And he certainly hadn't planned it that way. Here is how he might have described the situation as he rode the C&O train from Charleston, going to Sweet Springs:

At the age of seventy-six here I am on this train, traveling to Sweet Springs to resolve a situation that, had there been good judgment, should have never occurred. I get off at Allegheny Station, the next stop after White Sulphur. I left Charleston at 12:30 P.M. and arrived there at 7:15 P.M. I hope a coach is waiting to take me down to Old Sweet.

Son Cam has gotten himself in trouble, so I'm heading to Old Sweet to spend the summer and manage the place. Without my approval, he purchased the resort plus 1,200 acres. He was carrying a $35,000 debt, but it's gone beyond that now. I like the idea that Old Sweet is back under Lewis ownership, but not as an unprofitable enterprise. The popularity of the Virginia springs has long ceased. With the railroad and the coming of the automobile, people have more choices where to spend their vacations than they did fifty years ago. Doctors now question the curative powers of the springs. In addition, there is competition from Hot Springs and White Sulphur, both of which have rail service to their front doors.[17] It's fifteen miles from Allegheny down to Old Sweet.

Cam bought Old Sweet back from the Biernes, who originally purchased it from the William Lewis side of the family before the Civil War. Now the Biernes are taking Cam to court. He hasn't paid them, or the corporation taxes, or even the $15 to the state of West Virginia for a golf course license.

Cam is in Charleston.[18] I had him put an ad in the Gazette for Old Sweet and to ship me a case of hams from Lewis, Hubbard. He's worried whether we should buy 15 cent or 18 cent matting for guest room floors, but decided on the latter because it was a better color. He tells me to keep a close eye on White, the Superintendent, who he says is rather extravagant and a little loose overseeing the help. I have asked him to send me the Sweet Springs minutes, also the papers and books to close up the accounts. Five hundred shares of Tyree stock are missing. I'm dealing with past due accounts and a guest list that can't be found.

Some Richmond and Charleston people still come to Old Sweet. My children love the place; they each have a cottage near the hotel. Daughter Anne and her husband Howard Johnson bring their four little boys down for the summer. But none of this pays off the debt.

I've worked hard all my life to give my children financial security and now am involved in legal proceedings to save one of them. I'm having to deal with a cantankerous lawyer in Union down in

Old Sweet Springs, the Grand Hotel.

Monroe County. It will take considerable sums to keep the place from going back to the Biernes. I'm too damn old to be fiddling with something like this.[19]

C.C. Lewis saved the place. And the old resort still had some pizazz. An article, entitled "High Time at the Old Sweet," in the *Richmond Times Dispatch* reported that the largest crowd of the season "merrily walks its spacious halls. . . . The place is filled by newcomers in search of a breath of the mountains to complete their summer outing. . . . Everyone is agog with expectation over the crowning events of the season" –the golf tournament. There is a picture of "Beautiful New Yorker, Mrs. Charles Higgans wife of the Standard Oil magnate . . . a beauty and a belle . . . at Southern resorts . . . is spending some time at the Old Sweet. . . ." Another picture is of a "Charming Matron, Mrs. Charles P. Stacy. . . . As Miss Virginia Lewis she was a reigning bell in Charleston, W.Va. . . . She married a former Richmond boy . . ." She was C.C. and Bettie's daughter.[20]

C.C. described Old Sweet in a letter, perhaps to obtain insurance. He said the place had 1,825 acres in the whole tract. The Grand Hotel, built in the Jefferson style, had a dining room that could seat 1,000, a ballroom, 72 rooms with water closets down the hall, kitchen, bakery, and, in the basement, rooms for pool, billiards, and a bar. The Central Building contained another 72 rooms on three floors. There were five brick cottages with eight to fourteen rooms each, plus a number of frame cottages giving a total capacity of about 800 guests.[21]

Nevertheless, the financial problems continued. C.C.'s son John would take Old Sweet as his portion of his father's estate, believing that running it would be a nice life. A revenue agent, auditing John's tax return, asked the family accountant to drive him there, looking for a few days of good living at John's expense. As the revenue agent and the accountant sat in the luxurious dining room of the Grand Hotel, they watched owner and host, John Lewis, move from table to table, charming his guests. The revenue agent asked the accountant, "Does Mr. Lewis run this place for pleasure or for profit?" The accountant said he didn't know. "Well, go ask him," said the agent. The accountant came back with Lewis' answer. "I receive damn little of either and am going to sell to the first damn sucker that comes along." John sold Old Sweet in 1920.[22]

Charles Cameron Lewis, Sr. had died in 1917, the year after he straightened out Old Sweet's ownership. The Charleston papers reported that he passed away "in his home at 1202 Kanawha Street . . . at the age of 78 . . . from earliest manhood was prominent in banking, salt, coal and other large business enterprises but of late years had retired . . . outside of managing his large estate, including the famous Old Sweet Springs property." His was "one of the largest funerals ever held in Charleston."

An editorial stated: "Mr. Lewis was a link that bound the old to the new . . . Inheriting wealth, and quite the antithesis of many other men, he added to it . . . in his quiet, unostentatious way he was interested in every phase of city building and . . . in the moral and Christian growth of the people . . . A life long business associate . . . said: 'He is one of the most moral men I ever knew.' . . . He was a modest man, steeped in old fashioned ethics of personal conduct, which repel instinctively the desire for any form of publicity or notoriety. . . . It is no easy task to accumulate great wealth and do it honorably . . . to hand down to posterity great wealth without the sacrifice of character."[23]

C.C. Lewis Family, Christmas 1904. C.C. and Bettie are in the center. Back Row, L. to R.: John Lewis, Mrs. John Lewis, Ashby Lee Biedler, Elizabeth Josephine Lewis Biedler, Charles S. Stacy, Virginia Wilson Lewis Stacy, Howard S. Johnson, Laura Payne Lewis, Charles Cameron (Cam) Lewis, Jr. Center, L. to R. Elizabeth (Bettie) Wilson Lewis, Charles Lewis Johnson, Charles Cameron (C.C.) Lewis, Anne Dickinson Lewis Johnson. First Row, L. to R.: Elizabeth Josephine Stacy, George Palmer Stacy, Charles Lewis Stacy, Frank Payne Lewis, Rodolph Lewis Johnson (uncle and namesake of the author), Margaret Lynn Lewis, Andrew Payne Lewis, Ashby Lee Biedler, Jr., Charles Cameron (Cam) Lewis, III. *Author's Collection*

PART V

Governor George Atkinson, Republican (1845-1925)

CHRONOLOGY

1800 George Wesley Atkinson's grandfather moves to the Kanawha Valley.
1845 George Wesley Atkinson is born in Kanawha County.
1861 At age fifteen Atkinson enlists in the Union Army.
1865 Booker T. Washington comes to the Kanawha Valley as a young boy.
1870 George Atkinson graduates from Ohio Weslyan University.
1871 Democrats regain the state house from Reconstruction Republicans.
1876 Atkinson's *History of Kanawha County* is published.
1877 Atkinson loses a legislative contest and moves to Wheeling.
1879 Atkinson becomes a revenue agent, chasing moonshiners.
1881 Atkinson is the U.S. Marshall for the District of West Virginia.
1888 Stephen B. Elkins gains control of the state Republican Party.
1890 George Atkinson wins a contested seat in Congress.
1885 The state Capital moves from Wheeling to Charleston for the last time.

1897	In a Republican sweep Atkinson is elected governor.
1898	The Spanish American War begins.
1901	Atkinson becomes the U.S. Attorney for Southern West Virginia.
	President McKinley is assassinated. Teddy Roosevelt becomes President.
1905	Roosevelt appoints Atkinson to the U.S. Court of Claims.
1912	Woodrow Wilson is elected President.
	Atkinson's son-in-law, Brashear Avis, is elected to Congress.
1913	Constitutional change establishes the popular election of senators.
1914	World War I begins.
	Congress imposes the income tax.
1916	Atkinson retires from the Court of Claims.
1925	Atkinson dies in Charleston.

21

CHARLESTON

If the Johnsons revered C.C. Lewis, then the Avises revered Governor George Wesley Atkinson. The two men were contemporaries in Charleston, though each chose a different career-one in business, the other in politics. As I grew up, I was constantly aware of my link to the Governor through my grandmother, Florence Atkinson Avis, whom I called "Nana." Looking like a professor, my Great Grandfather Atkinson had been a lawyer and an author. In my mind, though, I had lumped him with the rest of the Avises, whom I considered to be lesser men than the Indian-fighting Lewises. I was wrong.

Another ancestral fact concealed by my southern, traditionalist grandmother was that her father, George Atkinson, had served in the Northern Army. This discovery shook my faith in my southern heritage. Why had Nana never mentioned this? Was this another situation like that of John Avis not being acknowledged?

As befitting a governor, a picture of the Atkinson coat-of-arms, hung in our house. My mother and grandmother searched mightily to trace the family back to England or, at least, to tie the name to the more esteemed Atkinsons of eastern Virginia. No luck. That coat of arms didn't fit our Atkinsons. They were farmers and could be traced only back to the governor's grandfather who arrived along the Kanawha about 1800.

On that raw November day when I traveled to Charleston to find C.C. Lewis' home, I was looking also for more information about my other great-grandfather. My ultimate destination was the Cultural Center near the Capitol. In 1876, at age thirty-one, George Atkinson wrote the *History of Kanawha County*, and I wanted to see what I could add to that history.

I drove by the Capitol and looked for the Cultural Center. The area had changed greatly from what I had remembered. Nana's house once had sat on the corner of Duffy and Virginia Streets across from the Capitol and behind the Governor's Mansion. Neither the house nor Duffy Street remained. Instead there is now a parking area and the Cultural Center. Thus, the long time homes of both sets of my grandparents no longer existed.

While Nana's two-story, brick house hardly matched the grandeur of my Grandmother Johnson's place on Kanawha Boulevard, the Avis house held some vivid family memories. My grandfather's body had been brought there after he was killed by lightning on the Edgewood Country Club golf course. A candle ignited my mother's veil during my parents' wedding ceremony. And across the street the construction of a new Capitol must have seemed to go on forever before finally being completed in 1932.

When I was eleven years old, I lived in Nana's house for a few wartime months in 1944. My father had retired from the Coast Guard, and we had returned to Charleston from Florida so he could help out at the family-owned Charleston Electrical Supply Company. During that time, I made friends with the grandson of Governor Matthew Neely and we had the run of the Governor's Mansion. I briefly attended Kanawha Elementary School. My mongrel dog, Chief, whom I had brought with me from Florida, chased squirrels on the Capitol lawn. I once went to the state museum in the basement of the Capitol to see Governor Atkinson's "bus." Instead, I found his bust and was disappointed.

Doing my part for the war effort, I kept track of the family's rationing stamps and rolled cigarettes for Nana. I sat at a table on the sun porch and cut out clippings about the Normandy invasion from the *Charleston Gazette* and the *Daily Mail* and pasted them in a scrapbook.

Occasionally, I would hop on the city bus and ride out to Kanawha City to visit Ike Smith. Ike's great-grandfather had been William MacCorkle, a Democrat who preceeded my Republican great grandfather as governor. On the other side of Ike's family, Isaac Noyes Smith had been in the Kanawha Riflemen with Great-Grandfather C.C. Lewis. Both Ike and his father served as president of Kanawha Banking and Trust, the bank that C.C. Lewis founded. Ike's mother was my godmother, and we lived next door to the Smiths before moving to Florida in the 1930s. Now, Ike and I have places on the same property in Lewisburg. Family relationships often go way back in this part of the country.

As I walked along the edge of the Capitol lawn to the Cultural Center, I saw squirrels that must have been the descendants of the ones Chief chased fifty years earlier. I entered the Archives Library. There, I quickly discovered a book George Atkinson wrote about his days as a revenue agent, raiding the moonshiners. One of the librarians brought me a file on the Atkinson family. It contained information on Atkinson finally winning a contested race for a West Virginia congressional seat in 1890 by a few votes.

I made more discoveries. The microfiche files of the *Charleston Gazette* furnished me with a 1912 obituary of my Great-Grandfather Braxton Davenport Avis, noting that he was a founder of Kanawha City, a suburb of Charleston. I knew that he had been involved because I had an 1890 map of Kanawha City that listed B.D. Avis as the General Manager. He, of course, was the "youngest drummer boy," the one I had been trying to find out about when I discovered his father's relationship to John Brown. Why or when Braxton left Harrisonburg, Virginia and came to Charleston I don't know. I did know from letters that his son (my grandfather), Samuel Brashear Avis, wrote that Braxton was not always a success as a land developer. In 1893 Brashear, while a law student at Washington and Lee, wrote, "I sincerely sympathize with Father in his present financial problems." The letters were to his mother, who with his little sister, was living in a boarding house in Washington, DC.

Continuing to scour the microfiche files, I found a 1924 *Gazette* front page article that described in graphic detail the death of my grandfather. Lightning struck him while he was playing golf. I had been warned all my life about lightning so I knew how he died, but no one talked about the details.

By mid-afternoon, I was tiring of my research and went to see the Lewis and Atkinson gravesites at Spring Hill Cemetery. Close to the Lewis plot was Atkinson Circle. The tall, thin obelisk in the center of the plot was a bit more imposing than the Lewis tree stump. At the foot of the obelisk lay two coffin-size markers, each with an embossed cross. One was Father - George Wesley Atkinson, 1845-1925, the other Mother - Ellen Egan Atkinson, 1842-1894. As a child, Ellen Egan had come to western Virginia with her family during the Irish potato famine. She married well, but died before her husband became governor. The governor's second wife was not buried with the Atkinsons, much to Nana's relief.

The governor's son-in-law, Samuel Brashear Avis (1872-1924), rested nearby. And next to him, I was surprised to see, Infant Daughter, 1906. This would have been my mother's older sister, but she had never been mentioned. Unpleasant family matters were swept under the rug, as my mother would say.

Nana was not there. She accompanied us to Florida in the 1930s and is buried in the Avis-Johnson plot in Vero Beach.

I thought about George Wesley Atkinson writing a history 130 years earlier. He had devoted a chapter to the Lewises. And he may have known of the cantankerous Patrick Gass, since he had lived for a time in Wheeling close to Wellsburg. Atkinson would have certainly been familiar with John Brown, but an Avis had not yet become his son-in-law, so he would not have known about John Avis. It would still be twenty years before he would become governor.

At Spring Hill Cemetery, there had been another marker, one placed between George and his wife, Ellen, by the Grand Lodge of West Virginia. It said, "he tried to be honest," he "would not lie," wouldn't "wrong his fellow man," was "a friend of the poor," "never stole a dollar," and that he did what he could "to make the world broader and better and nobler and grander because he lived in it."

Was he the statesman portrayed to me, or just another West Virginia politician in a time when disreputable politicians and industrialists ruled the state for their own self-interest?

I can't seem to tell George Atkinson's story without bringing Nana along. I will call her by her given name, Florence. After age four, she was the only grandparent that I had, and she was my bridge to the past. She told me much of what I know and held back what she thought I didn't need to know. I think I can guess how she would react and what she would say in certain situations during her father's life. Of course, she is not an impartial observer, and I'm trying to look for the truth.

G. W. Atkinson and family. Back row: Florence, Howard, George, Jr. and Nell. Center: Ellen Egan and George W. Atkinson. Front: Bess. *Author's collection*

22

AN IDEAL CANDIDATE

Nineteen-year-old Florence Atkinson walked out the front door of the elegant Victorian Ruffner Hotel in Charleston into the crisp air. There were people everywhere. Her daddy was already in his open carriage, wearing his top hat and grand clothes. Four bay horses twitched their tails, ready to pull his carriage up Capitol Street.[1] A drum and bugle corps stood at attention at the front of the parade, waiting for the signal to march.

Florence climbed into the second carriage with her two sisters and two brothers. She wore a dress that she bought herself. Had her mother been alive, she would have helped her pick it out. But Ellen Egan Atkinson had died four years earlier. Gazing up at the clear, blue sky on that March day, Florence wished that her mother were still with them.

The bugles sounded and the drumbeat began; the horses started off. The clomp of their hoofs was quickly drowned out by the noise and commotion of the people lining the street. Florence had never seen such a crowd. They applauded as her father's carriage passed. He waved. She could see only the top of his hat and his arm as he moved it back and forth. The people clapped even when the carriage she was in passed. She and her sisters smiled shyly and waved back.

Unlike the Lewises, the Gasses, and the Avises, there is no information when Atkinson's ancestors arrived in America. The first record is of his grandfather, George Atkinson, and his grandmother, Irish born Sarah McCoppin, moving into the Kanawha Valley from Pennsylvania. They farmed on Elk River where George's father, James, was born in 1811.

As a young man, James and two other men floated a barge with lumber down the Mississippi to New Orleans and spent two years working at the carpentry trade along the way. When he returned to the Kanawha Valley, he married Miriam Rader. She had a strong western Virginia lineage. Her grandfather, William McCoy was from Greenbrier County and fought at the Battle of Point Pleasant. A family biography described Miriam as being the most good-natured person that ever lived. If she had a fault, it was being overly generous. Florence, who had been given the middle name of Miriam, would have probably admitted to having a hard time living up to her grandmother's reputation.

After their marriage, Miriam and James bought a farm on the Elk River five miles from Charleston. George grew up on that farm with seven brothers and sisters. He described his early life in one of his speeches:

> My father owned a thousand acres of land in my boyhood, and it took a number of persons to cultivate it and keep the fences and houses in repair. I was set to work early in life and was not allowed my choice about it. . . . From my sixth year, up to the time I entered college at nineteen, I spent an average of five months in school every year. The country schoolmaster, in those days, advanced people more rapidly than now. I remember being put entirely through 'Ray's Third Part Arithmetic' in one term, and carried four other studies besides . . . .
>
> When I was not in school I was at work on the farm, and even while at school, I was required to steadily toil mornings and evenings at farm work. My father was also engaged in the lumber business for many years, and I worked at that, driving teams –oxen and horses. This was a happy rest from farm work. . . . These two occupations, coupled with athletics . . . gave me a whip cord muscle that has never left me . . . .
>
> My parents were religious people, and they saw to it that I was taught good morals and proper concepts of religion . . . .
>
> Before I entered college, I had one year's experience as a clerk in my father's dry goods store and also one year as a deputy under my father who was the high sheriff. These two years were invaluable to me in giving me an opportunity to mix with men and study human nature.[2]

Atkinson does not mention serving in the Union Army. However, records show that he was a private in Company F of the First West Virginia Cavalry.[3] He enlisted September 17, 1861 at Athens, Ohio for three years. His age is shown as "18" years. According to his birth date, however, he would have been fifteen. The only other record for him is a company muster roll dated December 31, 1861. Was he discharged for being too young? In a speech to some Union veterans many years later, he spoke lightly of his service:

> *I, though not yet sixteen, mustered up a super abundance of courage and enlisted in the 'Feather-bed service. . . . I was one of the great army braves who volunteered in the Quartermaster's department at $100.00 a month and rations. . . . Our suffering was for pay day to come—nothing else.*[4]

In 1861, the First West Virginia Cavalry gathered recruits from five counties in northwestern Virginia and two counties in Ohio. Thus, George had to leave Kanawha County, sympathetic to the Confederacy, and go north to join. In that first year, the West Virginia Cavalry did some scouting in western Virginia and guarded the B&O Railroad. Two years later, it fought at Gettysburg, presumably without young Atkinson.

A picture of George, probably in his late teens, shows a handsome, lanky boy with an intelligent face. His hair is neatly cut to his ears. He is in a suit with a vest, standing, holding a cap in one hand while resting the other on a chair. He is looking at the photographer intently with a serious expression. The picture had been given to an early sweetheart and was handed down through her family.[5]

During the Civil War, George's father, James, became sheriff of Kanawha County.[6] George apparently joined him as an assistant sheriff after his brief service in the Union Army. Mrs. Alberta Rebecca Littlepage Putney wrote about a deed Atkinson performed at the end of the Civil War. Her granddaughter passed the story on:[7]

> Just after the close of the Civil War . . . the Republicans, of course were in office. . . . Everyone who knew the Littlepages knew they [we] were 'Rebels' . . . they have not changed since, only now we are called Democrats. Well the Rebels were starved, not whipped, and my father was killed . . . in the Rebel Army, leaving my mother a widow. . . . The Rebels took supplies–grain, hay, horses, bacon, molasses, sugar . . . from my father's store. Father and Johnny, a boy 14, went with them. Then came the Yankee army and burned every building left standing but the store house . . . not a horse was left to send a bag of corn or wheat to mill in. The future looked black to

poor Mother. The children had to be fed. . . . Taxes were coming due . . . things were getting worse. With an aching soul she turned to God to help, but! One morning the sheriff came to . . . collect Taxes. The County was in need of money and Taxes had to be collected! My mother told the sheriff her circumstances and begged for time to get the money. Everything was wild and scattered. Confusion reigned! Business forever gone. Nothing but the house, the children and land! No money in them.

In a few weeks a young man—a deputy sheriff—he seemed nineteen years of age, came to the door, inquired for my mother. When she came to the door she recognized George Atkinson whom she had known since his childhood. He said, "Mrs. Littlepage, I have been sent to collect your taxes or sell some of your property to satisfy the claim."

My mother said, "George, this is hard! I am trying too, to sell my Suppers creek house but I can not. If you can possibly give me a little more time, I will do all in my power to raise the money, but do not let my property go delinquent, please. I will try very hard.'"

George Atkinson knew the circumstances and all about the death of my father, the loss of our goods and stock, and everything . . . . He could see and know all the consternation of war. He rose from his chair and said, "Mrs. Littlepage, I am sorry to have added anything to your distress, and, if your property is ever sold, someone else will see to it. I will not."

Tears of gratitude filled my mother's eyes. But she thanked him and said, "I will remember this." In a very short time Mother completed arrangements with . . . a lumber mill in Charleston that made barrels . . . and bought timber enough from the Suppers Creek farm to more than pay the taxes.

But young George Atkinson was not forgotten. My mother gathered her five sons and she told them that when they are old enough to vote and if George Atkinson ever ran for anything—though he is a Republican—"you must, everyone of you, vote for him for everything he runs for as long as you live." And every Littlepage, though Democrats to the man, have always voted for George—Governor, Judge Atkinson.

When General Wise came to the Kanawha Valley, he wanted to make the Littlepage's stone house his headquarters. The general attempted to enter the house. Rebecca Littlepage stood in the doorway with her seven children and refused his entrance. As one story goes, General Wise became so furious that he aimed his cannons at the house and ordered his men to fire. They refused. However, when Wise left the Kanawha Valley, he purportedly took everything moveable from the Littlepage home.[8]

With the war over, an awful mishap befell George's father. Riding along Elk River on his horse, on the way to Charleston, James dropped by his daughter's house to have dinner. After a hearty meal, he went down in the cellar to get a cool drink of cider. He picked up a jug and took a deep swallow. Instead of cider he drank caustic soda - lye. It's a wonder he didn't die on the spot, but he was never himself again. Bedridden, he wasted away from a big man of over 200 pounds to skin and bones. He died two years later in 1866. He was a religious man and George said he was a man of faith and was now with God.

Despite being raised on a farm and having parents with no formal education, Atkinson at nineteen enrolled at Ohio Wesleyan University, entering the preparatory class for two years before starting college. He studied Latin and Greek. How he came to go to college is not clear other than it was an Episcopal Methodist school, and all the family were strong Methodists.

When Atkinson entered in 1864, enrollment was heavy as Union Civil War veterans came to the college, some with amputated arms and legs. During the war, the student body had been mostly Republican, anti-slavery, and loyal to the Union. While he was there, a riot almost broke out between Republicans and Democrats around a flagpole at the center of the campus. A professor ran, screaming at the students to stop.

Many of the students, like Atkinson, were from the country and brought their own food with them. One student went through school and spent only $13 in a year. George probably paid fifty cents a week for a bed at a boarding house where he did chores.

Ohio Wesleyan had a female college, but the girls "were carefully guarded within the enclosure." The boys "sent up their cards, and the couple found two chairs among the crowd where they could spend the evening, or they could promenade the hall until the bell rang." The boys would watch the girls parading to church on Sundays in their Godey's fashions of the day with their overskirts, bustles, pullover knit shirts with crew necks, and hair coiled on the top of their heads.[9] By the time Atkinson graduated in 1870, he was twenty-five and had married Ellen Egan two years earlier.

Florence described her mother as beautiful. Family pictures of Ellen, as a young woman, showed this to be true. Her photographs reveal fine features, a lovely mouth, and dark hair parted in the middle. Ellen Egan had been born in County Cork, Ireland. When the Irish potato famine struck in 1842, her father came to America to seek work, leaving his wife and five children behind. Three years later he had enough money to return to Ireland and bring his family across the Atlantic. Ellen's father, however, died at sea. The family arrived in New York City, and, somehow, Ellen's mother earned enough money to move herself and her children to Charleston. Grandma Egan lived to see her children prosper. Ellen married a future governor. Her sister married Alvaro Gibbens, who started the first Republican newspaper in Charleston after the Civil War. And a brother, with a career in construction, built the Charleston town hall. Florence was ten years old when Grandma Egan died in 1888.

After finishing Ohio Wesleyan, Atkinson received a master's degree the following year from Mount Union College in Ohio. Somehow, during that time, he held the position of assistant superintendent of Kanawha County schools. How he fit that in while also attending college is not clear. At age twenty-four, he received his first political job. Governor William Stevenson appointed him collector of tolls for the Kanawha River Board. Stevenson served as the last Republican governor during the state's Reconstruction period, though he promoted the right of Southern sympathizers to vote. It would take twenty-six years and six straight Democratic governors before another Republican held the office. That governor would be Stevenson's toll-taker, George W. Atkinson.

In 1871, Atkinson received another patronage position, postmaster of Charleston. He held that job for six years, during which time he passed the bar and edited the local Republican newspaper, the *West Virginia Journal*. The Capital had just moved to Charleston from Wheeling. In response to some grumbling about the inadequacies of Charleston, Editor Atkinson wrote, "We have no doubt that even the (legislative) members . . . will find as good beef, whiskey, and wine with much genuine hospitality and refinement in Charleston, as they have been accustomed to in Wheeling."[10]

But Charleston was not as refined as the editor would have liked. Two lynchings took place. A group of white men broke two white murderers out of jail, took them up to Campbells Creek, and hanged them. Also in the Charleston jail was a white man who had cut the throat of a black shoemaker. Following in the footsteps of the whites, fifty blacks assaulted the jail, grabbed the throat-slasher and took him to Campbells Creek to hang as well. John Kenna, Jr., the state's attorney, attempted to prevent the lynchings. He was the son of the John Kenna who had been murdered by Lewis in-laws. Also present at the lynching was newspaperman George Atkinson. Atkinson said, "Being an eyewitness of the entire production, I hope I shall never be called upon to behold another sight so dreadful and appalling."[11]

In that same year, 1876, Atkinson completed his history of Kanawha County, the first of its kind about the area. However, his favorable sentiments about the area changed as Southern sympathizers again could vote, the Democrats resurrected themselves, and the Capitol moved back to Wheeling. In the Democratic sweep, Atkinson lost an election to represent Kanawha County in the House of Delegates. He, too, moved to Wheeling, a Republican stronghold. Of Charleston he now said, "This part of West Virginia is bankrupt both financially and morally."[12]

In Wheeling, he became the editor of the *Wheeling Evening Standard*. Shortly after the Atkinson family's arrival, George and Ellen produced Florence, their fifth child. She had two sisters, Bess and Nell, and two brothers, Howard and George, Jr. Their father might have told the children about the West Virginia capital that moved at will and how they had followed it from Charleston to Wheeling.

No sooner had they arrived in Wheeling than the legislature decided to let the state's voters determine in which of four cities the capital would reside. John Kenna, Jr., and Atkinson's one-time law partner and good friend, Romeo Freer, helped shape the decision. Ten days before the election, "a noted circus clown invited them [Kenna and Freer] to travel with the circus and speak for five minutes at each performance."[13] Their speeches were a factor in swinging the election in favor of Charleston. In 1885, Charleston became the permanent capital. The Atkinsons followed it back a few years later when George became governor.

Meanwhile, in Wheeling, George left the newspaper to become an internal revenue agent. Florence, just a baby, was unaware of her father's escapades. He wrote a book called *After the Moonshiners, By One of the Raiders*, which described it all. Often as a part of a government posse and one of the "Raiders," he captured moonshiners and destroyed their distilleries. These posses rode on horseback, armed with Springfield rifles, which, he wrote, could "carry a one ounce ball a thousand yards with precision." They also toted one or more revolvers. The raiding parties could be as large as fifty men. They would shoot, "running at full speed on foot, and also from their horses while in a sweeping gallop, and the exception was to miss." Raiders killed moonshiners; moonshiners killed raiders. After an attack, one of the raiders—called a "hatchet man"—would cut up the "copper stills, caps, worms, and tubs." Most of George's raiding activities occurred in the Cumberland Mountains of Tennessee. He held the title: "champion distance runner of the raiders." In one raid during the winter of 1879, he "pursued a moonshiner, on a continuous race, for upwards of four miles, caught him and brought him back to the place where they started." On another raid, moonshiners fired on Atkinson's party from the hills without effect. But the next day as they were "destroying a moonshine distillery, near Powells River [Tennessee], resistance was offered . . . which resulted in his [the moonshiner's] death."

Florence would have found it hard to believe that her loving, Christian father participated in such activities. Atkinson was in his thirties at that time, and, according to a drawing of him, wore a thick mustache and a bushy goatee that extended a few inches below his chin.

After his "revenuer days" the future governor settled down. He became a United States marshal for the district of West Virginia and practiced law. Meanwhile, the state was changing from one with a largely inaccessible population scattered among its mountains and up its hollows to one that began to congregate in the new towns that developed near the coal mines and the sawmills. These towns were being tied together by the railroads, which were spreading all over the state. The politics had changed from the pre-war Whigs and Democrats to the 1865 Reconstruction Republicans, and by 1870 back again to the Democrats. All this happened as the state capital floated back and forth between Wheeling and Charleston. As industrial changes swept across the state, the Republicans were regaining power. Workers from northern states, including blacks, migrated into West Virginia. And money poured in from out-of-state coal, gas, timber, oil, and railroad interests.

By 1880, George Atkinson led the Republican Party as chairman of the West Virginia Executive Committee. He was organizing the party to again be a force in state politics. He established committees in each county, extolling them to collect lists of voters and charging them with "visiting the doubtful, stimulating the indolent, and furnishing political information and documents to all voters in their districts."[14]

George Atkinson was becoming well known in West Virginia. In addition to his various careers, Florence noted that while she was young he held positions in the Methodist Episcopal Church and the Masonic Lodge. He talked at Sunday schools, temperance meetings, and philosophical and literary meetings. He authored books. He wrote poetry. He spoke at university and college commencements.

Atkinson became the ideal choice as a Republican candidate for political office. But the millionaire industrialists began moving into politics.

23

ELKINS AND ATKINSON

The governor's parade proceeded down Capitol Street, applause following George Atkinson's carriage. In front of the Capitol, Florence watched as her father dismounted and, escorted by other grand-looking men in top hats, walked into the Capitol. She had never seen a grander building. Its four stories rose above her with parapets on each corner and a tall clock tower on top, which seemed to touch the sky. Escorts led the Atkinson children to seats directly in front of the building. As she took her seat, Florence thought of her mother and of how proud she would have been on this day. Florence glanced down the row of seats and spotted Mrs. Myra Horner Camden. She feared her father would marry this woman. How could he?

Thousands of people stood about on the lawn. They spread across Capitol Street into the park on the other side of the street where the two-story house that served as the Governor's Mansion stood. This was about to become Florence's new home.

The crowd roared as Governor George Wesley Atkinson stepped out on the second-story porch. Florence felt goose bumps all over. When he accepted the nomination six months earlier, he had said, "This is the first time I was ever nominated for governor and you have scared me well nigh to death."[1]

George Atkinson's ascension to the governorship had not been easy, neither personally nor politically. Many things seemed out of his control. Foremost, Stephen B. Elkins, an outsider, had stepped in to wrest control of his party in an era when the outsiders were all but encouraged to take over the state.

Out-of-state control started with Henry Gassaway Davis. His family empire was in the northeastern part of the state, but he had ties to outside interests. He began by dispensing favors; particularly railroad passes. He worked for the B&O Railroad as a brakeman, conductor and lobbyist. He went into banking and built a coal, timber,

George W. Atkinson while Governor. *Author's collection*

and railroad empire, all the while bringing outside capital into the state to support his endeavors. He cared much more about national politics, than local politics: national politics had a much more direct impact on his business interests. Despite being inarticulate, rough, and hardly in the Virginia-statesman tradition, he established such favor with the state legislature that in 1871 they elected him the first West Virginia Democratic senator since the end of the Civil War. He remained in the senate for the next twelve years.

Johnson N. Camden joined Henry Davis as one of the Democratic powers in West Virginia politics. Camden owned railroads and coal, and began the oil industry in West Virginia in conjunction with Standard Oil. He, too, wasn't much of a speechmaker. Instead, he bought up newspapers to express, more elegantly, his point of view. Camden lost the governor's race to Republican William Stevenson in 1868. But his ambitions, like Davis', lay at the national level. In 1881, he became a senator, lost the position after one term, but returned for six more years in 1893.

It was neither Davis nor Camden who became George W. Atkinson's nemesis, but a fellow Republican, Stephen B. Elkins. In 1873, at age 32, Elkins arrived in West Virginia. Two years later he married Henry Davis' daughter. Born in Ohio, Elkins made his fortune in New Mexico; speculating in land, founding a bank, and representing the territory as a delegate to Congress. Within ten years of his arrival in West Virginia, Elkins controlled the state Republican Party. Like his father-in-law, Elkins sought a U.S. Senate seat to enhance his expanding coal, timber, and railroad interests. He maintained an office in one of New York City's first skyscrapers, side by side with corporations that held interests in West Virginia coal.

Nathan B. Scott joined Elkins as another money factor in the Republican Party. Scott's fortune came from the glass business in the Ohio Valley, a business that later expanded into banking and mining. He employed his money politically whenever necessary to defend his interests and to finance newspapers where it suited his goals. Like his contemporaries, he wanted to become a senator. "Whatever grease is necessary" was his attitude as he and his cohorts ensured that plenty of dollar bills and whiskey were available at the polls in return for the right votes.[2]

Self-interest motivated Johnson, Camden, Scott, and Elkins as they became the richest men in West Virginia at the close of the nineteenth century. Party loyalty was not always a factor in their actions. When the Democrats considered lifting tariffs on coal, Davis, his own party be dammed, supported the rise of Elkins and the Republicans, who wanted to maintain the tariff. When Republican McKinley beat Bryan for President, Democrat Camden said, "The compensation for this overwhelming defeat . . . is found in the fact that during the next four years we ought to make lots of money."[3] Under the influence of these men, the entire government apparatus, both Democrats and Republicans, began to concentrate on bringing "foreign" coal, timber, and railroad interests into West Virginia.

A tax commission was formed in 1884 to investigate the impact of "foreign" interests on West Virginia. The commission defined the state as progressing when those permanently living in the state were increasing in wealth. It was not referring to Davis and his associates. The commission said: "Twenty years have passed; the treasures untouched in 1865, have been considerably exhausted, vast private fortunes have been accumulated, but not by those who are permanent citizens and today the home population does not own one-half the property which it owned when the war ended."[4]

Elkins developed strong political relationships in Washington. He nominated Benjamin Harrison for President and later became his Secretary of War. Elkins' power came from his money and his control of federal patronage in the state. He was a chunky man with white hair, a round face, a wide girth, and an expansive mouth that turned down at the corners.

George Atkinson, too, wanted to be a U.S. senator or at least a federal judge. Elkins stood in the way. Atkinson knew that Elkins with his Washington connections decided who in West Virginia would or would not obtain a federal position. On the other hand, Elkins had to reckon with the future governor's popularity in the state.

One of Atkinson's poems about ambition seemed particularly pertinent:

> *Ambition all should cultivate.*
> *But curb it with rightful aim;*
> *Teach one another love of state*
> *At sacrifice of private gain.*[5]

In one of his first moves, Elkins replaced Atkinson as chairman of the Republican Executive Committee by bringing in William Dawson, a legislator and weekly newspaper editor. Dawson, who proved himself a skilled organizer, strengthened the party by effectively implementing at the precinct level the plan outlined by Atkinson in his 1880 circular.

Elkins still had a problem. The two most popular Republicans in the state were George Atkinson and Nathan Goff. Goff was a Union war hero, a legislator, briefly a secretary of the Navy, and a long-term U.S. congressman. He wanted to be a senator as well. Both Atkinson and Goff stood in the way of Elkins' ambitions. Elkins convinced Goff to give up Congress and run for governor in 1888. Atkinson would run for Goff's congressional seat. This got them both out of the way. However, Goff lost the governorship in a disputed contest. And Democratic Senator John Kenna, Jr. retained his senate seat. But President Benjamin Harrison looked after the two losers. Goff obtained a federal judgeship, and Elkins became secretary of war.

Meanwhile, Atkinson's race for Congress in the First District (northern West Virginia) ended in a dispute, much like his friend Goff's election. Atkinson won by fifty votes. His Democratic opponent, John Pendleton, demanded a recount. The recount showed the Democrat with 19,453 votes and George with only nineteen fewer votes. The Democratic Governor Aretas Brooks Fleming, a Davis crony and retainer for Standard Oil, certified Pendleton the winner. George protested, particularly against the results in two precincts, Martin's School House and Archer's Fork. A recount in those precincts still left him seven votes short. Atkinson continued to claim fraud and listed 256 votes for his opponent that were questionable. The votes represented men who were mostly nonresidents as well as a few that were minors, paupers or of "unsound mind." The last was hard to prove. One fellow, Minniwether Moss, was said by witnesses to have had "mind enough to go to the mill, chop wood, and while his mental capacity was not very strong, knew right from wrong." It was determined that he was qualified to vote.

In the two suspicious precincts, ballots showed evidence of tampering, having been scratched or erased and the name changed to that of Atkinson's opponent. The ballots had arrived at the county seat in unsealed paper bags and were placed in "Arbuckle's coffee box." They had sat on the county clerk's desk for several days before being taken to the vault. This wasn't much of an improvement as the vault was where the clerk and his friends kept the beer that they enjoyed while "spending pleasant evenings together between sessions of the court." This same court was overseeing the recount. A Mr. Earnshaw, the president of the court, further delayed the recount by stating that his wife was ill and that he must return home. Meanwhile, she was seen attending a "merry-making on the 22nd [of November] and seemed to be enjoying herself." Then, a man demanded $3,000 to tell what he knew of the ballot scratching.

George Atkinson brought the case before the U.S. House of Representatives, and with all the circumstantial evidence in his favor, Congress declared him the rightful winner.[6] It helped that Republican Benjamin Harrison had become President and that the House had a Republican majority. Atkinson was finally seated more than a year after the election took place. He served from February 1890 to March 1891.

Atkinson's term in Congress was busy. Five states were admitted to the Union: North Dakota, South Dakota, Montana, Washington, and Wyoming. Congress passed the Sherman Anti-Trust law and the McKinley Tariff Act. The anti-trust law made it illegal for combinations or conspiracies in the form of trusts to restrain trade or commerce. This legislation was passed in response to the practices of people like Vanderbilt, Rockefeller, and Carnegie. The tariff act raised duties on imported goods. This protected American corporations from the competition of lower-priced foreign goods, but it raised prices for the general population. Voting rights were also at issue. Wyoming had been admitted to the Union as the only state that allowed women to vote. And, finally, the House initiated a federal elections bill that attempted to enforce the "colored man's" right to vote in the South.

While in Washington, George Atkinson, according to records, enrolled in Howard University, a school for African Americans.[7] The school's history mentions him as one of its illustrious alumni. Why did Atkinson attend at age forty-six when he already held two degrees and was a practicing lawyer? Why did he pick Howard? There is no explanation. The fact that he would go to school with "blacks" is not a surprise. He had a far broader view of life than most of his contemporaries. Florence would certainly never understand her father doing such a thing, nor would she mention it later.

Atkinson declined to run for a second Congressional term. He may have been disgusted over what he went through in his initial election, or perhaps he desired something grander—the governorship. Elkins dominated the Republican nominating convention of

1892. Yet, Atkinson's popularity could not be discounted. Atkinson and Elkins were wary of each other. Elkins didn't want the governorship; he wanted to be a senator. But he didn't want Atkinson to have the governorship either, because it could be a springboard for Atkinson's senate ambitions. Atkinson respected Elkins' connections in Washington, realizing that only through Elkins could he get an eventual federal judgeship. The convention selected Thomas Davis (no relationship to Elkins Davis in-laws), a banker and legislator, and, as it turned out, a sacrificial lamb to run for governor. In fact, Atkinson nominated him.

The Democrats, with William MacCorkle as governor, swept the election, winning all four congressional seats and a majority in the legislature. MacCorkle with his "black slouch hat and red goatee" and his grand oratorical style appealed to Southern sentiments and railed at the Republicans for their appeasement of Negroes.[8] The Southern-leaning faction of the party, based in Charleston and known as the Kanawha Ring, had asserted itself. This group consisted of "circuit riding lawyers," who developed connections in the southern counties and who were much involved in assisting "outsiders" in land transactions.[9] The Ring's center included MacCorkle, Senator Kenna, and other Charleston lawyers. With Charleston as the capital, in 1885, money flowed into the city as the lawyers represented outside interests who were investing in the state's resources. MacCorkle would say later, "I smiled and the money came."[10]

The next year, 1893, Atkinson lost his wife. Ellen Egan Atkinson died at age fifty and was buried in Spring Hill Cemetery in Charleston. George and Ellen had been married twenty-five years.

Senator Kenna also died that year. As young men, George Atkinson and John Kenna had stood side by side outside a Charleston jail as they tried to prevent a lynching.

With the senator's death and with the aid of a Democratic state administration, Johnson Camden reinserted himself in the Senate and finished Kenna's term. Since Kenna had accumulated few financial resources, the industrialists saw to it that his wife received a federal appointment as postmistress of Charleston. That would last only until the Republicans gained control.[11]

In the election of 1894, Elkins had only one purpose, getting himself elected to the Senate. Earlier he subdued his competition by obtaining the judgeship for Goff and keeping Atkinson at bay with the promise of one. Elkins spoke in every county for the protection of labor and industry. Meanwhile, the Democratic Party was in disarray with factional infighting. With the assistance of M. E. Ingalls, president of the C&O Railroad and Henry Davis, who put self-interest before loyalty to his own party, money poured in. Republicans swept to victory in the legislature. The grateful legislators voted three to one for Elkins to replace Camden as senator. Camden stepped down gracefully, knowing that Elkins would represent their joint business interests in Washington. The victor said to his supporters, "My gratitude goes out to you as rivers flow to the sea."[12]

With Elkins at last established in Washington, he could now stand by quietly and let George Atkinson be nominated for governor in 1896. Elkins in essence had prepared the way as stated by a Wheeling newspaper: "When the next campaign begins, the Republican Party will be ready for the fray. There are no sores to heal; no differences to adjust. The leaders as well as the rank and file will be found ready to begin the battle with a zeal and determination which prove irresistible."[13]

The Democrats nominated the Kanawha Ring selection, Cornelius C. Watts, for governor. He was a Charleston attorney, a former state attorney general, and was in partnership with retiring Governor William MacCorkle. Reared in Virginia, Watts had served the Confederacy with Colonel Mosby's Raiders. But this time the Southern element lost.

George Atkinson, age 51, swept into the governorship, overpowering Watts by 12,000 votes.[14]

24

THE GOVERNOR'S TERM

To the political party to which I have the honor to belong, and I trust to all the people of the state, this is an auspicious occasion. For twenty-six years the Democratic Party has had exclusive control of our State Government. In a Republic it is not best that any political party should be kept in power too long . . . we have, politically speaking, after this long lapse of years, 'hung our gate on the other post.' I am sure that we will lose nothing, and I trust that all of us, both Republicans and Democrats, will profit by the change. . . . I shall serve my party first; but in the execution of the trusts placed, in my keeping by the people of the state, I shall know no party, class, race, or creed.[1]

So spoke Governor George Atkinson at his inaugural as Florence sat on the edge of her seat, listening.

The new governor spoke of the rift, which thirty years after the Civil War ended, still remained between North and South.

I am a Virginian, but at the same time, I am an American. . . . I stand for the United States first, and West Virginia secondly. . . . The whole is greater than a part. . . . I trust I shall always be big enough and broad enough to see beyond the integral to the whole.

He stated that he opposed trusts but favored corporations "for proper business purposes." During the election, the Democrats had made an issue of the Republicans favoring trusts. The governor praised the state's wonderful resources, but said that better schools, penal and charitable institutions, and roads were needed. "They pay for themselves every day," he said. He then asked for everyone's "aid and sympathies to enable me to discharge my duties faithfully and well," and wished for a "Divine blessing upon all of us in our public and private relations."

Applause thundered across the lawn. Florence was filled with pride.

More than just the governorship was on Atkinson's mind. Soon after his inauguration, and much to the displeasure of his daughter, he married Myra Horner Camden, the widow of Judge Gideon Draper Camden. The judge had been everything Atkinson was not: a wealthy Southern sympathizer and a Democrat. He had died at age eighty-six.[2] Myra was the judge's second wife and much younger than he. Family lore says that Myra Horner Camden married her first husband, Mr. Horner, for love, the judge for money, and the governor to stay out of jail. Some suspected that she may have tired of waiting for the judge to die and assisted the process.[3]

Florence's mother had died three years earlier, and she had no intention of accepting this woman who she felt had pursued her father. She did not wish to share the Governor's Mansion with a stepmother. Florence would always refer to Myra as "the old bitch."

The governor, as always, a prolific writer of verse, composed a poem, which may have reflected his grief over the death of his first wife, Ellen, and the joy that might come from a second marriage.

> As stars shine brightest in the night,
> And shed their radiance all around,
> So darkness yields to sweetest light,
> And joy from grief is often found.[4]

In his initial address to the legislature, the governor spoke about the issues of the state. He was concerned about the $700,000 a year wasted on highways while few improvements were being made. He wanted to make it unlawful to employ children under fourteen, because they worked the same long hours as " the strongest men and often for less than two dollars per week." Employers made no provision for the privacy of females. He spoke of the strong tendency toward industrial organization and concentration and the relations between capital and labor as seeming "to be a menace of the future [a prophecy of the mine wars to come]."[5]

He amplified his position on labor and capital in a later speech in Chicago:

> I stand for the working man, because he alone produces wealth. . . . Labor and capital are inter dependent. . . . The

laboring men have the same right to organize for their advancement and protection as have the capitalists. . . . We must . . . make it a penal offense against . . . men of great wealth to combine for the sole purpose of stifling and choking middle men and small dealers . . . . It is my desire . . . to prevent capital overslaughing [sic] labor, and to do my utmost . . . to aid the working man to earn an honest livelihood for himself and those dependent upon him.[6]

The governor expressed concern for the safety of West Virginia's 24,000 miners. During the six years prior to his term, mine accidents had killed 427 men. Yet there were only four mine inspectors to cover the whole state. He expressed concern about a "total absence of industrial legislation for the welfare and preservation of the life and health of the wage earners. . . ."[7]

The legislature did little, but the governor appointed Isaac Barton, a dynamic man, as labor commissioner. Barton made inspections himself and pushed employers and the legislature to improve safety. The governor's patronage decisions did not please Elkins and his cohorts. They looked on patronage as a major part of the political process. The governor tended to appoint the best men, like Barton, for the jobs.

When a circuit court judge issued an injunction against the United Mine Worker organizers, the governor ordered his attorney general to intercede, calling the injunction a violation of free speech and the right to assemble. He and union leader, Samuel Gompers, corresponded over the matter.

On the other hand, the governor was pleased that $25,000,000 of outside capital had come into West Virginia during his first year in office. Five hundred mining and manufacturing industries had started, creating 15,000 additional jobs. In three years wages increased more than twenty per cent.

While George Atkinson ran the state, Stephen B. Elkins sat in Washington, but never too far away. To keep a check on the governor, he placed his cohort, William Dawson, in the Atkinson administration as secretary of state. (This was the same Dawson that had replaced Atkinson as executive of the Republican Party.)

Despite his duties, Atkinson continued to harbor ambitions to become a U.S. senator.[8] Democrat Charles Faulkner had held the position for twelve years, but with the strong Republican showing in the election of 1896, he looked vulnerable.

Within the Republican Party itself, support split between Atkinson and Nathan Goff, both popular with the electorate. Elkins wanted neither as a Senate companion. He and his cohorts considered, "'Brother Atkinson'—who was, besides being a politician, a pious Methodist and prolific writer of prose tales of idyllic mountain life—as something of a ninny."[9] Goff had already been taken care of with a federal judgeship and showed little enthusiasm for a new position. Elkins tried to placate Atkinson by saying that if he could raise the money for the campaign himself, he (Elkins) would support him. Both men knew this was impossible.

Meanwhile, Nathan B. Scott drooled for the nomination. Scott was Elkins' kind—rich. They decided on a jolly arrangement to make members of both houses beholden to them. Scott would finance the Republican candidates for the legislature and Elkins, the candidates for the state senate. It was the state lawmakers that elected U.S. senators, not the people. This would change in 1913.

However, the Democrats settled their internal squabbles in the election of 1898, and made a strong showing. The majorities in both the legislature and the senate stayed in doubt. Many elections were still being contested. Elkins' Democratic father-in-law, Henry Gassaway Davis, saw the possibility of returning to Washington himself. Quietly, he attempted to gain control of the *Charleston Gazette* to push his own candidacy. He financed election recounts, as did Scott. Dawson, as secretary of state, worked to organize both houses into Republican majorities. Atkinson watched from the sidelines, believing that if the Republicans maintained control, he would have a chance. The contested state of affairs continued for two months. Rumors spread that the governor would call out the militia, presumably to maintain order when the legislature convened. The national dailies wrote of "colorful mountain warfare" in West Virginia.[10]

To keep things under control, Elkins took Atkinson to Washington for a chat with President McKinley. Atkinson reported that he had a "very satisfactory talk" with the President, who said he "was confident he could fix me [Atkinson] on the bench, in the District—if not in West Virginia."[11]

The Republicans finally won majorities in the State House. Nathan B. Scott became U.S. senator. Elkins took Scott and his wife to Washington in his palatial railroad car. The two Republican industrialists together represented West Virginia in the United States Senate for the next twelve years. In the forty-year period from 1871 to 1911, there was only one term that the industrialists (Davis, Camden, Elkins, or Scott) did not hold at least one of the two Senate seats. Meanwhile, Governor Atkinson carried on, looking forward to a federal judgeship rather than a Senate seat.

The state of West Virginia and its resources made the governor proud, and he delighted in speaking of its glories. As did all the fine politicians of the time, he liked to use elegant words and great metaphors.

> We think we have the richest and best located State in the Union. We have a salubrious climate, charming scenery, low taxes, cheap, fertile lands, good schools, well-executed laws, and a happy contented population. We have more coal, oil, gas, and timber than any other state. We are pumping oil in sufficient quantities every day out of our West Virginia hills to grease all the axles on the earth, and have enough left over to lubricate the North pole and the hinges of every politician's jaw from Maine to California. . . . Our population has gone beyond the one million mark and people from other states are coming to us rapidly.[12]

He referred to coal as the "dusky diamond that is greater in value than the gems of Golgonda or the sparkling jewels of South Africa or Peru."[13] He continued:

> Farmers were never so prosperous. . . . Timber grows on every hillside. . . . The famous blue grass . . . makes a veritable paradise for sheep and cattle. . . . There is no labor trouble. . . . Wages are being advanced everywhere and men who want to work have it. . . . I doubt if any other State in the Union is keeping apace with us in growth and development. . . West Virginia . . . is the hub of the universe in natural wealth . . . and is the favorite State for young men to live in and old men to die in.[14]

Florence often pointed out that the phrase about "young men" and "old men" was one of her father's favorites and he "used it to death."

The governor talked of progress, good and bad, and its impact on the environment.

> We have founded an empire within the limits of a State of which fifty years ago was practically a wilderness. . . . Where the whistle of the locomotive is heard, the shriek of the panther and the scream of the eagle are heard no more. . . . Come railroads—go ignorance and non-action. Come lightning express trains—go the haw-eater and the whippoorwill. Come electric lights—go the pine torch and the tallow dip. Come education and intellectual development—gone the moccasin, the hunting-shirt, the shot-pouch and the lop-eared hound. . . . Mountains are useful, healthful, beautiful, grand. . . . . Man naturally longs for mountains and mountain freedom. . . . Plow down your mountains and your hills, and the world will become a desert. They furnish fountains for our rivers, timber for our dwellings, stones for our quarries, fields for our herds, scenery for our people, minerals for our wealth.[15]

The Spanish-American War occurred during Atkinson's administration and West Virginia supplied two volunteer regiments. Though they never saw battle, these units provided a great source of pride for the state and the governor.

> War is pitiless and strikes to hurt. Pity is not for the enemy until he is conquered. Spain was a fool to allow the war to begin. . . . . when they blew up the *Maine* . . . . Before we get done with Spain for that awful crime, we will puncture her old hide so full of holes that it won't hold "shucks."[16]
>
> We were only allowed to furnish two regiments. . . . I could have furnished twenty-five regiments. . . . Our people literally climbed over one another to enlist in the Volunteer Army. . .[17]
>
> Although our conflict with Spain was short, it was marvelously decisive. Our boys from West Virginia were brokenhearted [sic]because peace came before they could get to the front.[18]
>
> History will register it, unqualifiedly, as one of the wonderful wars of the Centuries. Spain went to the rear - the United States as the friend of liberty, came to the front. God Almighty was behind the scene.[19]

With the legislature not in session, the governor arranged for the state to borrow $28,000 to equip the two volunteer regiments. He beamed with pleasure when at "Camp Atkinson" the men asked if he and his new wife, Mrs. Myra Atkinson, would be the godfather and godmother of one of the regiment's companies. Florence probably choked on that one. She undoubtedly thought that the Spanish-American War, about which her father seemed so enthusiastic and which was popularly referred to as "that Splendid Little War," was far from splendid. American men died in that war. Her future husband, Brashear Avis, had served as a captain in one of the West Virginia volunteer regiments. Fortunately, the unit came no closer to danger than a camp in South Carolina.

Soon, a second marriage took place in the Governor's Mansion between Florence and Samuel Brashear Avis. Many years later Florence described in a thank-you note her reaction to seeing Brashear when he first arrived in Charleston. The handsome young son of one of her friends had delivered a birthday gift to her. In thanking her friend for the gift, Florence wrote: "It seems rather foolish for an old lady to respond so overwhelmingly to masculine good looks but his [the son's] appearance thrilled me as Brashear Avis' manly beauty used to do. Brashear had a room at Lady Ruffner's, and I used to spend my time at a front window watching for him to pass. He paid a wee little visit and we had quite a chat."[20] Some time after that "wee little visit," Florence and Brashear were married.

The photograph of the wedding party shows Florence in an elegant gown with a veil descending on either side of her face from a tiara with tall feathers on top. The bodice of the dress is off her shoulders and is tucked to accentuate her tiny waist. She wears long kid gloves. On her left, standing erect, handsome in his tuxedo, is the groom. Their brothers and sisters are grouped around them. Her brother, George, Jr., sits on the floor in front holding what looks like the smeared image of a dog that moved when the photographer clicked the shutter. (The photographer must have owned the dog and must have also taken the picture of Howard and Anne Johnson in their Merry Oldsmobile, mentioned in Chapter 20, since the dog appears there also. Unfortunately, the photographer never taught his dog to sit still.)

On the right hand side of the picture stands the father of the bride, the governor, with a semi-walrus mustache and wearing small eyeglasses. Next to him is Myra Horner Camden Atkinson. Like the dog, she too had moved at the click of the shutter, and her face looks a bit fuzzy, though youthful. Despite a dark dress and a white

Florence Atkinson Avis, the governor's daughter. *Author's collection*

The Avis-Atkinson wedding party, 1893. Florence Atkinson and Brashear Avis are on the far left. Governor Atkinson (with mustache) and his second wife, Myra, are center right. *Author's collection*

bodice to the neck, she is apparently a fit woman with a trim figure. Two unidentified, elderly women stand to her right. Perhaps one is the groom's mother. She would have come from Washington. The groom's father, the former youngest drummer boy in the Confederate Army, is not in attendance or at least not in the photograph. As a land developer, he had incurred some financial difficulties.[21] He may very well have been at the punch bowl.

The governor continued to push the legislature to correct and improve working conditions, education, and black people's rights. "Toilet rooms needed to be provided for the exclusive use of females." He commended the legislature for "making eight hours a legal day's work." Well educated himself, the governor wanted to improve the state's level of education. "Every child between the ages of eight and fourteen must attend some public school for at least sixteen weeks a year. . . . Our young colored people seem anxious to secure higher grade educations," and he wanted their schools to be better. Concerning the Jim Crow law, he said, "West Virginia has never adopted a law which abridged the rights and privileges of any of its citizens, on account of race, condition or color, and I hope it never will. . . . Virginia and Kentucky have enacted statues which prevent colored people from riding in railroad cars along with white people. . . . I recommend that our existing statute be so amended as to prohibit such discrimination in the future."[22]

In contrast to her father, Florence would have preferred not to ride in a railroad car with "colored people."

The blacks in West Virginia, Republicans mostly, favored Atkinson as a supporter of their rights. Phil Waters of Charleston, a friend of Booker T. Washington's, called Elkins "the greatest Senatorial Ananias of modern times."[23] He was referring to the high priest in the Bible of whom Paul said in Acts, "You sit there to judge me in accordance with the law; then, in defiance of the law, you order me to be struck." Waters said, "It is he [Elkins] who has blocked Gov. Atkinson repeatedly." Waters later wrote to Booker T. Washington that he thought, "Atkinson's unwillingness to challenge Elkins proved that the governor was 'greater and stronger than his party.'"[24]

As temporary president of the Republican State Convention in 1900, the governor, reiterating the differences between the two national parties, said:

> The Democratic Party fought us with Free Trade . . . and well nigh bankrupted the Government. . . . Then they took up the free and unlimited coinage of silver, and they went down under that. . . . They promised us prosperity and gave us idleness and soup kitchens. They promised us a tariff . . . to fill the National treasury with money, and filled it instead with a vacuum. . . . Our party lives in the present—the other in the past . . . . The Democratic Party called the Republican Party an "Abolitionist, Negro-loving organization." They called it . . . a "Greenback" and when we turned the greenbacks into gold, they called us "Gold Bugs." And now, since we are holding the islands we won by the war we did not seek, they are calling us "Imperialists" . . . the Democrats say that McKinley ought to go out and Bryan ought to come in. . . . Our Democratic friends are claiming that the Republican Party belongs to the Trusts. . . . The Republican Party . . . believes that capital has the same right to organize as labor has to organize . . . a majority of the law-abiding, liberty-loving voters of this country . . . will stand by . . . the great Republican party which has, under God, made the

United States the foremost Nation of the world.[25]

A reporter from the *New York World* asked the governor if he thought a southerner should be placed on the Republican ticket for vice president. He replied, "Naturally," further stating that, "West Virginia has two men, Senator Stephen B. Elkins and Judge Nathan Goff. They are big caliber men that would grace the Presidency itself."[26] President McKinley chose Teddy Roosevelt.

McKinley again beat William Jennings Bryan. In his first term, McKinley had increased the import tariff to protect American industry and the wages of American workers from cheaper foreign goods. He led Congress to pass the Gold Standard Act of 1900 making the paper dollar or greenback worth a set amount of gold. Bryan had been for free silver, to issue an unlimited amount of silver dollars. Money shortages had been a factor in a series of economic slumps during the late 1880s. Free Silver was part of a populist move to put more money in circulation to help the farmers, but the Republicans believed it would weaken the value of the dollar.[27]

As his term ended, the governor established the state flower, saying, "I know none more beautiful, and none more common in West Virginia, than the Rhododendron." He was also proud that "the United States Government is now engaged in building and equipping several new cruisers, and among the number is one to be christened *West Virginia*."

He spoke of progress and changes as the nation and his state moved into the new century:

> We received the ox cart from the eighteenth century, and we bequeath to the twentieth century the locomotive, the trolley car, the automobile, and the bicycle. We received the goose quill and bequeath the fountain pen and the typewriter; received the sickle and bequeath the reaper, the mower, and the harvester; received the tallow-dip and bequeath the arc-light; received the horse-back and the stage-coach and bequeath the "lightning express" trains, the telegraph, and the telephone; received the hand press and bequeath the Hoe cylinder and linotype machines; received the sailing ship and bequeath the double-screw propeller; received the common stairway and bequeath the elevator; received the two story houses and bequeath the twenty-story edifices; received the raw-leather man and bequeath

the university graduate . . . . We received but twenty-two million English speaking peoples from the eighteenth century, and we bequeath one hundred and twenty million to the twentieth century. . . . In West Virginia we received a wilderness, the savage, the elk, and the buffalo and we bequeath to the twentieth century the richest 25,000 square miles of territory that has thus far been developed on terra firma . . ."[28]

William MacCorkle, the Democrat who preceded Atkinson, would say of him, "Whilst not a learned lawyer, he had the particular ability which he learned on the hustings [in court], of massing the testimony so as to throw it into the most effective force. He was an exceedingly fine governor, and by his sobriety of thought and power with the party, prevented any excess of party politics."[29]

In his farewell speech, George W. Atkinson talked about the state's growth in output of coal, oil, gas, and timber, that the treasury held "more money than ever before at this season of the year and all bills had been paid." He wished he had "done much more, but the times were not ripe for the many changes which to [him] appeared as ideals." He urged his successor to maintain the "high ideals in educational and moral work" as the "progress and prosperity of the State" depended on it. He said, "Let us look to God for courage, love and humanity, which will keep West Virginia in the national constellation of States the bright star that shall never set."

He concluded with: "I take unfeigned pleasure in introducing to you my successor as the governor of your State, the Honorable Albert B. White, of Parkersburg, an educated, broad-minded, able, generous, manly man, a patriot and a Republican in whom there is no guile."[30]

Governor White promptly fired all of Atkinson's holdover appointees. The new governor belonged to Elkins.

25

A SOUTHERNER WITH NORTHERN PRINCIPLES

George Wesley Atkinson departed the governorship with minor legislative accomplishments but with the respect of the people of West Virginia. He was always in demand as a public speaker both in and out of the state. These speeches defined the man and the times.

Following is an excerpt from a speech at an industrial conference in Alabama:

> I am a Southern man with Northern principles. . . . am a Virginian-born and reared on the 'sacred soil' of that great, old 'Mother Commonwealth.' Her interests are mine and I revere and love the name of Virginia and the dear Virginia people. But having been educated mainly North of 'Mason and Dixon's line,' I could not do other than oppose human slavery and make the best fight I could for the universal freedom of the human race.[1]

In a speech to Union war veterans, Atkinson defined the Civil War:

> For two hundred fifty years an increasing conflict has been going on between two ideas on this continent. One of those came on the May Flower and was planted by the Plymouth Rock settlement. . . . The other . . . was rooted in the Jamestown settlement. . . . One of these ideas was the God-given doctrine that all men ought to be free . . . The other . . . proclaimed that men might own their own fellow man . . . . In 1860 . . . the people . . . said the Plymouth Rock idea was right and the Jamestown idea was wrong, and they elected Abraham Lincoln to the Presidency. . . . The sword was unsheathed, and the clanking of musketry could be heard from Fort Sumter to Bunker Hill. . . . the shackles were broken from four million bondsmen, and they were made free. Who did it? God did it: but you

soldiers were the instruments. He used you to do His work. He always uses humanity for the furtherance of His purposes.²

It took four of the best years of our lives to do the work, but during that time they settled two great questions for all ages. First: That human slavery was not of God . . . second . . . that this is a Nation and not a Confederacy. . . . We want but one union, one flag, one Constitution, one country, one destiny. Our fathers had no other idea than this.³

Reflecting his feelings about slavery and the black race, Atkinson, wrote a poem, "The Life Story of a Slave."

> Within a lovely vale by waving pines,
> Sequestered, I first saw the light of heaven.
> A slave was I, and so was born, yet not
> To wrong or habit, but my master was
> A man; an old Virginia Planter he;
> The only difference between us two,
> A trifling one of color.⁴

Atkinson knew Booker T. Washington, whose parents were slaves. At the end of the Civil War, nine-year-old Booker T. walked with his family from eastern Virginia to Malden, a few miles from Charleston. There, he began work as a salt packer. Later, he became Mr. Louis Ruffner's house boy. Mrs. Ruffner helped him to learn, saying of him, "He seemed peculiarly determined to emerge from his obscurity. He was ever restless, uneasy, as if knowing that contentment would mean inaction. 'Am I getting on?' That was his principal question."⁵ He worked in the mines at Campbells Creek, and then attended Hampton Institute in Virginia before returning to Malden to teach school. He founded Tuskegee Institute in Alabama. When asked how he chose his name, he said, "The freeing of the slaves . . . gave me the right to choose a name for myself, and I therefore selected the best one [Washington] in sight."⁶

When Booker T. Washington spoke at the Opera house in Charleston, Atkinson, and then the governor, made the introduction, referring to him as "My friend, Mr. Washington:"

> has perhaps done more than any other colored man now living for the advancement of the educational interests of his race

in this country. His great school at Tuskegee is a massive monument to his ability, education, skill and enterprise. . . . Professor Washington has learned that the negro can rise in knowledge and prosperity only as the white race rises still higher. . . . Both races must move together, hand in hand. . . . One race in our country is absolutely dependent on the other. . . It has been my pleasure to know Professor Washington from his boyhood. Being a native of this Kanawha County, where both of us were reared, I have watched his career with unabated interest. . . . He stands tonight easily the foremost man of his race on this continent. . . . Ladies and gentlemen, Mr. Booker T. Washington, formerly of West Virginia, but now of the United States.[7]

Even Florence, attending Booker T. Washington's speech with her husband Brashear, would have had to admit that her father's "friend" was an impressive man. He was tall and muscular, with piercing eyes, and when he spoke he commanded attention.

Atkinson responded to a question from a Chicago newspaper about the "Negro Problem in the South:" He wrote the following:

It is one of the most important questions that confronts us as a nation. I have thought much about it, and I frankly confess that I can not solve it. . . . Southern people have an abiding prejudice against the negro . . . but when they say that it is folly to attempt to advance the negro race by education . . . that it is a waste of time, they . . . seek only to vent narrowness, prejudice and spleen against their "brother in black.". . . The very fact that Booker T. Washington has made his way from slavery and poverty to the high position he now occupies as a man of brains and education proves the assertion false.[8]

The problems were not all in the Deep South. A black man was lynched in Mercer County. A white man murdered a colored woman, and no attempt was made to arrest him. In a letter to the attorney general, the governor found both situations "appalling." He offered rewards for the apprehension of the lynchers and the white man. He was concerned about what lynchings did to the reputation of the state. He said, "If a white man kills a Negro, he should be prosecuted. . . . I shall recognize neither condition or race."[9]

George Atkinson believed in three things: First, he believed that

"Christianity is the unquestioned able friend of mankind." He believed second "in the Divinity of Christ," and third "in the surpassing potency of the civilizing influences that grow out of the teachings and principles of the Gospel of Christ."[10] About the Golden Rule, he said, "It means that every man shall deal honestly with every other man. . . . The best way . . . is one by teaching it to the children in our public schools and two by men in high places, and in all business, practicing it in their daily walks and conversations."[11] He thought that the Bible was "the greatest civilizing power of the centuries, and selections from its pages should be used in the public schools."[12] With regard to evolution he said, "I am aware that the learned skeptics and the highly cultivated scientists . . . give to other causes the credit for human development . . . . The impartial historian . . . if he has an honest desire to ascertain the mysterious forces which awaken the human mind . . . must give to Christianity the first and foremost place."[13]

When asked by the *Methodist Episcopal Times* if the United States was a Christian nation, Atkinson responded:

> I answer yes and no. It is a Christian Nation in fact, but not in law. Neither in the Article of Compact [the Mayflower Compact], the Declaration of Independence, nor the Constitution, is there a provision or requirement that makes the United States distinctively a Christian government . . . (but) I cannot refrain from believing this is a Christian Nation. Our people not only believe in God, but they believe also in the divinity of Jesus Christ.[14]

Florence noted that her father was forever giving advice on how to be a good and successful person. And because he was an excellent orator, he was frequently asked to speak to young people. One of his favorite sayings was, "When men cease to struggle, they invariably go down. This is the reason why the bottom in the learned professions is always crowded, and why there is invariably room at the top." His favorite sayings were: "Heart-power is more potent than brain-power;" "Education does for the mind what religion does for the soul;" "Be wise enough at all times to be yourself;" and "Men may be born rich, but they cannot be born great."[15]

Atkinson would speak at public schools, law schools, Sunday schools or reform schools. It didn't matter to him. At the Boys Reform School at Prunyville, he talked of the necessity "to make intelligent, useful men out of the apparently hopeless, hapless, reckless, thoughtless boys."[16]

Addressing young people at the Wheeling Business College, Atkinson gave his thoughts on marriage:

> God won't keep a man sober who has a quart of liquor in him all the time; God won't keep a young lady pious who has her waist encircled seven times a week by the arms of a spider-legged dude. . . . Very few men amount to anything until they get married. . . . No young man who is free, happy, and independent, however, need invest his money in a family, and carry a colicky baby seventeen miles and two laps in a single night, and pour down its windpipe three bottles of Mrs. Winslow's soothing syrup, unless he wants to. But with all the drawbacks many prefer it, and when we go into it with the right spirit, we do not regret it.[17]

In an age when wives subjugated themselves to their husbands and suppressed their own ambitions to foster their husbands' success, Florence would be the first to say that women were not often a subject of her father's speeches.[18] However, at the dedication of a cornerstone for a new school, Atkinson let his feelings be known:

> Although we have seen fit not to admit them [women] to our fraternity [Free Masons], we are willing to acknowledge that they, as a rule, are better than the men. A beautiful chaste woman is the perfect workmanship of God, the true glory of angels, the rare miracle of earth, and the sole wonder of the world. . . . Women decide and fix the morals of all countries. They reign supreme, because they hold possession of men's passions . . . . Women modify and soften the natures of men by gentleness, affection, and love . . . . A man seeks and demands a woman's first love. A woman feels most secure when she feels that she has a man's last love . . . . An honest avowal of love is always considered by a woman whether she reject or accept it, as the highest recognition of her womanhood.

The statement that man demands a woman's first love must have raised some questions with Florence. Her father had dismissed that philosophy in marrying Myra Horner Camden. He was her third love, at least.

In the same speech Atkinson gave his opinion on women's right to vote:

> I am not in favor of woman's suffrage, nor am I a friend of the so-called "new woman." I am in favor of real womanhood, because that is right; but I am opposed to the isms and nonsense of the new-fangled notions of some of our modern women. . . . I would rather be a dog and bay the moon . . . than to raise my voice for . . . the crankisims of the alleged "new woman" . . . . The fad will very soon fade away, and there will remain the God given womanly woman, who will continue to rule the man in the future as she has done in the past, in such a way that although she leads him, yet he hasn't sense to find it out.[19]

Florence's reply might have been: "That's disgraceful. I agree that the 'new woman' can be obnoxious, but women should be allowed to vote. Even colored men can vote. Some jackass of a politician said that women didn't want to vote. Well, he's wrong. I am as qualified to vote as any man."

Women would not gain the right to vote until 1920.

A favorite story of Atkinson's, which he told repeatedly, was one that he vowed came from a missionary in Africa.

> Two lepers were in a cornfield. One of them had no legs, the other no arms. The one with no legs was sitting on the shoulders of the one with no arms. Upon the back of the latter was the bag of seed-corn which he was dropping in a furrow, while the one with the legs was walking, carrying his load and covering up the grains with his feet. Thus the two cripples, by the unity of action, made a perfect man. Help one's self and then help one's neighbor to help himself.[20]

This story probably made Florence cringe. Would she have pictured a political cartoon with Stephen B. Elkins on the shoulders of her father or visa versa? This might have been the situation at one time, but no longer. However, the ex-governor still needed Elkins' help to achieve the long-promised judgeship.

26

JUDGMENT

On a summer day in 1916, playing solitaire Florence sat in the sunroom of her house on Virginia Street. The late afternoon light streamed into the room. She took her eyes off the cards and looked through the windows, across the vacant lot, at the Kanawha River and South Hills beyond.

Her father had just returned to Charleston after eleven years in Washington. At seventy-one and in good health, he had recently resigned as associate justice on the United States Court of Claims. Florence wondered what he would do after being so busy for so many years. Her daughter, Sissie napped upstairs. She knew the quietness would soon be interrupted when her son Buck returned from a friend's house.

She waited eagerly for the sound of her husband's Packard entering the garage, marking his arrival home from his law office downtown. She was glad that Brashear had decided not to run for Congress again. His one term had been hectic. His father, Braxton, had died during the election. Then Sissie was born during his first year in Washington. Tonight she would ask the maid, Erlina, to feed the children early so she and Brashear could have a quiet dinner together.

Florence began thinking about all the things that had happened since her father had been governor.

Shortly after Atkinson left office in 1901, Leon Czolgosz, a Polish anarchist, assassinated President McKinley at the Pan-American Exposition in Buffalo, New York. Strangely enough, both Czolgosz and McKinley had ties to the Kanawha Valley. McKinley served there during the Civil War; Czolgosz worked in a nail factory in Kanawha City before going to Buffalo. Atkinson, as governor, had financed from his own pocket the West Virginia exhibit at this exposition. Later, he had a difficult time getting reimbursed by the legislature.

After McKinley's death, Teddy Roosevelt became President. In 1904, Roosevelt was elected President in his own right. He ran against Democrats Alton B. Parker and, of all people, Henry Gassaway Davis. Henry Cabot Lodge commented, "To nominate a man 81 years old for vice president is strange, but I suppose it means money and a desperate bid for West Virginia." Parker and Davis lost decisively.[1] At the time, Atkinson was United States Attorney for Southern West Virginia.

In 1905, Teddy Roosevelt appointed Atkinson to the U.S. Court of Claims. The judgeship, the reward that Elkins had promised, finally materialized.[2] Atkinson and his wife, Myra, moved to Washington to assume the long-sought position.

Atkinson had been selected to the five-judge court as its twenty-second judge. The court, having been created in 1855, handled civil suits for monetary damages against the United States government. The new judge said the court had established a reputation as "the conscience of the nation." People "need protection against the excesses of big government, and the Government needs protection against the unreasonable demands of some citizens and that as government grows ever larger, it is essential that it should never become more powerful before the law than its most humble citizen."[3]

Judge Atkinson was involved with a variety of cases in the court. One case dealt with the "Drafted Men's Suites." During the Civil War, some men in Kentucky paid the Federal Government so that someone other than themselves would be drafted and serve in their place. Later, these men sued for the return of the $300 they had paid. Their position was that volunteers exceeded the quota required so they shouldn't have had to pay the $300. The Court considered their claim "bizarre and outrageous." It was amazing that this legal action would still be going on forty years after the Civil War.

The French Spoliation claims went back even further. France assisted the United States in the Revolutionary War and asked in return that the new nation defend France's West Indian Islands from the British. The U.S. had no means to do this. In retaliation, French privateers seized U.S. ships and cargo and sold them for profit. This almost led to war. In order to resolve the issue, the U.S. proposed giving up its claims against losses to the privateers if France would drop its claim about defending the islands. The Court ruled that under international law, despite the agreement and a subsequent treaty, many of the claims were valid and had to be resolved. Over

5,000 claims were handled with the final one completed, during Atkinson's judgeship, well over one hundred years after it had all started.

In the Boxer Rebellion in China in 1900, the U.S. and other countries stepped in to protect the Emperor. He agreed to compensate governments and private parties for damages suffered as a result of the Rebellion and furnished to the U.S. a $24 million bond. Congress, "as an act of friendship," returned the money, except for $2 million that was set up as the Chinese Indemnity Fund to pay for claims by U.S. interests. These cases were handled by the Court of Claims.

Also during the judge's tenure, there were significant claims over patents obtained by private individuals, which had been used by the government without compensation to the inventor.

As the new century began, Charleston continued to prosper, its population approaching 30,000. In addition to the state's coal and gas resources, oil had been discovered up Elk River. There was talk of great chemical companies moving into the Kanawha Valley. Labor strikes and coal mine wars, however, kept the state stirred up. Florence was glad these events occurred after her father's term as governor. She undoubtedly disapproved of the well-known labor agitator, Mother Jones, blaming her for the trouble that forced troops to be called out to quell the disturbances. Her father, based on his record, might have had some sympathy for the miners. He knew the coal mine owners were at fault as well. They paid the miners in scrip and forced them to buy at the company store and to live in company houses. Florence had heard and believed that the coal mine towns were awful, although she had probably never been anywhere near one.

In 1912, Brashear joined his father-in-law in Washington as a newly elected United States congressman. Just a few days before the election, his father, Braxton Davenport Avis, died. The *Charleston Gazette* reported on its front page that Braxton was "practically the founder of Kanawha City." Florence accepted the paper's praise of her father-in-law, as she might say "with a grain of salt," considering his financial troubles in the land business.

Even though Brashear was upset by the death of his father, he had no choice but to go on with the election. He beat Adam Littlepage, the Democratic incumbent, whose family Atkinson helped when they were destitute after the Civil War.

Brashear served in a Congress that had a three-to-one Democratic majority. Much of what occurred made the Republicans unhappy. Wilson forced a reduction in tariffs through Congress. Atkinson, Brashear, and the Republicans held the position that duties were necessary to protect U.S. businesses and labor. With the reduction in tariff revenue, Congress felt it necessary to impose an income tax ranging from one percent on incomes over $3,000 to seven percent for those over $500,000.

The nation passed a Constitutional amendment establishing the popular election of senators, rather than being chosen by state legislatures. By 1916, the "West Virginia millionaire senators" were no more. Elkins died in 1911, and Scott lost in the first state wide senatorial election.

During Brashear's term, Florence had enjoyed Washington the few times she visited. Becoming pregnant with Sissie just before Brashear's election, Florence gave birth to Sissie in June 1913. Brashear and Florence received a telegram from some friends who said they hoped "the daughter may become the First Lady of the land."

The month before Sissie was born, Brasher and Florence received an invitation to a reception at the White House. Florence, looking "a bit like a cannon ball," as she might have described herself, remained in Charleston. Brashear attended, and he would have described his hostess, Ellen Wilson, as a lovely, gracious, southern lady. He did not, however, have think as much of her husband, finding him self-righteous and arrogant.

Mrs. Wilson died the next year of cancer. Within months the president married again, this time to Edith Bolling Galt, who owned a fancy jewelry store in Washington. Florence was tickled by the story going around at the time: "When the President proposed to Mrs. Galt, she was so surprised that she fell out of bed."[4]

Like his father-in-law, Brashear chose not to run for a second congressional term. His first election had been stressful, with Florence pregnant and his father dying. Now that they had a baby girl, it was too hard with him being in Washington and Florence in Charleston. Besides, it appeared that Wilson would be reelected, and that Congress would remain Democratic. A Republican Congressman would have little chance of making an impact. Adam Littlepage ran and reclaimed the seat that Brashear had taken from him.

George Wesley Atkinson retired from the Court of Claims in 1916. At his farewell from the court, the assistant attorney general of the United States, I. Huston Thompson, said, "But with Judge Atkinson the look in his eye, the clasp of his hand, the smile of his countenance, have telegraphed to those of us who have mingled with him the 'sweetness and light' of his soul. It is this that has drawn friend and success to him."[5]

Solicitor General John Davis, a West Virginian and former Democratic congressman, said, "Speaking for the Department of Justice, . . . Judge Atkinson's duties here have been discharged with conspicuous fidelity and integrity. This great court is charged with the solemn duty of administering justice between the Government itself and the humblest of its citizens. Unawed by power and unmoved by pity, he has kept the scale of justice even."

Another West Virginian, Richard Randolph McMahon, said, "If I should be asked what is the secret of the great esteem in which he is so universally held I would give it in one word—kindness. . . . Judge Atkinson has held posts of power, of dignity, of responsibility, always with honor and credit to himself and to the advantage of State and Nation. West Virginia never had a better, if as good, a governor. . . . I have witnessed the evidence of the people of West Virginia's affectionate regard for him . . . . They know and trust him. He is a good man. He has robbed the earth of nothing but its sorrows."

George Atkinson responded simply by saying, "The eleven years I have spent on this court have been the pleasantest and to me and the most profitable years of my life."[6] He returned to Charleston and his family. His grandchildren called him Great Bompoo.

In 1923, Brashear Avis was killed. The headline in the *Charleston Gazette* would forever be seared into Florence's memory: "Bolt of Lightning Strikes Dead Two Prominent Local Attorneys While Playing Golf at Edgewood."

That tangible thing, a bolt of lightning, ricocheted through space on the links of the Edgewood Country club at noon yesterday, tore a hole through the roof of a summer house and struck dead two of the most prominent attorneys in West Virginia, and through the idiosyncrasies of nature left unscratched a third member of the golfing threesome. The dead are:

Captain S. B. Avis, former member of congress, and one of the most eminent attorneys of the state.

R.G. Altiser, vice president and general counsel of the United Fuel Company.

H.G. Scott, director of the United Fuel company, third member of the party, escaped after a close-up on death.

And while the players sought shelter in a dilapidated building, the current ripped its way through the decayed roof and destroyed two men. . . . Death was instantaneous . . . they lay on the earth and in their hands were the implements of play, mashies, which they were leaning on when the current struck. . . . The three had just played the first hole when rain began to fall. . . . Once under the roof . . . they watched the violent storm . . . . lightning illuminated the skies. . . . Altizer and Avis . . stood about two feet from the center of the post, leaning on their irons. Scott was four feet away . . . when suddenly there was crash almost cataclysmal in its intensity. Scott . . . says it . . . rocked him . . . was conscious of a smell, of something burning, an odor not unlike brimstone . . . he found his friends lying still . . . he hurried to Avis. The clothing on his shoulder was burning. . . . He pinched out the flames . . . seeing no one around he ran a quarter mile to the club house. . . . Dr. H.L. Robertson . . . had just driven in from the club house. . . . Robertson . . . hurried up the hill to find two dead men. . . . the golf professional with his crew started up the hill with sand screens upon which to carry the men down the hill as it was impossible for an automobile to make the ascent. . . . Mr. Scott called up Mrs. Scott and told the news to her who in turn notified Mrs. Avis. . . . The bodies of the dead men were taken to their homes . . . that of Mr. Avis to his home on the corner of Virginia and Duffy streets. . . . [the men] were to [have been] joined by their wives for luncheon at the club.[7]

Sissie was eleven years old. Over the years, she said little about the death of her father other than provide warnings about the danger of lightning.

Ten months later, Florence lost her father. He was eighty years old. A newspaper report said

George Wesley Atkinson, former governor of West Virginia,

died at his home here early today. Death came at four o'clock this morning after an illness of 36 hours. Pneumonia following an attack of acute indigestion was the cause of death.

The end was peaceful. Mr. Atkinson after sleeping throughout yesterday afternoon and evening, became conscious at midnight. He recognized those at his bedside at the Fleetwood Hotel, and spoke to his grandson, S.B. (Buck) Avis, warning Mr. Avis not to attempt to lift him. He complained of feeling tired, and the attending nurse administered an injection of morphine. Mr. Atkinson dozed off to sleep once more and was sleeping quietly when he breathed his last breath.[8]

Just a few days before he died, Atkinson had attended evening services at the Methodist Church. Since his retirement from the Court of Claims, he had been busy writing and serving as president of the West Virginia Bar Association. At the time of his death, he was still on the Board of Directors of his alma mater, Ohio Wesleyan College. During the last summer of his life, Atkinson suffered a stroke and stayed several weeks with his daughter, Nell Buery, and her husband at their country place in Lewisburg. He seemed to have recovered and returned to Charleston, spending the fall and winter there in fair health. Then he deteriorated rapidly.

On Sunday morning, April 5, 1925, Florence sat with a cup of black coffee in her sunroom with the two Charleston papers before her. Both editorials for the day spoke of her father. She picked up the *Gazette* and read the article.

> Born on Elk River, in Kanawha County, he has been prominent in the public and business life of this state. . . . He is probably as well known in every nook and corner of West Virginia as any man in the state. . . . There is probably no Republican in West Virginia who could count in the opposite party so many warm, devoted, personal friends.
> He was sixteen years of age when the great Civil War began. . . . he has seen the formation of this state, its development from a wilderness to its present greatness and importance. . . . He was a link between the days of Jackson, Calhoun, Clay and Webster and the very present; and not since 1863, when the state was formed, has there been a political contest, an impor-

tant constructive movement, or a session of the legislature, or a constitutional convention, in which there was not present his influence through his writing, speeches and immediate counsel. To go through the last sixty years as one of the most prominent citizens of West Virginia and pass from the scene full of honors and with the love and respect of citizens of all political parties and of all faiths is enough to show that he was a man of courage, brains and deep rooted character.[9]

Florence Atkinson Avis closed the paper and laid it on the table. She reached over and picked up her coffee. She took a sip. It was cold and bitter.

An era had ended.

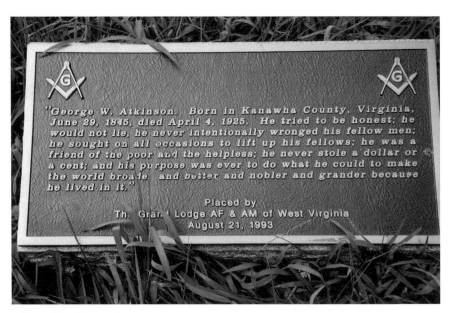

Photo by the author

ACKNOWLEDGMENTS

Cousin Charles Stacy, now deceased, the family expert on the Lewises, provided stories and made sure I had my facts straight. Lifelong friend Ike Smith talked about ancestors and constantly fed me information. Lewisburg neighbor Fred Jesser peppered me with West Virginia lore. Eugene Gass Painter provided a tour of Wellsburg and made his great-grandfather, Patrick Gass, come alive. Mimsi De Olloqui guided me through the Sweet Springs Valley where she spent her childhood summers. John Lewis Seidel graciously showed me the old Lewis home in Point Pleasant. Margaret Lynn Spellman, the last living Lewis descendant at Sweet Springs, talked about the valley and her family. Gloria Rousch at the Manson House Museum at Point Pleasant shared her interest in Charles Lewis. Mrs. Howard S. Johnson, my Aunt Pye, inspired me with her memories and family tales.

John Lily, editor of *Goldenseal* magazine, provided a start by publishing my article on Old Sweet Springs. Author Suzann Fox helped organize and narrow the scope of my project. Short-story writer Belinda Anderson and her Lewisburg writing group critiqued excerpts and forced me to be more creative. Retired history Professor Roland Layton read and corrected my manuscript as if I were one of his students. Cathy Pleska from West Virginia State, *Monroe Watchman* writer Maryann Franklin, and essayist and grammarian Dolly Withrow provided their editing expertise.

In the area of research, Christy Venham assisted with the review of the Lewis family papers at the West Virginia and Regional History Collection in Morgantown. Susan Collins, Carmen Cremer, and Katy Crane helped me discover John Avis files at the Jefferson County Museum in Charles Town. Archivist Bob Taylor provided assistance with the Atkinson files at the West Virginia Division of Culture and History's Archives and History Library in Charleston. Librarian Anne Farr presides over the Greenbrier County Library and its West Virginia Collection of old books through which I spent many hours rummaging. Archivist Jim Talbot at the Greenbrier County Historical Society's North House Museum helped in the search for Lewis-related material.

Staffs of other institutions provided important assistance, including the Research and Collections Department at the Museum of American Frontier Culture in Staunton in tracing the roots of John Lewis; the Rockingham County Historical Society Museum near Harrisonburg where I first found files on John Avis; the Staunton Public Library with its genealogical and historical files; the Monroe County Library in Union where I discovered a dissertation on Old Sweet Springs. The Virginia Historical Library provided Revolutionary-War data on William Lewis. The Lewis and Clark National Historic Trail Interpretive Center in Great Falls, Montana, made Patrick Gass and the Lewis and Clark Expedition more real.

I thank editor and publisher Bill Clements for his thoroughness and patience. And finally, Katharine Johnson with little regard for the sensibilities of her husband, objectively reviewed the manuscript with a critical and constructive eye.

APPENDIX

Descendants of Benjamin Gass

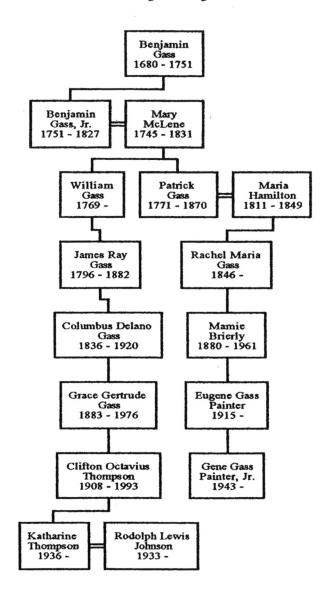

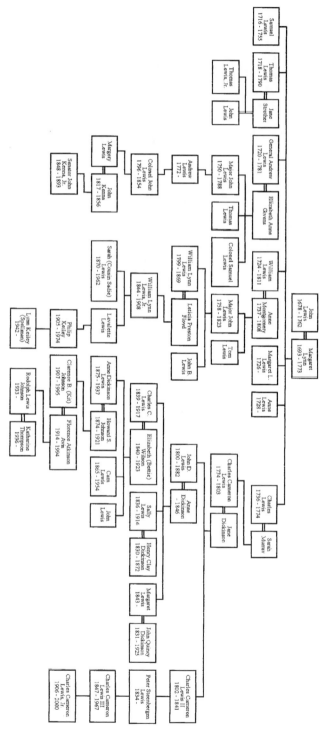

Selected Descendants of John Lewis

IN THEIR FOOTSTEPS

Ancestors of Rodolph Lewis Johnson

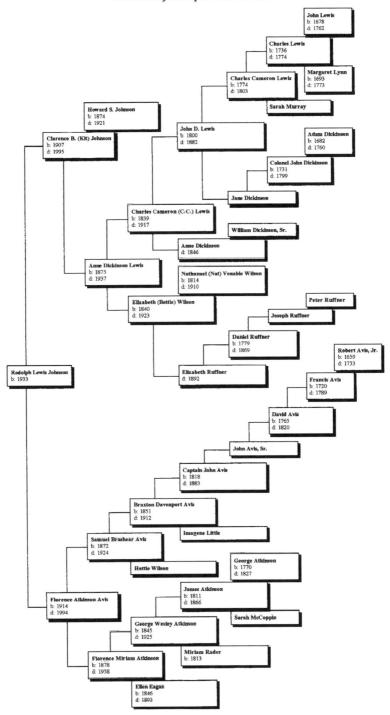

ABBREVIATIONS USED

    GAL   *General Andrew Lewis of Roanoke and Greenbrier*, Patricia Givens Johnson

    FJLP   *The Family of John Lewis, Pioneer*, Irvin Frazier and Lewis Fisher

    HAC   *History of Augusta County*, John Lewis Peyton

    HKC   *History of Kanawha County*, George W. Atkinson

    HJC   *History of Jefferson County*, Millard Bushong

    JB   *John Brown*, Robert Penn Warren

    KS   *The Kanawha Spectator*, Volume I, Julius deGruyter

    LFP   *Lewis Family Papers*, West Virginia and Regional History Collection.

    OS   *The Old Sweet*, Francis Logan

    PA   *Public Addresses of George W. Atkinson*

    WVCI   *West Virginia and the Captains of Industry*, John Alexander Williams

CHAPTER NOTES

1

1. The prime source for the details of John Lewis' life is John Lewis Peyton, *History of Augusta County*. Peyton was a great-grandson. Supplementing this source are: Waddell, *Annals of Augusta County* and Frazier and Fisher, *The Family of John Lewis, Pioneer*. Leyburn, *The Scotch-Irish* and Rouse, *The Great Wagon Road* provided the background of the times.
2. Burton, affidavit on Andrew Lewis Lineage.
3. There is conflicting detail on the Lewis arrival in Ireland from France. Frazier and Fisher state that they came in the early 1600s after the assassination of Henry IV, and the subsequent religious prosecutions. Other sources indicate that some of the Lewises came by way of England and Wales during the major Huguenot migrations after the Edict of Nance was lifted in 1685 and persecution began again. As John Lewis was born in Ireland in 1678, it is clear that his ancestors arrived in the earlier migration.

2

1. The story of John Lewis slaying the lord originated orally with John's son William, was written down by John Lewis Peyton's father, and incorporated in Peyton, HAC, 26-29. I have added dialogue and enhanced the description. The man slain has been referred to as an "Irish Lord." If he had been Irish there would have been little concern at the time about his death. It is more likely that he was an English landlord.
2. According to the *Charleston Gazette*, the Golden Horseshoe still lives. Since 1932 students who score well on a statewide test of West Virginia history are awarded a Golden Horseshoe pin.
3. While some sources spell it "Bellefonte," Peyton drops the "e."
4. HAC, 9.
5. GAL, 17.
6. HAC, 58.
7. GAL, 12.
8. This event is based on descriptions of frontier marriages in Peyton and Rouse.
9. FJLP, 5, is the source for the cudgel match. I have added some dialogue.
10. HKC, 87. This book, published in 1876, has a great deal of information on the Lewises. George W. Atkinson was my great-grandfather.
11. HAC, 34, provides the superlatives used at John Lewis' burial.

3

4

1. HKC, 86, tells the story of Charles' escape from the Indians and his encounter with the rattlesnake. I have added minor details.

2. GAL, 27.

3. John Lewis' first son Samuel is omitted from some family history. According to Frazier and Fischer, he never married and was indeed killed at Braddock's Defeat before family records were kept. John Lewis' gravestone mentions five sons, which would include Samuel. Sources indicate William and Charles were at Braddock's Defeat, but there are differing opinions whether Andrew participated. There is also some question about William's participation. He had recently returned to Bellefont from Philadelphia to look after his aged father's business matters, and he and his wife were expecting a child.

4. Stacy, *Tales of the Indian Wars*, from the Palladium 1829, 8, is the basis for the description of Braddock's Defeat. I have added some dialogue.

5. Hale, *Trans-Allegheny Pioneers* describes the death of Colonel Patton and the remarkable escape by this frontier woman. Hale is her descendant.

6. GAL, 50-54, tells the story of the Sandy Creek Expedition.

7. Ibid., 47.

8. Ibid., 97.

9. Lyle, "Sources of the Valley Manuscript," *Augusta Historical Bulletin*, Fall 1999, provides an evaluation of the "hoax."

10. Hale, *Trans-Allegheny Pioneers*, 212.

11. Charles Lewis had matured. George Washington wrote nineteen-year-old Charles, a captain in the Virginia militia, in 1756 after Braddock's Defeat: "Dear Charles . . . . Your courage and abilities were always equal to my wishes: But I dreaded the pernicious effects of liquor, especially as I know it bereft you of that prudent way of reasoning, which at other times you are master of. Such inconsistent behavior as liquor sometimes prompts you to, may be borne by your Friends, but can not by Officers; and in a camp, where each individual should regulate his conduct for the good of the whole, and strive to excel in all laudable Emulations. This comes from me as your friend, not as a Superior Officer; who must, when occasion requires, condemn as well as applaud: Though in sincerity I tell you, it would grate my nature to censure a person for whom I have a real love and esteem; and one, too, who I know has a capacity to act as becomes the best of Officers." Cousin Marion Johnson Henderson found this among the writings of George Washington in the Electronic Text Center at the University of Virginia Library.

12. Morton's *Annals of Bath County*, 93.

13. Ibid., 88.

14. Ibid. 89.

15. A painting, purportedly of Charles wearing the scarlet coat when he was killed, hangs in the Hubbard House museum in Charleston. The painting was owned by Lewis cousin Charles Stacy.

16. Bierne, *"Historical Sketches,"* Allegheny Historical Society, Covington, VA in 1982 shows M. Botts Lewis of Clifton Forge holding the rifle Charles Lewis carried at Point Pleasant. The photo was taken in 1957. Botts Lewis was a descendant of Thomas Lewis and was the former owner of the *Clifton Forge Daily Review*. In 1985, according to FJLP, the gun was in the National Guard Heritage Display in Washington, D.C.

17. Frazier and Fisher, FJLP, 74. The original source for Andrew's and Charles' dialogue before Charles died is Kercheval's *History of the Valley of Virginia* and is attributed to two battle participants who overheard it. Charles' final statement is from Peyton, HAC

5

1. The claim that the Battle of Point Pleasant was the "first Battle of the Revolution" by Mrs. Simpson-Poffenberger, who led the effort for the monument at Point Pleasant, and other with West Virginia leanings, is disputable. Otis Rice, a West Virginia historian, however, brings a more current and unbiased perspective. His research indicates that the Indians at the time were not allies of the English and that Dunmore was not the schemer that some desired. Despite disputing the "Revolution" claim, Rice says, "Point Pleasant was clearly one of the most important engagements in American frontier history." It opened the frontier to westward expansion and treaties resulting from the battle kept the Indians out of the Revolutionary War until 1777. Brand, "Dunmore's War," *West Virginia Historical Quarterly* states that Dunmore was treated as a hero in Williamsburg after the battle, that he, contrary to English policy, was with the Virginians in their desire to expand the frontier. Schlesinger, *The Almanac of American History* mentions Point Pleasant as only a battle against the Indians. Paul Johnson's *A History of the American People* contains no mention of it.
2. HKC, 88, says, "Charles was esteemed the most skillful of all the leaders of the border warfare, and was as much beloved for his noble and amiable qualities as he was admired for his military talents."
3. Brand, "Dunmore's War," *West Virginia History Quarterly*, Fall 1978, 45.
4. Ibid., 42.

6

1. Hale, *Trans-Allegheny Pioneers*, 195. Quoted from Peyton.
2. HKC, 40.
3. The story of the Battle of Point Pleasant is well covered by all sources. The original information came from Colonel John Stuart who participated and wrote an account. Hale found a Belfast, Ireland newspaper article based on a letter from Williamsburg, November 10, 1774.
4. Brand, "Dunmore's War," *West Virginia History Quarterly*, Fall 1978, 45. This source is the basis for Andrew's meeting with Dunmore and Cornstalk after the battle of Point Pleasant. I have added some details.
5. HAC, 172.
6. FJLP, 63, is the source for William Lewis's military record:
Lewis, William (Va.): 1st lieutenant, 1st Regiment, 2 Oct. 1775; Captain, 4 Sept. 1776: Brigade Inspector, Muhlenberg's Brigade, 7 Apr 1778; Major, 10th Virginia Regiment, 12 May 1779: taken prisoner at Charleston 12 Feb. 1781, and was prisoner to close of war. (Died 1811.)
Family history other than Tarleton's attack on Staunton does not mention William as an officer in the Revolutionary War. However, the above record is undoubtedly his (correct death date). The source is Heitman, *Historical Register of Officers of the Continental Army During the War of the Revolution*. The date taken prisoner at Charleston was more likely May 12, 1780 when 5,400 men of the American garrison were captured. Excerpts from "Virginia Continental Infantry," a document provided by the Virginia Historical Society further substantiates William's Revolutionary War record.

7. GAL, 25, is the source for the battle of Gwynn's Island and Andrew's other Revolutionary War activities.

8. Stokesbury, *A Short History of the American Revolution* and William's war record stated above is the basis for William's Revolutionary War experiences. Dabney's *Virginia, the New Dominion* provides the Virginia perspective on the Revolution.

9. William's unit was at Valley Forge. FJLP places his son and his nephew there as well. I have added dialog.

10. Work by Andrew and Thomas Lewis on the treaty with the Delaware Indians and their negotiation with Pennsylvania to settle the boundary dispute with Virginia are described in GAL.

11. Tarleton was the basis for the villainous British officer in the 2000 movie *The Patriot*.

12. Stokesbury, *A Short History of the American Revolution*.

13. HKC, 89, tells the story of William's sons riding off to protect Augusta. I have added the dialogue except for Anne's parting cry that comes from Atkinson.

14. Ibid., 89.

7

1. Lay, *Architecture of Jefferson Country*, 102. Kidd, *The History of Sweet Springs* states that the Jefferson Building at Sweet Springs resembles an untitled sketch lettered by Jefferson that is in the archives of the Alderson Library at the University of Virginia. She learned that someone in the Lewis family supposedly had the original set of plans labeled by Jefferson, but since 1900 their whereabouts have been unknown. However, nowhere in Nichols, *Thomas Jefferson's Architectural Drawings* is a drawing of a structure similar to the Jefferson Hotel listed. Elmwood, the old Caperton home in nearby Union, West Virginia, according to present owner, Chris Zolek, was also constructed by "principal brickmason," William Phillips.

2. Monroe County Historian Ron Ripley is the source for the difference in brickwork at Lynnside.

3. Per Burton, affidavit on Andrew Lewis lineage, the Floyds, like Margaret Lynn Lewis, were descendants of the Pattons.

8

1. The narrative on William's activities at Sweet Springs is based on a 1958 West Virginia University master's thesis written by Barbara Kidd, *The History of Sweet Springs*. Another prime source is Francis Logan's booklet, *The Old Sweet*.

2. FJLP, 68.
3. OS, 2.
4. Ibid., 3.
5. Ibid., 16.
6. OS, 24.
7. Ibid., 24.
8. Ibid., 25.
9. There has been some speculation that the families of Meriwether Lewis' and John Lewis descended from Huguenot brothers that fled France in the 1600's and, therefore, are cousins. However, John Lewis' birth in Ireland before that time refutes the theory. Another theory purported by Rosalind Williamson Lewis in her 1969 book states that Meriwether Lewis was a descendant of a Robert Lewis who was Johns Lewis's brother.

9

1. In Chapters, 11 and 12, the expedition is described from Patrick's point of view, using quotes, where possible, taken from his journal as presented in either *The Journals of Patrick Gass of the Lewis and Clark Expedition*, edited by Carol Lynn MacGregor or *Gass's Journals*, edited by James Kendall Hosmer. I have used Gass's words extensively because of their wonderful simplicity and clarity. Where this is done, the sentences and phrases are in quotations.

The sources for Gass' early life are: J.G. Jacob, *The Life and Times of Patrick Gass*, which I reviewed in the archives of the West Virginia Cultural Center, Forrest, Patrick Gass, *Lewis and Clark's Last Man* given to me by Patrick's great-grandson Eugene Gass Painter, and Carol Lynn MacGregor's work. Background on the Lewis and Clark Expedition and its historical significance is based on Stephen Ambrose's *Undaunted Courage*. Also useful was Ken Burns' PBS video, "Lewis & Clark. The Journey of the Corps of Discovery."

Fifer and Soderberg, *Along the Trail with Lewis and Clark* provided detailed maps in sequence, area by area, conveying the magnitude of the journey and giving a wonderful sense of time and distance.

Bernard DeVoto in *The Journals of Lewis and Clark*, writes in his introduction that Gass' journal "was put into elegant English by a West Virginia school master . . ." He goes on to state about Gass' journal: "The early authentic account, it became very popular and has been reprinted many times, but though most useful to scholars it is wooden and lifeless." There has been a tendency with editors of the Lewis and Clark journals over time to discredit Gass as some kind of country bumpkin and opportunist because his journal was published seven years before Lewis and Clark's. Ms. MacGregor, as editor of Gass' journal, attempts to prove otherwise. Let the reader be the judge. There is certainly no indication that Gass made any money from his journal. Hosmer in his 1904 Introduction to Gass' journal says that as published the journal is "something a tough, untutored frontiersman could have never attained" and "under McKeehan's (the editor) hand the document was thoroughly school-mastered."

10

1. *Gass's Journal of the Lewis and Clark Expedition*, 1.
2. The white pelicans have always fascinated me. They spend the winter on the Indian River near my Florida home. I was never sure where they came from. While exploring the Lewis & Clark Trail in 2001, I saw them on the Missouri River, near Great Falls, Montana.
3. MacGregor, *The Journals of Patrick Gass*, 226.

11

1. "Foundation Members Ride Idaho's Lolo Trail," *We Proceeded On*, November 1985, 29.
2. Fifer and Soderberg, *Along the Trail with Lewis and Clark*, 161.

12

1. Patrick's fictitious dialogue is based on Hosmer, Jacob, McGregor, and Forrest. Details in this chapter on Patrick's War of 1812 experiences and the quote "I'll try,

13

1. Hattie Wilson was a descendant of Rev. Christian Streight, the chaplain for Col. Muhlenberg's regiment in the Revolutionary War. This was the same regiment in which William Lewis served.
2. Wallace, *5th Virginia Infantry*, 92.
3. *Valley of the Shadow*, a University of Virginia Internet history project about two towns during the Civil War, Staunton, Virginia and Chambersburg, Pennsylvania.
4. Avis, *My Avis Family in America*.
5. My Uncle Buck Avis was proud of the Avis military heritage. His father, Samuel Brashear Avis, son of Braxton, was an army captain in the Spanish American War, and he was a captain in World War II. Somehow, the family missed World War I. Buck Avis would have been pleased to know that, I, his nephew, was a reserve army captain in the 1950s and his namesake, my son Buck, a captain in the 1980s.
6. *Valley of the Shadow*.
7. Avis, *My Avis Family in America*, states that Braxton Avis served "as a drummer boy at age 11 and served for three years. He was the youngest known enlisted soldier in the Civil War." I found his service record in *Valley of the Shadow*. The record stated, "Avis, Braxton D., Musician, Capt. Avis' Co., Provost Guard, Staunton. I came across a clipping on a book, William Styple's *The Little Bugler*, about a twelve-year-old boy who served as a musician in the 40th N.Y. Infantry. Braxton was a year younger so, perhaps, my mother's, my grandmother's, and James E. Avis' claims are true.

14

1. I found no information on John Avis' wife, Imogene Little. His second wife Mary O'Neil, born in 1835, was seventeen years younger than he was. She died in 1889 and is buried next to him in the cemetery at Charles Town. There are no dates for either of his marriages. County records were lost in the destruction of the courthouse during the Civil War. Mary's birth date would indicate that Imogene was the mother of John Avis' sons, James, Braxton, and probably Edward.
2. The museum in Charles Town provided a picture of the jail building where the Avis family lived. Stan Cohen, *John Brown, The Thundering Voice of Jehovah* has an interior sketch of the building. The building was torn down years ago.
3. Everhart and Sullivan, *John Brown's Raid*, 27.
4. Keller, *Thunder at Harper's Ferry*, 66. Floyd would later be an unpopular Confederate general, during the early battles of the Civil War in western Virginia. He had another western Virginia connection; his sister lived in Sweet Springs and was married to a Lewis.
5. Banks, *Cloudsplitter* portrays in historical fiction John Brown through the eyes of his son Owen.
6. HJC, 91-93, tells about the Mexican War and the Charles Town militia's participation.
7. Johnson, *A History of the American People*, 388. He should have included General Stonewall Jackson, then a lieutenant.

8. Everhart and Sullivan, *John Brown's Raid*, 36, and JB, 365, describe the positioning of the Charles Town militia including Avis' unit's location on Shenandoah Street and the subsequent action.

9. JB is the prime source for Brown's life and the raid on Harpers Ferry.

10. John Wayland, The Washingtons and Their Homes, as reported in *The Journal of the Jefferson County Historical Society*, 242. The story was told to Wayland by Captain Avis's son, James, in 1916.

15

1. I have assumed the Avis family might have had a discussion about their safety. Son James, indeed, was a jail guard.

2. HJC. In the appendix Braxton Davenport is listed as a 1st lieutenant, John Avis as a private in a militia company of 1814. This is John Avis, Sr. It is my assumption that Captain John Avis named his second son, Braxton Davenport Avis after one of his father's officers.

3. JB, 397.
4. Ibid., 400.
5. Ibid., 402
6. Ibid., 434
7. Ibid., 287

8. *Valley of the Shadow* displays John Avis's military records, showing that he was a slave dealer before joining the Confederate Army.

9. Avis, *My Avis Family in America* states: Before the war a freed slave, Mary Phelps, petitioned the court in Winchester " . . . by posting notice on the courthouse door for one month that she move the court to direct that she and her children become the property of the wife of John Avis."

10. JB, 274.
11. JB, 280.

12. HJC, Appendix C, 400. The statement is from the appendix and is in "Affidavit of Captain John Avis, the jailer, as to association with John Brown and concerning taking Brown from the jail to the scaffold on the day of his execution." It was dated April 25, 1882 and was in response to a book that made claims that Avis considered false.

13. Ibid.
14. JB, 438.
15. Ibid., 438.
16. Ibid., 439.
17. HJC, 401, Appendix C.
18. JB, 439.

16

1. Keller, *Thunder at Harper's Ferry*, 236-237, 242, covers both escape attempts.

2. Wallace, *5th Virginia Infantry* plus Selby's *Stonewall Jackson as Military Commander* are the source for details about the general.

3. Wallace, *5th Virginia Infantry*, 9. Why Avis became a captain in a Staunton militia unit rather than one from his own area is not clear.

4. Wallace, *5th Virginia Infantry* describes the Battle of Falling Waters and subsequent battles at Manassas, Romney, and Kernsville.

5. Wayland, *Twenty-Five Chapters on the Shenandoah Valley*, 226-227. James Avis related the story to Wayland in 1916.

6. Wallace, *5th Virginia Infantry*, 17. Maps in Hill, *The First Battle of Bull Run* illustrate the battle and show the position of the Fifth Infantry. Early one morning I stood by the statue of Stonewall Jackson at the Manassas National Battlefield Park near, perhaps, the spot John Avis and the Fifth Infantry had started their attack on Henry Hill. The neatly maintained fields with the Henry House in the distance had an ironic peacefulness.

7. Waddell, *Annals of Augusta County*, 469-479.

8. *Valley of the Shadow* displayed James Avis' military dossier that mentions his service in Staunton. The University of Virginia project is also the source for young Edward's broken leg, which appeared in an article in the July 8, 1864 *Republican Vindicator*, a Staunton newspaper.

9. Johnson, *A History of the American People*, 486, says that the only battle the South won after Jackson's death was Chickamunga.

10. HJC, 172.

11. HJC describes Charles Town after the Civil War and Jefferson County becoming part of West Virginia.

12. Wayland, *Twenty-Five Chapters on the Shenandoah Valley*, 227.

13. HJC Appendix C, 402.

17

1. Ingles, *Escape from Captivity*, 10.

2. Laidley, "Samuel Lewis and John Lewis and the Genealogy of the Lewis Family," *West Virginia Historical Magazine*, April, 1904, 140-141.

3. Cohen and Andre, *Kanawha County Images*, Vol. 2, 8-9.

4. KS, 202. The original source was HKC.

18

1. KS, 196.

2. Stacy letter.

3. Ibid.

4. Cohen and Andre, *Kanawha County Images*, Vol. 1, 34.

5. LFP. A typed survey for the heirs of John D. Lewis describes the property: ". . . below Campbells Creek, Thoroughfare Gap. . . . Beginning where once stood a sycamore corner to a tract of land purchased John D. Lewis of William Shrewsbury and Tobias Ruffner on the old John Dickinson line . . . where once stood a gum corner to the division of David Ruffner's heirs . . ."

6. Laidley, "Samuel Lewis and John Lewis and the Genealogy of the Lewis Family," *West Virginia Historical Magazine*, April, 1904, 140.

7. Rice, *Charleston and the Kanawha Valley*, 20.

8. Stacy letter.

9. The salt situation on the Kanawha was similar to the Organization of Petroleum Exporting Countries' (OPEC) attempts to control oil prices today.

10. Kurlansky, *Salt*, 256.

11. Hale, *History of Charleston and Kanawha County*, 128.

12. Carpenter, "Henry Dana Ward: Early Diary Keeper of the Kanawha Valley," *West Virginia History Quarterly*, October 1975, 34.

13. Stealey, *The Antebellum Kanawha Salt Business and Western Markets*, 15. A bushel is equivalent to a container approximately 2 feet by 2 feet by 3 feet.

14. MacCorkle, *Recollections of Fifty Years*, 114.

15. *KS*, 240.

16. *The New York Times*, April 4, 2002, reported: "Few Risks Seen to the Children of 1st Cousins." The article was based on an issue of the *Journal of Genetic Counseling*. Twenty-four states still have laws forbidding first cousins marrying.

17. deGruyter, *Kanawha Spectator Part II*, 4, 76-77. Mrs. Elizabeth Kenna of Charleston verified in a telephone conversation that her husband's ancestor was murdered by Lewises. In a follow up note she said, "I would like to know why Margery's brothers killed Edward (Kenna) - drinking, gambling, women, or all three!"

18. LFP.

19. MacCorkle, *Recollections of Fifty Years*, 99.

20. Skyles was well known on the frontier. He had been captured by and escaped from the Indians, and he was the father-in-law of James Rumsey, who built the first steamboat.

21. deGruyter, *Kanawha Spectator Part II*, 359.

19

1. Lowry, *22nd Virginia Infantry*, 3.
2. *KS*, 487.
3. Lowry, *22nd Virginia Infantry*, 3.
4. deGruyter, *Kanawha Spectator Part II*, 198.
5. John F. Lewis of Rockingham County and a descendant of Thomas Lewis "was the only delegate from within the present boundaries of Virginia who ultimately refused to sign the Ordnance of Secession" per LFP. After the Civil War he was elected a senator from Virginia.
6. Laidley, "Samuel Lewis and John Lewis and the Genealogy of the Lewis Family," *West Virginia Historical Magazine*, April, 1904, 140.
7. Lowry, 22nd Virginia Infantry, 14.
8. Stacy letter. This quote was passed down in the family.
9. KS, 383.
10. Stacy letter.
11. OS, 28.
12. Kesavan and Paulsen, "Is West Virginia Unconstitutional?," *California Law Revue*, March 2002. Two law professors analyze the statehood question. Dabney Chapman in an article for the *Potomac Review*, Spring, 1997, quotes a Virginian's description of West Virginia as "the bastard whoreson of a political rape."
13. Cohen and Andre, *Kanawha County Images*, Vol. 1. 43.

20

1. Drennen, *One Kanawha Valley Bank*, 30.
2. Lewis, *Transforming the Appalachian Countryside*, 86.
3. Cohen and Andre, *Kanawha County Images*, Vol. 2, 20. "A City of Charleston Democratic Municipal Ticket, Election, March 14, 1882," shows "For Treasure, C.C. Lewis."
4. Stealey, *Kanawha Prelude to Nineteenth Century Monopoly in the United States—The Virginia Salt Combinations*, 40. It incorrectly states that John D. Lewis is from Bedford County, Virginia. The picture originally appeared in the *West Virginia Historical Quarterly*, Apr. 1904.
5. LFP.
6. John D. Lewis's funeral program.
7. Laidley, "Samuel Lewis and John Lewis and the Genealogy of the Lewis Family," *West Virginia Historical Magazine*, April 1904, 139.

8. Scholz, *Memorandum on the lands now owned by Lewis Holding Corporation.*
9. Settle, *Addie*, 88.
10. Cohen and Andre, *Kanawha County Images*, Vol. 2, 482.
11. Henry Lewis became president followed by Isaac Noyes (Smut) Smith, son of Harrison. At the time of the merger with United National Bank, Isaac Noyes (Ike) Smith, Jr. was president.
12. The Dickinson family retained control of the Kanawha Valley Bank for 134 years. In 2001 it was acquired by BB&T. The Kanawha Banking and Trust Company merged with United National Bank in the 1980s.
13. LFP.
14. Stacy letter.
15. Ibid.
16. About the same time, the president of the C&O Railroad, M.E. Ingalls, led a syndicate that purchased the nearby Homestead, the Hot Springs resort initially developed by Andrew Lewis. My wife Katharine's mother was an Ingalls and a distant cousin of M.E.'s. It is likely that C.C. Lewis and M.E. Ingalls knew each other.
17. M.E. Ingalls arranged for a track to be run up to the Homestead. The C&O would soon own the Greenbrier Hotel. The C&O is now absorbed by the CSX Railroad. At one time there was consideration given to running the C&O tracks down the Sweet Springs Valley up Second Creek to the Greenbrier River rather than through White Sulphur Springs. If that had happened, Old Sweet might still be in existence as a resort.
18. LFP. Details are based on letters written between Cam Lewis and C.C. Lewis
19. Kidd, *History of Sweet Springs*, notes that the cost to C.C. Lewis was $60.000.
20. LFP.
21. Ibid. The description of Old Sweet is from a letter from C.C. to Zerban Brown of Philadelphia in 1909. Brown was a friend of C.C.'s son-in-law Howard Johnson and may have been in the insurance business.
22. Johnson, "A Lewis Family Legacy - Old Sweet Springs," *Goldenseal*, Summer 2000. Story attributed to Lewis descendant Charles Stacy.
23. LFP.

21

22

1. Morgan, *West Virginia Governors*, 61.
2. PA, 209.
3. Photocopies of the military records of George Atkinson provided by Broadfoot Publishing Company.
4. PA, 89.
5. This picture was sent to me by Jeff Lawrentz of South Charleston. It had come down through his family. The back reads: "Governor Wes Atkinson my mother's sweetheart." Jeff believes the mother was Catharine Heyer who later married Francis Haptonstall.
6. deGruyter, *The Kanawha Spectator, Part II*, 126, states that James Atkinson and John D. Lewis were Kanawha County magistrates together and both voted for an increase in the per diem for the presiding justice.
7. The granddaughter was Rebecca Putney Morgan. She gave the story to my mother saying, " It is a true story in Mrs. Putney's life at the Old Stone Mansion at

Two Mile creek, now West Washington Street in Charleston. Mrs. Littlepage often told this story to her children, one of who was Birdie who wrote it down."
  8. Lowry, *The Battle of Scary Creek*, 65-67.
  9. The description of Ohio Wesleyan in George Atkinson's time is based on Hubert, *Ohio Wesleyan's First Hundred Years*.
  10. Rice, *Charleston and the Kanawha Valley*, 52.
  11. HKC, 336.
  12. WVCI, 12.
  13. "West Virginia and the Capitol," *West Virginia Call*, A monthly newsletter of The C&P Telephone Company, June 1969.
  14. Circular No.1, West Virginia Republican Executive Committee, Wheeling, July 10,1880.

23

  1. Morgan, *West Virginia Governors*, 60.
  2. WVCI, 126.
  3. Ibid.
  4. Lewis, *Transforming the Appalachian Countryside*, 64.
  5. Herringshaw, *Poetical Quotations*, 209.
  6. All the information is based on the Government Printing Office, *Contested Election Case of George W. Atkinson vs. John O. Pendleton*.
  7. "Atkinson's Association with Howard Still a Mystery," *Charleston Daily Mail*, November 26, 1987.
  8. WVCI, 55.
  9. Lewis, *Transforming the Appalachian Countryside*, 213.
  10. WVCI, 10.
  11. Ibid., 132.
  12. Ibid., 67.
  13. Lambert, *Stephen Benton Elkins*, 18.
  14. Morgan, *West Virginia Governors*, 60.

24

  1. PA, 12.
  2. Atkinson, *Bench and Bar of West Virginia*, 123.
  3. This depiction of Myra Horner Camden comes from a descendant of the Horner family.
  4. Herringshaw, *Poetical Quotations*, 204.
  5. PA, 211.
  6. Ibid., 348.
  7. WVCI, 99.
  8. MacCorkle, *Recollections of Fifty Years*, 480, wrote that it was impossible for a West Virginia governor to become a senator. the governor made too many enemies to be elected to the Senate by the state legislature. MacCorkle said, ". . . I had thirty-seven hundred and sixty regularly written applications for office whilst I had less than one hundred offices to give. Thus there were more than three thousand people who were offended at me. . . . They were generally politicians who had the power and the will to punish."
  9. WVCI, 84.
  10. Ibid., 91.
  11. Ibid., 95.

12. PA, 211.
13. Ibid., 212.
14. Ibid., 466.
15. Ibid., 466.
16. Ibid., 184.
17. Ibid., 207.
18. Ibid., 202.
19. Ibid., 207.
20. Florence Avis to Statia. Letter from family papers.
21. The status of Brashear Avis' parents is contained in two letters from family files that he wrote in 1893, the year he graduated from law school.
22. PA, 523.
23. WVCI, 103.
24. Ibid., 280.
25. PA, 453.
26. Ibid., 319.
27. *World Book Online*. Topics on McKinley, Money, Free Silver.
28. PA, 491.
29. MacCorkle, *Recollections of Fifty Years*, 479.
30. PA, 606.

25

1. PA, 366.
2. Ibid., 178.
3. Ibid., 85.
4. "Atkinson's Association with Howard Still a Mystery," *Charleston Daily Mail*, November 26, 1987. The poem appears in this article but was taken from Atkinson's book of poetry, *Chips and Whetstones*.
5. Cohen and Andre, *Kanawha County Images*, Vol. 1, 47.
6. PA, 343.
7. Ibid., 343.
8. Ibid., 317.
9. Ibid., 139.
10. Ibid., 297.
11. Ibid., 425.
12. Ibid., 167.
13. Ibid., 172.
14. Ibid., 110.
15. PA, taken from various speeches.
16. Ibid., 505.
17. Ibid., 398.
18. A book review in the *New York Times* of *Some Memories of a Long Life, 1854-1911* by Malvina Harlan, wife of Supreme Court Judge John Marshall Harlan, describes a wife's role at the turn of the nineteenth century.
19. PA, 390.
20. Ibid., 148.

26

1. *WVCI*, 146.
2. Morris, *Theodore Rex*, p 429 - 435, describes differences between Elkins and

Roosevelt's over railroad rate legislation. However, as both were Republicans they could reach agreement on appointing George Atkinson to the Court of Claims. Morris describes Elkins as "affable, unreliable, energetic, a chronic schemer personifying the West Virginia notion that all scenes and situations could be profitably mined."

3. Retirement of George W. Atkinson from the Bench of the United States Court of Claims, Government Printing Office.

4. Johnson, *A History of the American People*, 656.

5. *Retirement of George W. Atkinson* from the Bench of the United States Court of Claims, Government Printing Office.

6. Ibid.

7. "Bolt of Lightning Strikes Dead Two Prominent Local Attorneys," *Charleston Gazette*, June 9, 1924.

8. "Former Governor G. W. Atkinson Dead," *Charleston Daily Mail*, April 4, 1925.

9. Editorial, *Charleston Gazette*, April 5, 1925.

BIBLIOGRAPHY

BOOKS

Ambrose, Stephen. *Undaunted Courage.* New York: Touchstone, 1997.
Andre, Richard and Cohen, Stan. *Kanawha County Images, Vol. 2.* Charleston, WV: Pictorial Histories Publishing Co., 2001.
Atkinson, George W. *History of Kanawha County.* Charleston, WV: West Virginia Journal, 1876 (Reprinted by West Virginia Genealogical Society, 1994).
Atkinson, George W. *After the Moonshiners.* Wheeling, WV: Frew & Campbell, 1881.
Atkinson, George W., Editor. *Bench and Bar of West Virginia.* Charleston, WV: Virginian Law Book Company, 1919.
Atkinson, George W. and Gibbens, Alvaro F. *Prominent Men of West Virginia.* Wheeling, WV: W.L. Callen, 1890.
Banks, Russell. *Cloudsplitter.* New York: Harper Collins, 1998.
Blumenson, John. *Identifying American Architecture.* Nashville, TN: American Association for State and Local History, 1981.
Bushong, Millard. *A History of Jefferson County West Virginia.* Charles Town, WV: Jefferson Publishing Co., 1942.
Carter, Hodding. *Westward Whoa.* New York: Simon & Schuster, 1994.
Cohen, Stan. *John Brown, The Thundering Voice of Jehovah.* Missoula, MT: Pictorial Histories Publishing Co., 1999.
Cohen, Stan and Andre, Richard. *Kanawha County Images.* Charleston, WV: Pictorial Histories Publishing Co., 1987.
Cohen, Wilson, Chief Justice. *The United States Court of Claims, A History, Part I and II.* Washington, DC: Court of Claims, 1978.
Conley, Phil. *History of the West Virginia Coal Industry.* Charleston, WV: Education Foundation, Inc., 1960.
Dabney, Viriginius. *Virginia, The New Dominion.* Charlottesville, VA: The University Press of Virginia, 1983.
Dayton, Ruth Woods. *Pioneers and Their Homes on Upper Kanawha.* Charleston, WV: West Virginia Publishing Co., 1947.
deGruyter, Julius A. *The Kanawha Spectator, Volume I.* Jarrett Printing Co., Charleston, WV 1953; *Part II.* Charleston, WV: William H. Irwin, Jr., 1976.
DeVoto, Bernard, Edited by. *The Journals of Lewis and Clark.* Boston: Houghton Mifflin Company, 1953.
Everhart, William C. & Sullivan, Arthur L. *John Brown's Raid.* Washington, DC: Government Printing Office, 1990.
Fifer, Barbara and Soderberg, Vicky. *Along the Trail with Lewis and Clark.* Great Falls, MT: Montana Magazine, 1998.
Frazier, Irvin; Fisher, Lewis F. *The Family of John Lewis, Pioneer.* San Antonio, TX: Fisher Publications, 1985.
Gass, Sergeant Patrick. *Gass's Journal of the Lewis and Clark Expedition.* Re-

printed from the edition of 1811, edited by James Kendall Hosmer. Mansfield Centre, CT: Lone Wolf Press, 1999.

Gwin, Hugh S. *Bicentennial History of Bath County, 1791-1991.* Warm Springs, VA: Bath County Historical Society, 1991.

Hale, John P. *History of the Great Kanawha Valley.* Gauley Bridge, WV: Gauley and New River Publishing Co. 1994. First Printing 1891.

Hale, John P. *Trans-Allegheny Pioneers.* Third Edition. Radford, VA: Roberta Ingles Steele, 1971, originally published 1886.

Harrison, Houston J. *Settlers of the Long Grey Trail.* Harrisonburg, VA: C.J. Carrier Co., 1983.

Heitman, Francis. *Historical Register of Officers of the Continental Army.* Baltimore, MD: Genealogical Publishing Company, 1982.

Herringshaw, Thos. W., edited by. *Poetical Quotations.* Chicago: American Publishers, Assc., 1892.

Hill, John. *The First Battle of Bull Run.* Fairfax, VA: CartoGraphics, 1991.

Hubert, Clyde. *Ohio Wesleyan's First Hundred Years.* Delaware, OH: Ohio Wesleyan University, 1942.

Ingles, John, Sr. *Escape from Indian Captivity.* Radford, VA: Roberta Ingles Steele and Andrew Lewis Ingles, 1969.

Jacob, J.G. *Life and Times of Patrick Gass.* Wellsburg, WV: Jacob and Smith, 1859.

Johnson, Patricia Givens. *General Andrew Lewis of Roanoke and Greenbrier.* Blacksburg, VA: Southern Printing Co., 1980.

Johnson, Paul. *A History of the American People.* London: Orion Books, 1997.

Keller, Allan. *Thunder at Harper's Ferry.* Englewood Cliffs, NJ: Prentice-Hall, 1958.

Kercheval, Samuel. *History of the Valley of Virginia.* Strasburg, VA: Shenandoah Publishing House, 1925.

Kurlansky, Mark. *Salt, A World History.* New York: Walker and Company, 2002.

Laidley, W. S. *History of Charleston and Kanawha County and Representative Citizens.* Chicago: Richmond Arnold Publishing Co., 1911 (Reprinted by West Virginia Genealogical Society, 1994).

Lambert, Oscar D. *Stephen Benton Elkins.* Pittsburgh, PA: University of Pittsburgh Press, 1955.

Lay, K. Edward. *The Architecture of Jefferson Country.* Charlottesville, VA: University Press of Virginia, 2000.

Lewis, Ronald L. *Transforming the Appalachian Countryside.* Chapel Hill, NC: The University of North Carolina Press, 1998.

Leyburn, James. *The Scotch Irish.* Chapel Hill, NC: University of North Carolina Press, 1962.

Lowry, Terry D. *22nd Virginia Infantry.* Lynchburg, VA: H.E. Howard, Inc., 1988.

Lowry, Terry. *The Battle of Scary Creek.* Charleston, WV: Quarrier Press, 1998.

MacCorkle, William Alexander. *The Recollections of Fifty Years of West Virginia.* New York: G.P.Putnam's Sons, 1928

MacGregor, Carol Lynn, Edited by. *The Journals of Patrick Gass.* Missoula, MT: Mountain Press Publishing Company, 1997.

Morgan, John G. *West Virginia Governors.* Charleston, WV: Charleston Newspapers, 1980.

Morris, Edmund. *Theodore Rex.* New York: The Modern Library, 2002.

Morton, Oren F. *Annals of Bath County.* Staunton, VA: The McClure Co., 1917.

Nichols, Fredrick Doveton. *Thomas Jefferson's Architectural Drawings.* Charlottesville, VA: Thomas Jefferson Memorial Foundation, Inc., 2001.

Peyton, Lewis J. *History of Augusta County, Virginia.* Staunton, VA: Samuel Yost & Son, 1908.

Public Addresses of George W. Atkinson, 1897 – 1901. Printed by the Public Printer, State of West Virginia, 1901.

Rice, Otis K. *Charleston and the Kanawha Valley*. Woodland Hills, CA: Windsor Publications, Inc., 1981.
Rice, Otis K. *History of Greenbrier County*. Parsons, WV: McClain Printing Co., 1986.
Robertson, James L. *The Stonewall Brigade*. Baton Rouge, LA: Louisiana State University Press, 1963.
Rouse, Jr. Parke. *The Great Wagon Road*. Richmond, VA: The Dietz Press, 1995
Selby, John. *Stonewall Jackson as Military Commander*. New York: Barnes & Noble Books, 1999.
Settle, Mary Lee. *Addie*. Columbia, SC: University of South Carolina Press, 1998.
Simpson-Poffenberger, Livia Nye. *Battle of Point Pleasant, "First Battle of the Revolution."* Point Pleasant, WV: The State Gazette, 1909, republished 1998.
Schlesinger, Arthur, Jr. *The Almanac of American History*. Greenwich, CT: Brompton Books, 1993.
Stealey, John E. III, *The Antebellum Kanawha Salt Business and Western Markets*. Lexington, KY: University Press of Kentucky, 1993.
Stealey, John E. III, edited by. *Kanawha Prelude to Nineteenth-Century Monopoly in the United States, The Virginia Salt Combinations*. Richmond, VA: Virginia Historical Society, 2000.
Stokesbury, James L. *A Short History of the American Revolution*. New York: William Morrow and Company, 1991.
Tams, W. P., Jr. *The Smokeless Coalfields of West Virginia*. Morgantown, WV: West Virginia University Library, 1963.
Tunis, Edwin. *Frontier Living*. New York: Lyons Press, 1960.
Waddell, Jos. A. *Annals of Augusta County*. Harrisonburg, VA: C.J. Carrier Company, 1986, originally published 1901.
Walker, Gary C. *Hunter's Fiery Raid Through Virginia Valleys*. Roanoke, VA: A&W Enterprises, 1989.
Wallace, Lee A. *5th Virginia Infantry*. Lynchburg, VA: H.E. Howard, Inc., 1988.
Warren, Robert Penn. *John Brown, The Making of a Martyr*. Nashville, TN: J.S. Saunders, 1993.
Wayland, John W. *Twenty-Five Chapters on the Shenandoah Valley*. Harrisonburg, VA: C.J. Carrier Co., 1989.
Williams, John Alexander. *West Virginia, A History*. New York: W.W. Norton & Company, 1984.
Williams, John Alexander. *West Virginia and the Captains of Industry*. Morgantown, WV: West Virginia University Library, 1976.

MANUSCRIPT COLLECTIONS

Atkinson Family Files, Archives, West Virginia Cultural Center, Charleston, WV.
Lewis Family Papers, West Virginia and Regional History Collection, Morgantown, WV.
Lewis File, Greenbrier County Historical Association, Lewisburg, WV.

ARTICLES, BOOKLETS, AND DOCUMENTS

Avis, James E. "My Avis Family in America." Washington, DC, 1997.
"Absentee Land Ownership." *Charleston Gazette,* Oct. 13, 2000, editorial page.
Bickley, Ancella. "Atkinson's Association with Howard Still a Mystery," *Charleston Daily Mail*, November 26, 1987.

Biern, Horton. *"Historical Sketches."* Allegheny Historical Society, 1982.

"Bolt of Lightning Strikes Dead Two Prominent Local Attorneys." *Charleston Gazette.* June 9, 1924.

Brand, Irene, "Dunmore's War," *West Virginia History Quarterly.* Archives and History Division, Charleston, WV, Fall 1978.

Brown, Rev. John C. "Sermon at the Funeral of John D. Lewis." *Kanawha Gazette*, Charleston, WV, 1883.

Burns, Ken. Lewis & Clark, "The Journey of the Corps of Discovery.' PBS Home Video, WETA, Washington, DC, 1997.

Burton, Patricia, Affidavit on Andrew Lewis Lineage. 1977.

Carpenter, Charles. "Henry Dana Ward: Early Diary Keeper of the Kanawha Valley." *West Virginia Historical Quarterly.* October, 1975.

Circular No. 1, West Virginia Republican Executive Committee, Wheeling, July 10, 1880.

"Contested Election Case of George W. Atkinson v. John O. Pendleton." Government Printing Office, Washington, D.C. 1891.

Extracts from *The West Virginia Historical Magazine* concerning the Lewis Family. Family files.

"Former Governor G. W. Atkinson Dead." *Charleston Daily Mail*, April 4, 1925.

Forrest, Earle R. *Patrick Gass - Lewis and Clark's Last Man.* Pamphlet published by Mrs. A.M. Painter, Independence, PA, 1950.

"Foundation Members Ride Idaho's Lolo Trail." *We Proceeded On.* November 1985.

"George Wesley Atkinson." *Charleston Gazette*, April 5, 1925.

Johanns, Katherine. "Stretch of I-81 Commemorates Revolutionary War General," *The Roanoke Times*, Roanoke, VA, May 29, 2001.

Johnson, Rody. "A Lewis Family Legacy - Old Sweet Springs." *Goldenseal Magazine*, Charleston, WV, Summer 2000.

Kesavan, Vasan and Paulsen, Michael Stokes. "Is West Virginia Unconstitutional?" *California Law Review*, Volume 90, Number 2, March 2002.

Kidd, Barbara. *The History of Sweet Springs.* Thesis for Masters Degree at West Virginia University, 1953.

Laidley, W. S. "Samuel Lewis and John D. Lewis and Genealogy of the Lewis Family," *The West Virginia Historical Magazine.* Charleston, WV, April, 1904.

Lewis, Rosalind Williamson. *Lewis*, self published, 1969.

Lyle, Katie Letcher. "Sources of 'The Valley Manuscript': The Creation of Historical Fiction," *Augusta Historical Bulletin.* Fall 1999.

Logan, Francis. *The Old Sweet.* A booklet. 1949.

Price, Andrew, Introduction by. *The Commonplace Book of Margaret Lynn Lewis.* Family files.

Military Records of George W. Atkinson, Broadfoot Publishing Co., Wilmington, NC.

"Retirement of Judge George W. Atkinson from the Bench of the United States Court of Claims," Government Printing Office, Washington, D.C. 1916.

Scholz, Carl. "Memorandum on the Lands Now Owned by Lewis Holding Corporation." Charleston, WV, 1942.

Sons of the Revolution in the State of West Virginia, Bulletin No. 8. Scholl Printing Company, Parkersburg, WV, 1941.

Stacy, Charles. "Tales of the Indian Wars from The Palladium 1829." Charleston, WV, 1988.

Virginia Society, Colonial Dames of America, Application for Membership for Mrs. S.B. Avis, May 31, 1935.

"West Virginia and the Capitol," *West Virginia Call*, a publication of the C&P Telephone Company, June 1969.

INTERNET

The Valley of the Shadow, University of Virginia Internet History Project, jefferson.village.virginia.edu.
Historic Valley Forge, Written by Joan Marshall-Dutcher, ushistory.org.
Biographical Directory of the American Congress. Ancestry.com.
World Book Online. Cssvc:worldbook.compuserv.com.2002.

LETTERS

Avis, Florence Atkinson to Statia (Payne), undated, mentioning Brashear Avis.
Avis, Samuel Brashear to his mother while a student at Washington and Lee , 1893.
Morgan, Rebecca Putney to Sis (Florence Avis) Johnson, May 1988, about George Atkinson.
Stacy, Charles to the author dated Sept. 2, 2002, concerning Lewis family history.

INDEX

Adams, Pres. John 69, 78
Albemarle County 79
Altiser, R.G. 234
Anderson, James 17
Anglican (Episcopal) Church 14, 17, 19, 152
Anne, Queen II 6, 7
Atkinson, Bess 191, 199
Atkinson, Ellen Egan 189-191, 193, 198, 199, 209, 212
Atkinson, Florence - *see* Avis
Atkinson, George (grandfather) 193
Atkinson, George, Jr. 191, 199
Atkinson, Gov. George Wesley 178, 187-236
Atkinson, Howard 191, 199
Atkinson, James 193
Atkinson, Miriam Rader 193, 194
Atkinson, Myra Horner Camden 203, 212, 217, 219
Atkinson, Nell 191, 199
Atkinson, Sarah McCoppin 193
Augusta Academy 17
Augusta County 15-20, 28, 29, 33, 34, 39, 50, 51, 57
Avis, Braxton Davenport 109, 110-113, 135, 137, 189, 229, 231

Avis, David 111
Avis, Dorcas - *see* Shirley
Avis, Edward 135, 137
Avis, Florence - *see* Johnson
Avis, Florence Atkinson (Nana) 109, 187, 190-194, 198-200, 201, 203, 208, 211, 212, 215, 217-220, 225-229, 231-236
Avis, Francis 111
Avis, Hattie E. Wilson 109
Avis, Imogene 121
Avis, James 109, 111, 122, 130, 131, 135, 137
Avis, Jim 110
Avis, Capt. John, Jr. 109-138, 187, 190
Avis, John, Sr. 111
Avis, Robert 110
Avis, Samuel Brashear 110, 189, 190, 217, 219, 225, 229, 231-234
Avis, Samuel Brashear, Jr. (Buck) 235

Baltimore and Ohio Railroad (B&O) 114, 168, 195
Banks, Gen. N. P. 133
Bath County 24, 144
Beaver Dam Falls 65
Bee, Gen. B. E. 132

Bell, John 162
Bellefont (Bellefonte) 12-15, 17, 18, 27, 30, 32, 34, 36, 57, 58, 66
Beverly, William 14, 15, 17, 19
Beverly Manor 14-16, 18
Big Levels 33
Bitterroot Mountains 74, 91, 94, 98, 99
Blacksburg 28
Boone, Daniel 146
Booth, John Wilkes 128
Borden, Benjamin 15, 19
Botetourt County 34, 39, 50, 58
Botts, Lawson 114-117, 122, 123
Bouquet, Col. Henry 34-36, 39
Boxer Rebellion 231
Braddock, Gen. Edward 28, 30, 32
Braddock's Defeat 31, 34, 39, 69
Brown, Fred 116
Brown, John 109-130, 136-138, 160, 161, 165, 178, 189, 190
Brown, Mrs. John 126
Brown, Rev. John C. 173, 175
Brown, Owen 121
Brown, Watson 117, 121
Bryan, William Jennings 206, 220, 221
Buchanan, Pres. James 78, 103, 114, 115, 165
Buffalo Gap 23
Buffalo Salt Licks 41
Bull Run 131, 132
Bullitt, Thomas 24, 145
Burning Springs 150, 151
Burr, Aaron 67

Calhoun, Mary - *see* Lewis
Camden, Johnson N. 205, 206, 209, 210, 215
Cameron, Charles 44
Camp Dubois 76, 80, 81
Camp Fortunate 90, 99
Camp Union 26, 39, 41
Campbell, Sheriff James 126, 128, 138
Campbell, Mungo 9, 10
Campbells Creek 41, 141, 142, 145, 147, 149-151, 154, 156, 158, 164-166, 172, 176, 198, 199
Cedar Grove 41, 177
Charbonneau, Toussaint 87
Charles Town 109-112, 114, 115, 117-119, 121, 122, 124, 125, 129, 134, 136-138, 168
Charleston, South Carolina 56, 58, 66
Charleston, West Virginia 39, 41, 42, 45, 141-147, 150-156, 159-169, 171-173, 177, 178, 180-183, 187-189, 193, 194, 196-200, 209, 210, 214, 217, 220, 224, 229, 231-233, 235
Charleston Electrical Supply Company 180, 188
Charlottesville 56, 57, 60
Cherokee Indians 31, 33, 37
Chesapeake Bay 52
Chesapeake and Ohio Railroad (C&O) 171, 172, 176, 177, 180
Chilton, Samuel 123
Cincinnati 149, 151, 155
Clark, Capt. William 69, 80, 83, 84, 86-90, 94, 96, 99-101, 103, 105

Clendenin Family 143, 145, 150
Clendenin Fort 143-145, 171
Coal River 155, 163
Coleman, Warren 60, 61, 63
Columbia River 76, 80, 90, 91, 94-99
Continental Congress 50, 51-53, 56, 58
Continental Morgan Guards 130
Cook, John 124, 129
Copeland, John 121
Coppoc, Edwin 121, 129
Cornstalk, Chief 24-26, 33, 35, 44, 47, 48, 50, 54, 55, 145
Cornwallis, Gen. Charles 56, 58
Corps of Engineers 171, 176
Council Bluffs 82
County Cork 198
Court of Claims (U.S.) 229-231, 233, 235
Covington, Virginia 23, 24, 33, 162
Cowpasture River 15, 23, 24, 35, 38, 65, 144
Cox, Gen. Jacob 163-165
Craig, Rev. John 17, 18
Crow, William 35
Cumberland 77, 133
Czolgosz, Leon 229

Darneal, Elizabeth - *see* Lewis
Davenport, Braxton 122
Davis, Henry Gassaway 203, 205-207, 209, 210, 214, 215, 230
Davis, Jefferson 115, 168
Davis, John 233
Davis, Thomas 209
Dawson, William 206, 213, 214

Delaware Indians 55
Delaware River 53
Dickinson, Adam 24, 144
Dickinson, Anne - *see* Lewis
Dickinson, Henry Clay 154, 167, 172, 173
Dickinson, Jane - *see* Lewis
Dickinson, Col. John 24, 42, 141, 142, 144, 147, 149, 150, 153
Dickinson, John J. 156
Dickinson, John Q. 155, 167, 172, 178
Dickinson, Margaret Lewis 153-155
Dickinson, Sally Lewis 153-155
Dickinson, William, Jr. 152, 155, 172
Dickinson, William, Sr. 150, 155, 158, 159
Dinwiddie, Gov. Robert 28, 31
Donegal, County of 4, 6, 9
Drapers Ferry (Meadow) 28, 30, 31
Dunlap Creek 65
Dunmore, Gov. (Lord) John 38, 39, 42, 48, 50-52

Early, Gen. Jubal 136
Edgewood Country Club 177, 188, 233
Egan, Ellen - *see* Atkinson
Elk River 39, 42, 145, 150, 158, 166, 172, 180, 193, 194, 197, 235
Elkins, Stephen B. 203, 205-210, 213-215, 220-222, 228, 230, 232

Fairfax, Lord 15, 16, 111
Falling Springs 77
Falling Timbers, Battle of 144
Falling Waters, Battle of 131
Faulkner, Charles 213
Fifth (5th) Virginia Infantry 130, 132, 136
Findly, Michael 35
First (1st) West Virginia Cavalry 194
Fleming, Gov. Aretas Brooks 207
Fleming, Col. William 39
Floyd, Sgt. Charles 82, 83
Floyd, Gov. John 62, 63, 68
Floyd, John B. 63, 114, 165-167
Floyd, Leticia Preston - see Lewis
Fontville 67
Forbes, Gen. John 32
Fort Clatsop 74, 76, 97
Fort Dickinson 24, 35, 144
Fort Donnally 54
Fort Duquesne 28, 32, 33, 39
Fort Fredrick 77
Fort Lewis (Cowpasture River) 24, 35, 38, 144
Fort Lewis (Staunton) 13, 14, 20
Fort Mandan 76, 86-89
Fort Necessity 28, 39
Fort Pitt 33, 38
Fort Savannah 26
Fredrick County 16
Freer, Romeo 199
French and Indian War 15, 21, 31-33, 45, 48, 55, 69, 157

Gage, Gen. Thomas 35, 36
Gallipolis, Ohio 160, 162
Gass, Annie 103
Gass, Benjamin 77
Gass, Benjamin, Jr. 77
Gass, Grace - see Thompson
Gass, James 103
Gass, James R. 77
Gass, John 105
Gass, Maria Hamilton 75, 76, 105
Gass, Mary McLene 77
Gass, Patrick 73-106, 111, 190
Gass, Rachel 73, 105
Gass, William 78, 105
General Lewis Inn 25
George II, King 14
Gettysburg, Battle of 136
Gibbons, Alvaro 198
Gibson, Col. John 115
Givens, Elizabeth Anne - see Lewis
Goff, Nathan 207, 209, 214, 221
Golden Horseshoe 12
Gooch, Gov. William 15, 17, 19, 28
Grant, Maj. John 32
Grant, Gen. Ulysses 136, 137
Great Falls 74, 75, 88, 89, 99
Great Meadows 28
Green, Lt. Israel 119
Green, Shields 121
Green, Thomas 122, 123
Greenbrier Company 15-17, 33, 68, 157
Greenbrier County 44, 54, 168, 194
Greenbrier Hotel 24, 61
Greenbrier River 15, 16, 23, 25, 35, 39, 171
Greenbrier Valley 23, 25, 26, 33

Griswold, Hiram 123
Gwynn's Island 52
Gypsy Hill Park 3

Hampton Institute 224
Hampton Sydney College 169
Hancock, John 53
Harding, Charles 123
Harper, Col. Kenton 132
Harpers Ferry 78, 88, 109, 111-115, 117, 121, 122, 125, 126, 129, 130, 136, 137, 160, 165
Harrison, Pres. Benjamin 206-208
Harrisonburg 109, 111, 189
Hart, Senator Thomas 152
Hazlett, Albert 124, 129
Henry, Patrick 50-52
Hidatsa Indians 87, 89
Hogg, Capt. 31
Homestead Hotel 24, 61
House of Burgesses 34, 36, 37, 48, 50
Hot Springs, Virginia 24, 33, 61, 65, 68, 181
Howard University 208
Hoyt, George 123
Hubbard House 145
Hunter, Andrew 123, 124, 136, 137
Hunter, Gen. David 136, 167
Hunter, Harry 123

Ingalls, M.E. 210
Ingles, Mary Draper 31, 141, 145
Iroquois Indians 37

Jackson, Pres. Andrew 169

Jackson River 15, 33, 35, 65
Jackson, Gen. Thomas Stonewall 130-136, 166
Jacobs, J.G. 106
James II, King 6
James River 25, 157
Jefferson, Peter 16
Jefferson, Pres. Thomas 16, 52, 56, 58-60, 63, 67-69, 79, 82, 83, 101
Jefferson Building (Grand Hotel) 59, 60-63, 182, 183
Jefferson County 110, 112, 113, 122-124, 126, 137, 168
Jefferson Guards 113-115
Jefferson River 89, 99
Johnson, Pres. Andrew 137
Johnson, Anne Lewis 3, 144, 147, 178, 180, 181
Johnson, Charles Lewis 147, 178, 180
Johnson, Clarence B. (Kit) 144
Johnson, Florence Avis (Sissie) 229, 232, 234
Johnson, Howard 144, 178, 180, 181
Johnson, Howard S. (Uncle) 62, 147
Johnson, Mrs. Howard S. (Pye) 62
Johnson, Katharine 41, 42, 44-46, 73-75, 77, 78, 110, 112
Johnson, Sir William 37

Kanawha Banking and Trust Company 143, 178, 179, 188
Kanawha City 150, 169, 176, 178, 188, 189, 229, 231,

Kanawha County 67, 135, 146, 160, 162, 169, 175, 178, 187, 195, 198, 199, 225, 235
Kanawha and Michigan Railroad 176
Kanawha Riflemen 159, 160, 162-164, 177, 178, 188
Kanawha River 23, 25-27, 37-39, 41, 42, 44, 47, 141, 142, 145, 146, 149, 151, 152, 156-158, 162, 163, 165, 171, 172, 176, 177, 187, 198, 229, 231
Kanawha Salt Company 151
Kanawha Valley 24, 25, 141, 145, 146, 150, 152-156, 159, 161-164, 166, 169, 171, 173, 177, 193, 196, 197, 229, 231
Kanawha Valley Bank 172, 178
Kansas 113, 114, 116, 117, 125, 129, 161
Kaskaskia 79, 80
Kelly, Walter 145
Kelly's Creek 41, 158, 176, 177,
Kenna, John 155, 156
Kenna, John, Jr. 156, 172, 199, 207, 209
Kenna, Margery Lewis 155, 156
Kentucky 23, 31, 42, 44, 45, 50
Kernsville, Battle of 133
Kerr Creek 33

Lake Erie 32
Lake Ontario 32
Lee, Gen. Robert E. 130, 132, 133, 136, 165, 167, 168
Lemhi Pass 90, 91
Lenhart, Charles 129
Letcher, Gov. John 129
Lewis, Andrew 5, 6, 11, 15, 16, 23-26, 27-58, 59, 65, 69, 145, 146, 151, 155, 157
Lewis, Andrew (John's father) 4, 6
Lewis, Andrew D. 155
Lewis, Anne 11, 13, 14, 35
Lewis, Anne Dickinson 147, 150, 153
Lewis, Anne Montgomery 34, 54, 57, 58, 63, 68
Lewis, Bettie (Elizabeth) Wilson 147, 159, 169, 171, 177, 178, 180, 182
Lewis, Charles 5, 14-16, 18, 23, 24, 26-28, 30, 32, 34-47, 51, 59, 61, 69, 141, 144
Lewis, Charles Cameron (C.C.) 41, 61, 141, 142, 144-147, 149-184, 186-188
Lewis, Charles Cameron (Cam) 61, 180, 181
Lewis, Charles Cameron (son of Charles) 38, 44, 45, 144, 187
Lewis, Charles Cameron, Jr. 45, 46
Lewis, Columbus 167
Lewis, Cousin Sadie 62, 63
Lewis, Elizabeth Anne Givens 32, 34
Lewis, Elizabeth Darneal 153
Lewis, Henry 178
Lewis, James (descendant of Andrew) 155
Lewis, James (descendant of William) 162
Lewis, Jane Dickinson 144, 147
Lewis, Jane Strathers 34
Lewis, Joel 150, 162
Lewis, John 3-7, 9-20, 23, 24,

27, 32, 34-36, 43, 57, 69, 73, 111, 144, 153, 157
Lewis, John (son of Andrew) 34
Lewis, John (son of C.C.) 183
Lewis, John (son of Thomas) 58
Lewis, John (descendent of William) 167
Lewis, John B. 54, 55, 67, 68
Lewis, John D. (Dickinson) 42, 141-145, 147, 149-169, 171-175, 176
Lewis, Julia 154
Lewis, Leticia Preston Floyd 165, 167
Lewis, Margaret L. (daughter of John) 11, 13, 17
Lewis, Margaret Lynn 5, 6, 10-20, 24, 30, 32, 34, 36, 37, 153
Lewis, Mary Calhoun 4, 6
Lewis, Capt. Merriweather 69, 73-75, 79-101, 103, 105
Lewis, Sally Lee Shrewsbury 150
Lewis, Sally Spears 173
Lewis, Col. Samuel (son of Andrew) 25, 54, 57
Lewis, Samuel (brother of John) 9
Lewis, Samuel (son of John) 11, 14, 28, 30, 36
Lewis, Sarah Murray 35, 38, 43, 44
Lewis, Thomas 5, 11, 15, 16, 17, 20, 23, 24, 33, 35, 50, 69, 111
Lewis, Thomas (son of Andrew) 146
Lewis, Thomas, Jr. (son of Thomas) 54, 58
Lewis, Tom (son of William) 66
Lewis, Virginia 182
Lewis, William 5, 11, 16, 17, 28, 50, 51-54, 55-69, 162, 165, 167, 178, 181
Lewis, William Lynn 166, 167
Lewis and Clark Interpretive Center 73, 75
Lewis Creek 4
Lewis Grant 15
Lewis, Hubbard and Company 177, 181
Lewis Spring 16, 26
Lewisburg, West Virginia 16, 23, 25.26, 33, 39, 41, 44, 54, 59, 67, 154, 165-167, 188, 235
Lexington 33, 136
Lincoln, Pres. Abraham 128, 137, 159, 162, 169
Lincoln, Gen. Benjamin 56
Littlepage, Adam 231, 232
Littlepage, Alberta Rebecca - see Putney
Lodge, Henry Cabot 230
Lolo Pass 74, 91, 93, 99
Long, William 18
Loring, Gen. W.W. 166, 167
Lost Trail Pass 91
Louisiana Purchase 79, 100
Loyal Company 15, 16, 33, 37, 157
Lundy's Lane, Battle of 104
Lynchburg 136
Lynnside 63, 166, 167

MacCorkle, Gov. William 188, 209, 210, 222
Madison, Pres. James 34
Manassas 131-133, 135
Mandan Indians 84, 86, 87, 101

Malden 142, 147, 149, 151-153, 161, 162, 167, 175, 224
Marias River 89, 99, 100
Martinsburg 118, 130
McClellan, Gen. George 115, 135, 164
McCoppin, Sarah - see Atkinson
McCoy, William 194
McDowell, Gen. Irvin 131
McKeehan, David 105
McKinley, Pres. William 206, 214, 220, 221, 230, 229
McLene, Mary - see Gass
McMahon, Richard Randolph 233
Medical College of Virginia 135
Mercer Academy 158-160, 166
Mercer County 225
Methodist Episcopal Church 161, 166, 197, 201, 214, 226, 235
Mexican War 109, 111, 115, 130
Milton, Maria - see Gass
Mississippi River 16, 24, 27, 30, 33, 42, 44, 58, 78-80, 82, 137, 156
Missouri River 76-82, 86-89, 91, 96, 97, 99, 100, 103, 106
Monroe, Pres. James 69
Monroe County 61, 182
Montgomery, Anne - see Lewis
Monticello 60
Montreal 33
Mother Jones 231
Mount Union College 198
Muddy Creek 25, 33, 41
Muhlenberg, Gen. Peter 53
Museum of American Frontier Culture 5

National Road 77
Neely, Gov. Mathew 188
New River 15, 25, 41
Newby, Dangerfield 116
Nez Perce Indians 94, 97, 98
Nicholas County 175
North Elba 116, 126
Northwest Passage 79
Noyes, P.H. 177

Old Wagon Road (Great) 17, 23
Ohio River (Valley) 12, 20, 23, 25-28, 31, 33, 34, 37-39, 42, 44, 46-48, 50, 55, 56, 66, 67, 74, 76-78, 80, 104, 105, 114-116, 123, 142, 144, 151, 156, 157, 160, 162, 166, 171, 177, 205
Ohio Wesleyan University 197, 198, 235
Orange 67, 135

Painter, Eugene Gass 73-78
Painter, Gene 74
Pan American Exposition 229
Parker, Alton B. 230
Parker, Judge Richard 123
Patton, George 160, 163, 166, 167
Patton, Col. James 15, 17, 18
Pendleton, John 207
Philadelphia 10, 11, 13, 50-55
Phillips, William B. 60, 63, 68
Pierce, Pres. Franklin 103
Pittsburgh 28, 80
Point Pleasant 37-39, 41, 42-44, 47, 48, 50, 54, 57, 69, 141, 144, 145, 150, 160, 163
Polk, Pres. James 115

Pomp 87, 98, 101
Pontiac, Chief 33, 34, 35
Potomac River 12, 15, 17, 111, 115, 116, 118, 130, 132, 135
Pottawatomie Creek 116
Presbyterian Church 7, 17, 152, 175
Preston, William 38
Putney, Alberta Rebecca Littlepage 195-197

Quebec 33, 50

Richmond 49, 50, 51, 58, 128, 131, 134, 135, 160, 162, 164, 165, 171, 181, 182
Roanoke 34
Roanoke River 34, 54
Rockies (Rocky Mountains) 79, 80, 87, 89, 97
Rockingham County 69, 109
Romney 132
Roosevelt, Pres. Teddy 178, 230
Rowan, J. W. 114, 115
Ruffner, Daniel 150, 169
Ruffner, David 150
Ruffner, David L. 158
Ruffner, Elizabeth - *see* Wilson
Ruffner, Henry 160, 169
Ruffner, Joseph 141, 149, 150
Ruffner, Gen. Lewis 169
Ruffner Hotel 177, 193
Rush, Dr. Benjamin 83, 86, 94

Sacagawea 74, 87, 89, 90, 98, 101
St. Louis 79, 80, 81, 87, 102, 105
Salmon River 90, 91

Sandy Creek (Expedition) 31, 37, 39
Scary Creek (Battle of) 146, 163, 165
Scotch-Irish 6, 7, 10, 11, 13, 14, 17-19, 175
Scotland 6, 19, 144
Scott, H.G. 234
Scott, Nathan B. 205, 214, 215, 232
Seaman 81, 98
Shawnee Indians 28, 30, 33, 35, 38, 39
Shenandoah River 12, 116-118, 121
Shenandoah Valley 3, 5, 11, 17, 23, 33, 34, 53, 69, 129-132, 134, 137, 150, 166-168
Sheppard, Howard 114
Shirley, Dorcas Avis 110
Shirley, Sir Walter 110, 111
Shoshone Indians 87, 89-91, 99
Shrewsbury, Joel 150
Shrewsbury, Sally Lee - *see* Lewis
Sioux City 82
Sioux Indians 83, 84, 102
Skyles Survey 157, 158, 176
Slidel, John Lewis 45, 46
Smith, Harrison 178
Smith, Isaac Noyes 178, 188
Smith, Isaac Noyes (Ike) 188
Soule', Silas 129
Spanish American War 216, 217
Spears, Sally - *see* Lewis
Spellman, Lynn 62, 63
Spotswood, Gov. Alexander 11
Spring Hill Cemetery 146, 147, 189, 190

Stacy, Mrs. Charles P. 182
Starry, Dr. John 113, 114, 118, 121
Staunton 3-5, 7, 13, 17-20, 23, 24, 27, 28, 34, 51, 57, 65, 112, 130, 134-136
Staunton, Lady 17
Stevens, Aaron 121, 122, 129
Stevenson, Gov. William 198, 205
Stewart, John 37
Stonewall Brigade 136
Strathers, Jane - see Lewis
Stuart, Gen. J. E. B. 118, 119
Summers, George 162
Sweet Springs (Old) 34, 58-68, 143, 154, 166, 167, 180-183

Tarleton, Col. Banastre 56-58
Taylor, Gen. Zachary 115
Tennessee 33, 37, 44, 162
Tenth (10th) Virginia Regiment 56
Thompson, Grace Gass 78
Thompson, I. Huston 233
Thompson, Sean 4
Tinkling Spring 17
Toby (Old Toby) 90, 91, 93, 94, 99
Tompkins, Henry 157, 177
Treaty of Paris 33
Tug Fork 31
Turner, George 117
Tuskegee Institute 224, 225
Twenty-second (22nd) Virginia Infantry 163, 165-167, 169

Ulster 5, 6, 9, 11, 14, 17

Upshur, Mary Jane Seith (Fanny Farmer) 37

Valley Forge 54, 55, 58
Virginia, University of 60
Virginia Military Institute 127, 130, 160

Walker, Tom 37
War of 1812 103-105, 116
Ward, Henry Dana 153
Warm Springs, Virginia 23, 24, 33, 38, 61, 65
Washington, Booker T. 220, 224, 225
Washington, Dick 117
Washington, Pres. George 12, 17, 28, 30, 32, 34, 36, 39, 49, 51, 53-58, 61, 67, 69, 78, 103, 111, 114, 146, 150, 157
Washington, Col. Lewis 114, 117, 119
Washington, D.C. 83, 101, 103, 110, 114, 117, 118, 123, 131, 132, 136, 156, 189, 206, 208-210, 213-215, 219, 229-232
Washington and Lee University (Liberty Hall) 189
Watts, Cornelius C. 210
Wayne, Gen. Anthony 66
Wellsburg 73-78, 103-106
West Virginia University 142
Wheeling 77, 162, 167, 172, 173, 190, 198-200
Wheeling Convention 168, 169
Whiskey Rebellion 78
White, Gov. Albert B. 222
White Sulphur Springs 61, 68

William and Mary, College of 11, 19
William of Orange 6
Williamsburg 11, 12, 15, 18-20, 28, 31, 34, 36, 37, 48, 50, 51
Wilson, Bettie (Elizabeth) - *see* Lewis
Wilson, Edith Bolling Galt 232
Wilson, Elizabeth Ruffner 169, 178
Wilson, Ellen 232
Wilson, Hattie E. - *see* Avis
Wilson, Capt. James 143, 144
Wilson, Nathaniel Venable 169, 178
Wilson, Pres. Woodrow 3, 232
Winchester 115, 125, 131-133, 135, 167
Wise, Gov. Henry (Gen.) 121, 124, 126, 129, 161-165
Wolfe, Gen. James 33

Yellowstone River 87, 91, 99-101

LIST OF ILLUSTRATIONS

First Settlers Grave 5
John Lewis Home 13
West Virginias and Surrounding Territory 21
Lewisburg 26
Portrait of Andrew Lewis 29
Fort Lewis 35
Detail of painting of Charles Lewis 36
Point Pleasant Battle 43
Col. Charles Lewis, 1736 -1774, Killed in Battle 43
Statue of Famous Virginians at Capitol Square, Richmond 49
Sweet Springs 62
Gass 75
Map of the Lewis and Clark Expedition 85
Portrait of Patrick Gass 102
Captain John Avis 125
John Brown 127
John D. Lewis 174
C.C. Lewis 179
Old Sweet Springs, the Grand Hotel 182
C.C. Lewis Family, Christmas 1904 184
G.W. Atkinson and family 191
George W. Atkinson while Governor 204
Florence Atkinson Avis 218
The Avis-Atkinson wedding party, 1893 219
George W. Atkinson 236

ABOUT THE AUTHOR

Rody Johnson was born in Charleston, West Virginia and grew up in Vero Beach, Florida. He is a graduate of the University of Virginia. He spent his career in the aerospace industry and later became publisher of a weekly newspaper. His first book, *Different Battles,* tells the story of a German U-boat attack off Florida during World War II. He and his wife, artist Katharine Johnson, live in Vero Beach and spend their summers in Lewisburg. When not writing, he kayaks and fly fishes.